Doorways to Christian Growth

Jacqueline McMakin
with Rhoda Nary

Harper & Row, Publishers, San Francisco
Cambridge, Hagerstown, New York, Philadelphia
London, Mexico City, São Paulo, Singapore, Sydney

Cover design: Terry Dugan

Library of Congress Catalog Card Number: 83-51390

ISBN: 0-86683-818-X

Printed in the United States of America

5 4 3 2

Acknowledgments

In a communal effort such as this, there are many people to thank. Lois Donnelly was the first to say yes to the idea of creating the Partners Community. Pat Davis followed shortly afterward. They, together with Mid Allen, Jean Sweeney, Dave Scheele, Sally Dowling, Cathie Bates, Susan Hogan, and Sancy Scheele worked with us in the major task of designing, offering, and critiquing these courses. All of us are especially indebted to Gordon and Mary Cosby of the Church of the Saviour and to Elizabeth O'Connor's writings about that community. Each of the other members and participants in the Partners Community these eleven years, our husbands, Dave and Bill, and our children—all have had a hand in conceiving this book and encouraging us along the way. Mim Dinndorf, Sonya Dyer, Mary Elizabeth Hunt, Maggie Kalil, Gertrude Kramer, and Billie Johansen read and gave us suggestions for the manuscript. Typing and research help was offered by Calista DiGiulian, Sally Dowling, Ricci Waters, Mary Pockman, Janet Rife, Mary Scantlebury, and Gretchen Nannon.

Grateful acknowledgment is made for permission to reprint the following materials:

From Robert McAfee Brown, *Creative Dislocation: The Movement of Grace,* Abingdon Press. Used by permission of the publisher.

From Walter Brueggemann, *Living Toward a Vision.* Copyright © 1976, 1982 by the United Church Press. Reprinted by permission of the publisher.

From Sidney Callahan, "Seesawing Through," reprinted by permission of the *National Catholic Reporter,* P. O. Box 281, Kansas City, Mo. 64141.

From Carl Jung, *Modern Man in Search of a Soul,* Harcourt Brace Jovanovich, Inc. Used by permission of the publisher.

From Thomas Kelly, *The Eternal Promise.* Copyright © 1966 by Richard M. Kelly. Reprinted by permission of Harper & Row, Publishers, Inc.

From Frank Laubach, *Letters by a Modern Mystic,* used by permission of Robert S. Laubach, son of the author. The book, now in its twentieth printing (first published in 1937) is published by New Readers Press, P. O. Box 131, Syracuse, N.Y. 13210, $1.25.

From Agnes Sanford, *Sealed Orders.* Copyright © 1972 by Bridge Publishing, Inc. Reprinted by permission of Bridge Publishing, Inc., South Plainfield, N.J. 07080.

From Dorothy Soelle, *Choosing Life,* copyright © 1981 by Fortress Press. Used by permission.

Contents

Preface

As we think about why these courses came into being and why we want to share them more widely, we hear some of the spoken and unspoken questions of those close to us.

My life is before me. Faced as I am with a dizzying array of choices and a confusing world, what kind of help is available?

—A college student

Recently I discovered I have cancer. All of a sudden, life looks very short to me. Are there ways I can make the most of the time I have left?

—An older woman

I work incredibly hard and come home exhausted. Part of an awesome decision-making complex, I have no time to look at things from perspectives other than military. Am I too narrow?

—An army officer

Life has been good to me. My children are raised. My husband and I are in good health. How can I invest myself for this next period of life in something worthwhile?

—A housewife

We hear these kinds of questions all around us—about jobs, children, illness, future. Social questions abound as well—about peace, environment, poverty, population.

Is there a place where such people can go for help in addressing these questions?

Many people look to the church for direction and empowerment. They see it as a place of wisdom, guidance, and companionship, a spiritual center where they can raise questions in company with others and thereby expand their ability to cope with their own problems and help transform society.

Unfortunately, none of the people we have just quoted sees the local church as such a place; it is simply not a part of their lives. However, many others have found that the richness and resources of the Christian experience are alive and available, whether in churches or in books, spiritual movements, intimate study sessions, weekend retreats, and social-justice activities such as picket lines, peace rallies, and battles for a clean environment. These and similar activities are often permeated by basic Christian attitudes and practices, and they awaken faith responses in people who do not think of themselves as Christian.

It was our awareness of those three realities—people's spiritual hunger, the strategic importance of the local church, and the rich resources of the Christian experience—that led to the design of these courses. In 1972, three of us started a small community called Partners, whose purpose was to serve the church in some way. (Our name is taken from Paul's Letter to the Philippians, 1:3-5, RSV: "I thank my God in all my remembrance of you, . . . thankful for your partnership in the gospel from the first day until now.")

Partners began at a time when the post-Vatican II enthusiasm for ecumenism had waned. In order to witness to our vision of Christian unity, whenever possible we work in ecumenical pairs and divide our time between Protestant and Catholic churches, drawing from both traditions in our life together and in our work. We began by responding to requests for retreats or workshops, but soon we became frustrated because our work seemed fragmented. In addition, it was impossible to meet people's needs within the number of hours that had been allotted for each event. Then we were tossed this challenge: "OK. If responding to our requests seems too piecemeal and if you had all the time you needed, what would you design for individuals and churches that would accomplish what you think needs doing?"

What a challenge! We decided to put our heads together to try to meet it. The yearnings of those we met in churches were our starting point. Beneath the surface friendliness and the many activities and committees held in churches, here is what we heard people say they were really looking for:
• "real spiritual nourishment, not simply more facts and knowledge";
• "experiences of God";
• "motivation and meaning for life work";

- "deep personal caring among a few people in good times and hard";
- "empowerment and direction about how to make a positive contribution to global betterment."

Next we reflected on the experiences and practices that had aided our own Christian growth. Much that was positive had occurred in local churches and in the various renewal or social-justice efforts that formed our combined experience. Yet many "peak experiences" had happened away from home on renewal weekends, and we knew the difficulty of reentry and the problem of communicating to those at home what had happened. Therefore we wanted to design ways for people to have these growth experiences in their home church with neighbors and friends who would then become spiritual companions and supporters of one another. We decided that whatever we designed would be offered in local churches within time frames accessible to most people. That is how we came to specialize in giving six-week courses on weekday mornings and evenings.

The theme song of our design team could have been Disney's "The Bare Necessities." We tried to determine and then present the essentials of Christian experience in the simplest, most direct, engaging way we knew. Many important things had to be left out. There is no church history, no denominational emphasis, no attempt to offer thorough study of certain biblical books, and no systematic review of historic or contemporary theological trends. We see our courses rather as *doorways to the essence of Christian life*. Our emphasis is how this relates to real people in real situations. Our hope is that once through the doorway, people will go on in dozens of ways to expand, enhance, and deepen these introductory experiences.

Introduction

Keeping in mind the yearnings of persons we knew both inside and outside the church, and *hoping to see local churches become vital centers of spiritual growth and mission,* we designed four courses, each with its own purpose:

Discovering God in the Old Testament provides a way to explore the understandings of God realized by people in the Old Testament. This introductory course starts from scratch and is suited to participants who have no prior experience or knowledge of faith as well as to longtime churchgoers who are taking a second look at the meaning of faith.

Meeting Jesus in the New Testament offers opportunities to learn about the Jesus of history and to make faith decisions today in response to the living presence of the Spirit. It is for those who want to be more than observers of the ministry of Jesus, who want to explore being companions in that ministry.

Tools for Christian Growth is for those who are committed to the way of Jesus and who would like to strengthen that commitment through experiencing classic resources for growth such as prayer, meditation, healing, and reconciliation.

Discovering Your Ministry and Gifts is for persons who are concerned about the pain and disharmony of the world and who want to help implement God's vision for the world. It offers a discernment process for discovering one's gifts and calling as well as a model for effective ministry.

These four courses are progressive in that they build on a deepening relationship with God and provide opportunities to do four basic activities:
• *explore* experiences of God;
• *decide* about one's relationship to God;
• *deepen* those decisions;
• *discern* life direction and purpose.
These are activities to be encouraged and supported in all churches. Our

1

courses are one attempt at a concrete model for doing these four things. We hope that they will encourage the development of other models.

Method as well as content is important in these courses. The style of learning we use is called "discovery" or "experiential" learning. This means that the participants are given opportunities to work with the concepts presented and then to reflect on their experience. For example, our courses describe a way of prayer using scripture as a springboard, then offer people a chance to practice the method and finally to report on what happened. They do not offer intellectual rationales for prayer or comparisons of different prayer techniques. Similarly, in dealing with the Bible, which we use a great deal in our courses, we do not offer thorough analyses of biblical history or comparisons of critical or interpretive approaches. Rather, we suggest specific ways to enter into some of the faith experiences described in the Bible and to share what they mean for us. We do not see our courses as presenting Christian doctrine but rather as *opening up Christian experience.*

As in teaching and learning science, lab work is essential. This we build into group sessions and into the individual work between sessions. Thus we use both theory and practice.

What results might individuals and churches expect? It is dangerous to be too concerned about specific results in spiritual matters; the Spirit always blows where it will. Yet like the writer of 1 John, we can tell what we have heard and seen in the churches and individuals with whom we have worked.

Churches. As people have taken our church-based courses, *they have experienced the church as a center where they can find others who will take their journey seriously, who will listen to and value their story, who will offer encouragement and stimulation for further growth.* As groups of people have gone through our process in churches, *they have developed ministries* that have made a difference. A home for battered spouses, a center for the elderly poor in the inner city, Jungian testing for self-understanding, a welcoming program for newcomers, a teaching ministry in the local jail, a parish training program that forms staff and teachers into a praying community as a base from which to share faith with others—these are some that come to mind.

Individuals. It is easier to see what happens to individuals who take these courses because they hand in personal evaluations upon complet-

ing each course.
- "My faith is more alive."
- "I see how important it is to combine prayer, caring, and mission, and I want to try to do that in my life from now on."
- "I have discovered and strengthened my sense of calling."
- "Jesus sends us forth to make friends for him in all the world. I now know my piece of the action and am eager to be about it."

Of course, not everyone has a life-changing experience, and some people are disappointed. Usually, however, for those who are beckoned by the purposes and methods of the courses, learnings occur. And for some, a basic change occurs. They choose to be not only participants in an important world organization called the church, but co-laborers and companions with One they have come to know and love very much.

As people were helped by what happened through the courses, they suggested putting them into a form that could be sent to family and friends not in our area. We both began working on this in 1979 while continuing with vocational and family commitments. We would discuss a particular section, how the material had worked in the group sessions and in individual lives. Then Jackie would write a first draft and Rhoda would edit, and we would have more discussion and revision. Although Jackie was the writer (the "I" passages scattered throughout the book describe her personal experience), we really produced the book together. We needed the perceptions of both of us to capture in writing the years of design and revision work that each member of Partners had contributed.

The courses were offered initially in white, middle-class, suburban churches to people who were hungry for spiritual growth and were attracted to exploring Christian resources for that growth. These busy, committed individuals wanted to take time out to reflect on life's meaning and direction.

We have found the material also helpful for those who do not fit this description. Young people searching for direction and nourishment, those who are not particularly committed to Christian understandings, and those not in suburban settings find that the material contains tools that can aid the search for meaning in their lives.

As we have been writing and facilitating these courses, a theological revolution has been going on. Liberation, Black, creation, and feminist theologies have shown us how bourgeois, white, and male-dominated are contemporary thought patterns and organizational structures. These theologies are stressing the gospel's "preferential option for the poor," the importance of valuing and incorporating the experience of non-white, third-world, female, oppressed, and marginalized persons into what we think and do.

Increasingly we have been affected and involved in these new theological understandings and want to incorporate them into our courses. When we facilitate them ourselves it is possible to do this since we have a sense of the group and can custom-design new material. But to do this in writing is another matter. In such a theologically fertile period, when new understandings are being lived, shared, and written about at an amazing rate, each choice of word, phrase, or emphasis has theological implications. Whatever we write, in a sense, is quickly dated. Yet, in another sense, we are trying to capture and describe some of the timeless aspects of Christian faith. This book would serve a good purpose if our attempts to preserve the old and incorporate the new stimulated each reader to do this personally.

How to Use This Book

This material is designed for individuals and groups. If you are going to use this book alone, you can gain much from "doing" the book in your own way and in your own timing. Adapt the group exercises to yourself and try them out. Do the individual work. Perhaps you can find another person with whom to share the course or to discuss some of its aspects. If you are motivated to work with the material alone, honor that feeling within yourself and have confidence that your efforts will bear fruit.

Groups that could benefit from the course are already-convened groups such as existing Bible-study, life-sharing, or task groups who want to grow together, or groups especially convened for the particular training offered through these courses.

A. How the Material Is Organized
Each course has four sections:
• Introduction: the background and rationale for each course;
• Session Text: basic introductory material on the topic;
• Group Design: practical ways for a group to work with the material in the session text;
• Individual Work: suggestions on how to apply the material to our own lives as individuals.

B. Using the Material in Groups
In order to get the most from the courses, it is important to do three things:

1. *Read and digest the text.* Before coming to the first session of any course, read the introduction and the first session text in preparation for the first group session. Then read the next session text in preparation for Session 2 and so on through the six sessions of each course. It is best to devote most of your time to the individual work related to the preceding session before reading the new session material. Leave the new material for the day or so before you meet.

2. *Participate in the group design.* Our experience shows that when

5

people relax, participate in the group activities, and try things out, much growth occurs. There is no perfect design nor any design that works equally well for all groups. Feel free to modify these designs in any ways that work well for you. Don't be bound by these design ideas, but do take some time to understand their underlying purpose. Then you can perhaps accomplish the same goals in other ways. Feel free also to modify the timing on the designs. We estimate that our timing works very easily for groups of about twelve people. Smaller groups will have more time; larger groups may have to shorten or omit certain activities.

Each group design has several parts that we will look at in detail.

a. *Gathering Time:* The purpose of this period is to assemble the group and ready yourselves for the session. We have built in some ways to share personal information gradually. You will know one another rather well by the end of each course. This happens as a result of all the activities, so it does not have to be accomplished fully in the gathering time. Usually ten minutes are allowed for this gathering time. A lot can happen if you divide the time equally among all participants and really listen to each person. It is often tempting to allow more time for this section or to be undisciplined in its use. Our experience is that groups usually regret this if it becomes habitual.

b. *Sharing Groups:* The purpose of these is to share in a small setting what you did with the suggestions for individual work and also to support one another as you take the course. These sharing groups of four are formed in the first session of each course. The same group meets at least once during each session to share individual work, to come to know one another better than is possible in the larger group, and to pray for one another. We find there are many benefits when the same group meets consistently. Of course, you will want to get to know others in the larger group, so in other parts of the design when smaller groups are formed, we recommend that you be with people not in your sharing group.

c. *Discussion of the Session Text:* We have included discussion time only occasionally because we felt it useful to give more time to a particular activity. However, if your group would like to include a period of reviewing and discussing the main points of the session text, feel free to do so. A sample discussion question: What learning from the text was most important for you?

d. *Lab Exercise:* The purpose of this is to enable the group to experience one aspect of the topic and to reflect on this experience. The activities in this section vary a great deal. Some are lighthearted and others more serious, but we have found them all to be valuable.

e. *Closing:* The purpose of this time is to give people an opportunity to reflect on the session and to have a feeling of closure. Sometimes we offer a suggestion about how to do this; at other times we leave it to you. Some groups like to vary their closing exercises; others like the consistency of the same ending each time, such as a favorite song or a circle of prayer.

f. *Materials:* We suggest that each participant bring a Bible and a notebook for each session. Where additional materials are needed, we have indicated that in the design.

g. *Breaks:* According to your group's needs, schedule a 5-to-10-minute break in the middle of each session. Our estimated timing does not include breaks, so adjust your timing accordingly. People like to know at the beginning of the session when the break will be.

3. *Do the individual work.* This work is designed to be done at home between sessions and is a vital part of the courses. It is a bridge between group sessions and provides ways for individuals to work with the material personally. Our participants find this one of the most worthwhile parts of the whole experience and urge us to underscore its importance.

The individual work usually involves 15 to 30 minutes of quiet time set apart for reading, reflecting on the reading, and noting your thoughts in a journal, usually a looseleaf notebook. In this notebook we suggest that you jot down insights or questions about the material each week plus your responses to the questions posed. At the end of each week it is very useful to write a short one-paragraph summary of what you did, the particular learnings and difficulties, and any questions. This summary can be shared with the group.

We suggest that you devote the quiet times during the first part of your week to the individual work and that you use the last few days before your group session to read the new session text in preparation for the next session.

People are always tempted to give too little attention to the individual work. This can shortchange everybody. You are then not engaging with the material personally, and are coming empty or poorly prepared to the group. This weakens the group experience. Try to take this time seriously. For the six weeks of the course, budget the time you need to do the individual work. It can be very rewarding.

C. What About Leadership?

The course will go more smoothly for the group if one or two people offer some leadership for the sessions. These can be the same people each time or a rotating leadership with a different person or pair leading each session.

The basic responsibility of the leaders includes:
* reading the session text, group design, and individual work in advance;
* gathering the necessary materials for the next session;
* convening the group at the start of the session;
* leading it through the group design, taking care not to let the session exceed the planned two hours;
* closing the meeting with a reminder of the time and place of the next session.

Here are additional ways leaders can help the group if they want to but these should not be seen as an added burden. The leaders could:
* Do some additional background reading.
* Go over the group design and make it your own, adding your creativity to it, tailoring it to the needs of the group.
* Consider making an inner commitment to pray for each person in the group.
* Consider starting group sharing times by offering your own experience. This is called modeling. The way this is done is crucial. If you make a long response to a question, others often follow suit and your timing may be thrown off. If you share personally, others will feel freer to be personal. If you as leader are willing to share examples from your life that could be described as negative, others will feel free to talk about such feelings as anger or jealousy. Similarly, positive sharing frees people to share joys. By your example you give others permission to be real and honest, to share both positives and negatives. Our participants tell us that when they hear leaders share authentic pains and joys, they feel encouraged to face similar feelings in their own situations.
* Be attentive to the nonverbal communication in the group. You as a

leader can foster an atmosphere of caring, genuineness, and openness through a smile, a word of encouragement, a touch on the arm.

Gathering a Group

Suppose you are not a member of an existing group but would like to gather a group in order to take the courses together. Find another person who will work with you and who has enthusiasm about doing the courses. There are several things you can do:

1. Spread the word as widely as possible. Start with family and friends, neighbors, members of groups active in the church and community, newcomers. Try to contact these people personally. Tell them about the purposes of the courses: to provide spiritual nourishment; to build a caring supportive group; and to discover which part of God's work we are called to foster. To become clearer about the purposes of each individual course, read the introductory material in the beginning of that course.

People respond to an invitation to join the course for a variety of reasons. Some are looking for a sense of belonging; others want purpose or direction in their lives; others are hungry for spiritual nourishment. Find out what people are looking for and then explain how the courses can help meet that need.

2. Be sure to go over the procedural matters such as the dates, time, and place where the course will be held. If possible, try to hold the course in a home since that is often the most comfortable. Explain that the course depends on the commitment of everyone to come regularly, be on time, to do the individual work, and, when circumstances prevent this, to let someone know so that one can be brought up to date before the next session. Let people know that the method used will be *discovery learning* that depends on the participation of each person and not on the expertise of a leader. You will be learning by doing, and each of you is an expert on your own experience. Each of you will proceed at your own pace and in your own way. Some will have important insights during the group meetings; others may have them at home; others may see results from the course only after it has ended.

This style of learning contrasts with traditional ways of teaching: offering truth as a body of material shared by an authority (theologian, pastor, teacher) to a disciple whose main job is to assimilate and apply the material but not to question it in any major way. It is important to touch on these matters because many people still expect this traditional approach and ask questions such as "Who's teaching the course? Who's the leader? Do you have permission to do this?" Sometimes we offer this explanation: The traditional approach is useful for imparting doctrine (the wisdom and teachings of the church throughout history). Experiential learning enables us to examine some of those doctrines and make them a living part of our lives.

3. It is not easy to gather a group, but people find it worth the effort when they see valuable results occur in individuals and churches. We find that praying together for the group often makes the crucial difference between gratitude and frustration in this work of gathering. So as you discuss whom you have contacted, remember to pray for one another and for the whole group. Often you are given inspiration about new people to contact or new ways to do it.

4. Size and makeup of the group. We believe the material works well with groups numbering from ten to twenty, people of all ages, clergy and laity, men and women.

One

Discovering God in the Old Testament

This course focuses on six of the major discoveries people in the Hebrew scriptures made about God and enables us to verify some of these experiences for ourselves. God was to the Hebrew people and can be for us *Creator, Caller, Deliverer, Covenant-Maker, Suffering Servant,* and *New Song.*

"How did you choose the six?" someone asked. "Are they the ones you think most important, or did they just drop out of the sky?" Both possibilities are in a sense true. They did occur to us quickly, and we have found them full of meaning for ourselves and for others.

Many other images for God are important and enhance the ones we chose as well as other aspects of the fullness of God. For example, in *The Divine Feminine,* Virginia Mollenkott focuses on feminine images for God in scripture such as nursing mother, midwife, mother eagle, and Dame Wisdom. These recover aspects of the nature of God that are often lost when only male images are used.[1] Matthew Fox uses another emphasis. In *Original Blessing* he celebrates the God of blessing, creative energy, and motion in contrast to more static understandings of God.[2]

For each of the images we chose, we have selected sections of the Hebrew scriptures for study and response. By working with key biblical passages, persons, and experiences, we are introduced to the history, theology, poetry, and faith found in this astounding set of books. And by allowing ourselves to enter into some of these experiences with God, we can discover the reality God can have for us today.

For example, it is one thing to see that in some mysterious way God the *Creator* formed the universe in the beginning of time. It is quite another to know God as Creator of me, a unique person with my own particular conglomeration of traits and talents, and to see that I am invited by God, the *Caller,* to be a co-creator, continuing the life-giving

11

work already begun.

Surely, in a world of frightening instability and tension, to be a creative, loving contributor to "building the earth," as Teilhard de Chardin put it, involves risk, moving out, leaving the old and comfortable ways. We can feel insecure and troubled in such a partnering with God. It is then that it is necessary and comforting to know God as *Deliverer,* "a very present help in time of trouble."

Is there anything tangible to hang onto in this changing world? God seemed to know our need for that. We are invited into a deep relationship with God, the *Covenant-Maker.* In the first days, this covenant between God and humankind was marked by tangible signs—blood, stone tablets, and the shepherding figure of Moses. Today we are still invited into a covenant with God and others and are challenged to make that covenant tangible through deeper experiences of support and service.

As we become more involved with others through support and service, we come up against the reality of evil. Old Testament people wrestled with the mystery of the goodness and love of God that existed alongside the evil and sin in the world. The picture of God as *Suffering Servant* evolved as a mysterious concept whose meaning we will never wholly grasp. But surely if it means anything, it is that God does not love us in a casual, fair-weather sort of way. The love of Yahweh gives everything, even life itself, to seek the lost, mend the broken, go after and woo the faithless. The experience of being loved with this steadfast and just love is a fundamental experience of the Old Testament people.

We complete this course with God as *New Song.* When Hebrew people reviewed their own story, they often broke into song. This is a personal and realistic note on which to end. Sometimes our songs are happy, sometimes sad, bewildered, lonely. Like the Hebrew people, we can learn to sing to God of our deepest feelings and experiences. We can know God as freshly present, creative, calling, helping, and steadying in all kinds of spiritual weather.

Notes

1. Virginia Mollenkott, *The Divine Feminine* (New York: The Crossroad Publishing Company, 1983). Here it is important to state our com-

mitment to using inclusive language in this work. There are problems with this. Language has not yet caught up with our conviction that exclusive use of male images for God limits our appreciation of God's fullness. Inevitably the writer is faced with awkward or unfamiliar usage. It is impossible to find language to speak about God that works for everyone. Further, there is as yet no inclusive language version of the Bible, although portions have been translated inclusively. On the whole we use four translations: the Revised Standard Version (RSV), the New American Bible (NAB), the Phillips translation (Phillips), and the Jerusalem Bible (JB), all of which use only masculine pronouns to refer to God. In the interests of quoting each translation accurately, we did not change the language. Some writers whose scholarship includes linguistic skills have included their own inclusive translations in their work. This was beyond the scope of our work. In addition, we have quoted other works written before people were sensitized to this issue; with these as well, we have not changed the language.

2. Matthew Fox, *Original Blessing* (Santa Fe: Bear & Company, 1983).

Session 1

Creator

The opening chapters of the Bible contain some wonderful and striking ideas about God and people. The very first description used of God is that of Creator: "In the beginning God created. . . . " It is as if the writers wanted to reaffirm their faith in God as the origin of life regardless of the apparent hopelessness of their immediate circumstances.

We must remember that the opening creation accounts (Gen. 1:1—2:4a and Gen. 2:4b-25) in their present form date from the Exile, that period when the Jewish nation had been conquered and many of its people sent in exile and defeat to Babylon. They had seen Yahweh as a god of victory, a bringer of grandeur, power, and unity to Israel. How tempting to think in exile that the defeat of the blessed nation meant also that God was dead! But no, the opening note is one of hope—God, first of all, is Creator.

Second, the opening chapters in Genesis affirm that everything created is of God and is good. The author of the first creation account (1:1—2:4a) portrays God as creating the world in six days and resting on the seventh. During those six days, out of chaos God formed light and darkness, night and day, land and sea, sun and moon, all living creatures on land and in the sea and air, and finally humankind. Four times in the passage, God is portrayed as looking at what had been created and finding it good. And at the end of the account, God declared that everything that had been created was "very good." A tremendous affirmation of faith in the goodness of all that is created by God and given to us as gift! And further, an implied but crucial corollary: No one nor any living creature is left out.

Third, all people are seen as created in the image of God. This creative energy of God, this ability to bring form out of chaos, is given to all people, who in turn are instructed to be fruitful. People are made co-

14

creators with God, to continue the creative process, to have a part in completing the "building of the earth."

The second creation account begins with the creation of persons and proceeds to wrestle with the questions of personal freedom, choice, and the problem of evil. People are free to be fully human and can cooperate with God's creativity. Or they can open up chaotic or destructive possibilities, out of harmony with the order envisioned by God.

Matthew Fox, in discussing these destructive possibilities, says that sin is misusing our potential to join God as co-creators. It is the abuse or neglect of our creative imaginations and thereby our potential for good. To use our creative potential in any way that destroys or harms our planet and all the life on it is a violation of the divine invitation to fruitfulness.[1]

If we want to cooperate with God's creativity, it is helpful to understand how the process of creativity works. In *Courage to Create,* Rollo May writes about many of its components. He describes the creative breakthrough in terms of gratification, joy, and "participating in an experience of elegance." This breakthrough also entails rebellion and often rage against things as they are. It involves valuing the nonrational as well as the rational. Anxiety is a prime ingredient, as our previous ideas and relationships are shaken up.

The creative act involves an encounter of the individual with the world, an encounter that involves real engagement, absorption, and commitment. Paradoxically, the precise moment of the creative breakthrough often occurs in a period of letting go, relaxation, solitude, or disengagement, and sometimes in opposition to the conscious idea to which one is clinging.

Contrary to the generally held notion that unlimited freedom is essential to creativity, May contends that "creativity arises out of the tension between spontaneity and limitations!" Indeed, limitations can often be a catalyst for creativity, as can ambiguity.

May concludes that this sometimes frightening array of ingredients requires courage in the creative person. It is the "courage to discover new forms, new symbols, new patterns on which a new society can be built."[2] From this description we can see the challenge of God's invitation to be fully human and creative.

The accounts of creation in Genesis 1 and 2 were written during the Exile by two different authors and were used for the same purpose: to form a prologue to the history of the Hebrew people. These people were seen as distinctly selected by God to be the ones through whom the relationship God desires with the whole created order is revealed. As Robert McAfee Brown points out, biblical writers were not trying to prove the existence of God. Rather, they were describing how God is revealed and what that has to do with people. They were "not talking about an idea of a 'something somewhere' that might or might not exist. They were talking about the living Reality who had confronted them, changed their lives, entered into relationship with them."[3] God's existence is not proved but taken for granted, since the writers feel they know God and are known by God. "Put another way," says Brown, "what we find in the Bible is not an accumulation of data about God, but rather a living God in living relationship with living people. These people have not lifted themselves by their own bootstraps into the presence of God. They testify that God has taken the initiative and sought them out."[4]

This gives us clues to how the biblical material can make an enormous difference in our lives. If we keep it at arm's length and use it for objective study only, we will come away simply with more knowledge about Hebrew encounters with God. But if we see the story of the Hebrew nation as the story of Everyone, including us, and seek to enter into a given biblical experience from within, we may find changes occurring in us as dramatic and as creative as any described in the Bible.

Here are two illustrations of what we mean. When Sally Smith, a young woman in her thirties, first heard about the concept of being a co-creator, it was new and important to her. With a husband and two toddlers to love and care for, she had her hands full. Yet meditating on her gift of creativity, she got back in touch with her original desire to become a writer of children's books. As she did the individual design work for these courses, she slowly nurtured this desire, rearranging time and commitments by giving up what she calls "the ministry of availability." She has produced one book, almost finished another, and has begun research on a third. She had thought that being God's person meant doing all the church and community work that was asked. Now she believes that by using her creative gifts fully, she makes a unique contribution to continuing the creation.

What about people with less obvious gifts of creativity? One Sunday service was made memorable by the participation of a young high schooler with severe learning handicaps. At two points she greatly enriched our time together. With warmth and enjoyment she took up the collection and then simply prayed, "Here is our money, Lord. Please do what you want with it." Later, during the time of intercessory prayer, she again prayed very directly, "Please be with the hostages, Lord." Somehow her simplicity and directness cut through all our wandering thoughts and placed us in the presence of God. She was a principal creator of that worship service in a way that more apparently talented people often cannot be.

What is being said here does not really have to do with talent at all, but choice: choosing to honor the essence of every person, including ourselves, and offering over and over again to work and live on the side of creativity and hope rather than that of chaos and despair.

Practically, how do we increase our ability to choose the creative rather than the destructive option? One way is to absorb God's compassionate love for all creation and gain God's perspective on life and events. Bible praying or pondering is a way to open ourselves to and deepen a relationship with God. This is different from Bible study where we attempt to master a book of the Bible or understand the biblical material on a certain theme. Such study is vitally important as a background for Bible pondering but not a substitute for it. Bible pondering involves a more personal and prayerful approach. It involves choosing a short passage, a phrase, or a word and then allowing it and its implications to penetrate our lives, thoughts, and feelings. Then out of that pondering, we might have a conversation with God. It is a way of hearing God's word personally and then responding.

In all our courses we suggest that people arrange to have a quiet time regularly for at least fifteen minutes. This is the crucial lab segment where we open ourselves personally to the experiences related in the Bible. This type of Bible pondering can be done both alone and in a group. During our first group session we will try it together, using a paraphrase of the material in Genesis 1 and 2. That part of the session is a demonstration of the kind of pondering and writing we can experience regularly in our times of quiet.

Group Design

Purpose: To get acquainted, share our hopes for the course, discuss our past experience with scripture, and meditate on and respond to God as

Creator.·
Materials: Marking pens, 8½ x 11 paper.

A. Gathering Time   (10 minutes)   Large Group
Using roughly one minute apiece, share anything you like about your name—first, last, married, maiden names. For example, "My name is Phillip Parker. I feel pretty good about both names. I like Phil because it's not too common, yet most people are familiar with it. Parker is all right, too. It's easy to spell and pronounce. Of course, as a kid I took a lot of ribbing as one not to be trusted by the girls if I asked them to take a spin in my dad's car."

B. Sharing Groups   (20 minutes)
Move into groups of four so that you are with people you do not know well. You can count off to do this, or do it by letters of the alphabet (those with names A-E; F-M; N-R; S-Z) or by any way that will mix you at random. If you happen to end up with spouses or good friends, switch around to find people you know less well. Exchange names and phone numbers, and write them in a notebook for ready reference. Then briefly share hopes and expectations for the course. You might want to jot down the hopes of each person so you can hold those in prayer.
   Note on sharing: A ground rule for sharing is that we should share what is personal and to the point at hand, but we should always feel free to refrain from sharing whenever we prefer to "pass." It is important to remind one another occasionally of this.

C. Our Experience with Scripture   (30 minutes)   Sharing Groups
Take five minutes of silence and think about your past experiences with the Bible—positive, negative, neutral, or nonexistent. As thoughts and memories occur, take some marking pens of your choice and sketch on a piece of 8½ x 11 paper some simple line drawings that depict some of this experience. Put your drawing on the floor in the center of your sharing group. When all have finished, briefly discuss what you drew and why.
   Note on materials: Any simple materials that are needed will be listed on the first page of each group design. It is suggested that the group leaders for any given session provide the materials needed for that session.

D. Experience of God as Creator   (50 minutes)   Sharing Groups
(with same people as above)

1. *Meditation read by one person in a slow and relaxed fashion:* "The following meditation on creation is designed to introduce the group to meditation or Bible pondering. It is a paraphrase of Genesis 1 and 2 that summarizes the message in those chapters. It is written as if it were the voice of God speaking directly to you.

"Before beginning the meditation, get in a comfortable position, with paper and pencil in hand. (Pause while people do this.) Take a few minutes of silence to quiet down. (Pause.) Be still outwardly and inwardly; closing your eyes might help. (Pause.) Imagine God in the room with you. (Pause.) Listen not just for the words that are read but for what message there is for you from God. (Pause.)

"I will read the first paragraph of the meditation twice. When finished, I will say, 'Respond.' At that time I will pause and give you time to respond inwardly and to jot down your responses. When people have finished writing, I will read the second paragraph slowly, ending with 'Respond.' Then there will be a pause for reflection and writing. Don't worry if some people write a lot and others don't. The main thing is to listen, reflect, and respond honestly in your own way. Sometimes that response might be a blank. That is OK. Now I will begin."

Meditation on Creation

Creation has begun. In the beginning there is darkness everywhere. See the darkness. Everything is a wasteland. It has no form. But it is *mine*. I am a creator. I create out of chaos. I create out of nothingness. Respond. (Reader pause for several minutes, allowing time for reflection and writing.)

Let there be light. I separate day from night. The wasteland becomes fertile, full of green. There is water, fish, animals. Day by day I create. There is order here. I am an orderly God. I have a harmonious creation. And it is good. Respond. (Reader pause as above.)

I have formed you—out of clay, out of earth. I have breathed my breath into you. Breathe now, deeply. Hear the sound of my breath in you. Just breathe. My breath is all around. It mingles with my creation. In my image I create you. Male and female I create you. Companionship is good. Respond. (Reader pause as above.)

I bring the animals before you. You name them. You co-create with me. You name things, know things, are fruitful. Your love names and creates. You have responsibility in this good place. I give you these things . . . to care for. Respond. (Reader pause as above.)

I settle you in a fertile land. I am fertile. I walk with you. I talk with you. I feed you. There is union with me if you wish it. Respond. (Reader pause as above.)

Now let us end our meditation.

2. *Sharing instructions read by the one who read the meditation:* "If we wish, we can share some of our responses in our groups. Go around the circle, each sharing our response to the first paragraph. Then go around again and share the second, and so on. Remember, if you prefer not to share, that is fine. Just say 'pass.'"

E. Closing   (10 minutes)   Large Group

Choose a way to close that is appropriate for your group. Possibilities:

1. Evaluate this session. (In a few words, what was helpful? What was not helpful?)

2. Sing.

3. Pray (give thanks to God who creates us and invites us to join in that creation).

4. Discuss details of the next session if necessary (time, place, leadership responsibility).

Individual Work

Purpose: To establish a regular time to be alone with God and to meditate on the meaning of creation for us personally.

As previously indicated, we suggest that you arrange to have a quiet time regularly for fifteen minutes (or more). Don't be discouraged if it is difficult to find a daily time. It is hard for everybody, but do not give up too easily. See this as a gift to yourself, an oasis of quiet, peace, and creativity.

1. *Read:* We suggest that you use your quiet time the first day for some Bible study. This week concentrate on Chapters 1 and 2 of Genesis. Get the full sweep of these passages. Try to understand what they are saying about God as Creator, about God's design for the world and for you in it. You also might review the session text.

2. *Meditate:* During each quiet time after your initial study day, select a theme, word, or phrase in these passages that draws you, stirs you, or freshens creativity in you. Sit with it quietly, allowing its meaning to deepen within you.

3. *Write:* Jot down in your journal any insights that occur to you. Consider writing on these questions: In what ways do I personally cooperate with creation? In what ways do I thwart it?

4. *Pray:* Respond to God out of your ponderings. Also use a few minutes to hold the people in your sharing group before God. You might want to look at their names in your notebook and visualize them receiving some of the blessings of creation.

5. *Bring:* Bring to class an object that symbolizes your experiences of God as Creator this week.

6. *Summarize:* At the end of the week, write a paragraph summarizing what you did with this assignment. Be brief, honest, and to the point. This will help you consolidate your feelings and learnings and prepare you for the next session.

Notes

1. *Original Blessing* (Santa Fe: Bear & Company, Inc., 1983), p. 231.
2. (New York: Norton, 1975).
3. *The Bible Speaks to You* (Philadelphia: The Westminster Press, 1960), p. 39.
4. Ibid., p. 41.

Session 2

Caller

It is one thing to believe in God as Creator. It is quite another to realize that all people and nations have been called into a special relationship with this loving God. All have been invited to share in the work of extending God's love and justice. This is spelled out in great detail in the stories of Sarah, Abraham, and Moses.

Picture Abraham and Sarah enjoying retirement life. One day Abraham announces that he has heard a special call from God:

> Go forth from the land of your kinsfolk . . . to a land that I will show
>   you.

> I will make of you a great nation,
>   and I will bless you:
> I will make your name great,
>   so that you will be a blessing.
> I will bless those who bless you
>   and curse those who curse you.
> All the communities of the earth
>   shall find blessing in you.

>   (Gen. 12:1-3, NAB)

Abraham's vocation was to receive and extend God's blessing to all the communities of the earth—an important vocation indeed. He was to do this by establishing a nation whose way of living could truly be described as "blessed" and which would, like Abraham, extend this blessing to all.[1]

Scripture does not detail the responses of this remarkable old couple. It simply records that Abraham and Sarah gathered up their household and possessions and set out for the new land of Canaan. Once there, they pitched a tent, built an altar to Yahweh, and worshiped. After some time,

22

God made the promise to Abraham clearer: "All the land that you see I will give to you and your descendants forever. I will make your descendants like the dust of the earth; if anyone could count the dust of the earth, your descendants too might be counted" (Gen. 13:15,16, NAB).

The story of Abraham and Sarah in the land of Canaan is well known. When Abraham asked God how he could have descendants, since he and Sarah were childless, God assured him that the heir would be "of your own blood." By the time Abraham was eighty-six, nothing had happened, so he and Sarah took matters into their own hands and arranged for Abraham to conceive a child with Sarah's maid, Hagar. Finally when Abraham was ninety-nine, God again approached him, reiterated the promise, and changed Abram's name to Abraham. God assured Sarah that she would bear a son, which she did when Abraham was a hundred years old. Sarah's reaction to all this was deep amusement: "God has given me cause to laugh; all those who hear of it will laugh with me." And so the child was named Isaac, or "God has laughed."

This improbable story carries some important truths. Abraham has always been described by the Jewish people as "faithful." Why? Certainly not because of his belief in God: He kept questioning the promises of Yahweh. It was not because of his moral rectitude: He had tried to palm his wife off as his sister in order to save his own neck and look out for Number One. It was not because of his superior knowledge of God: He seemed to need things repeated a number of times. It was because of what he did, how he acted, how he obeyed God's command to leave one place and move to another. Most important, Abraham was willing to enter into a relationship with God, to be a part of a covenant with God—a living, working partnership.

Throughout the Bible, God is portrayed as choosing to enter into a personal relationship with individuals and nations (at first the Jewish nation, later all nations). They are called to do a special work with God, to participate in a covenant with God.

For Abraham and Sarah, this meant saying yes to God's unlikely plan, moving to a new place, and parenting a son and heir.

For Moses, it involved returning to his people and leading them out of oppression in Egypt. When Moses heard what God had in mind, he was less than thrilled. In fact, he wanted no part of it. His mutterings and resistances are spelled out in detail in Exodus 3. Moses had five objections to God's call, but Yahweh was ready with five responses. Here they are, slightly paraphrased:

Moses:	"Who am I to go to Pharaoh and bring my people out of Egypt?"
God:	"I will be with you . . . and as a sign of this, offer worship on the mountain" (the promise of presence).
Moses:	"What shall I say to my own people when I go to them?"
God:	"Tell them who I am, that I have seen their oppression and want to deliver them" (the promise of a mission).
Moses:	"People won't believe me or listen to me. They won't believe you've called me."
God:	"I will give you signs along the way that will provide meaning and reassurance" (the promise of support).
Moses:	"I'm not a public speaker—I can't think on my feet."
God:	"Go! I'll be with you and teach you what to say" (the promise of guidance).
Moses:	"Can't you send someone else?"
God:	"All right. Here's Aaron. Take him. I'll instruct you what to do, and then he can speak for you as your mouthpiece" (the promise of companionship).

Together, the stories about Sarah, Abraham, and Moses have much to tell us about God and persons. God is seen not simply as one who creates the world, winds it up like a watch and lets it go on running by itself, but as one who chooses continually to be in a loving, creative relationship with persons, one who calls them to special work. In the Bible, naming has great significance. Often a relationship with God is sealed with a special name. God is seen not only as loving humankind in general, but also as wanting a special relationship with individuals. Isaiah portrays God as saying, "I have called you by your name, you are mine. Should you pass through the sea, I will be with you. . . . Do not be afraid, for I am with you" (Is. 43:2-5, JB).

When one gets low, two thoughts occur: I'm worthless, and I don't fit anywhere. People often ask, "What does my life mean? Why am I here?" The promises to Abraham strike basic chords in all of us: the desire to be fruitful, to have our lives count for something, and to have a place, a home, our spot in the universe.

Both stories illustrate some important points about our response to God's choosing us and calling us into a loving, fruitful relationship. The example of Abraham and Sarah assures us that no one is too old or too barren to become fruitful when touched by God. Moses shows us that past failure (he had killed an Egyptian in a fit of anger) does not disqualify us for present or future usefulness. Even inner resistance can be overcome if one listens for the word of God in specifics. What seems to be required is not great talent, intelligence, or attractiveness, but a willingness to say yes to God's invitation to collaboration and companionship.

People today hear and respond to God's call in different ways. Sometimes it comes in a direct, definitive way: "Ever since I was seven, I knew I was to be a doctor." But for many the process is gradual, beginning with a "whisper," as one person described it, rather than a definite call. Dag Hammarskjöld described this beautifully when he wrote:

> I don't know Who—or what—put the question, I don't know when it was put. I don't even remember answering. But at some moment I did answer Yes to Someone—or Something—and from that hour I was certain that existence is meaningful and that, therefore, my life, in self-surrender, had a goal.[2]

Moses' experience gives us further clues as to how this works out in real life. For many people, hearing and responding to the call of God comes when they are absolutely alone. It was so with Moses when he was tending his sheep at the mountain of Horeb. He reported seeing a burning bush that was not consumed by the flame. He heard a voice call from the center of the bush, "Moses! Moses!"

"Here I am," he answered.
  "Come no nearer. . . .

Take off your shoes, for the place on which you stand is holy
ground" (Ex. 3:5, JB).

Afraid to look, Moses covered his face. He was told that God knew of the
oppression of his people in Egypt and was sending Moses to bring them
out of that land.

"A moment of disclosure" such as this is not as rare today as one
might suppose. A recent Gallup poll found that many people have
comparable experiences of God's presence. This is borne out in our work
with groups. We encourage people to look back over their lives and
remember times that they might describe as "holy ground"—moments
when an awareness of God was particularly keen, or when a burning
issue within was somehow felt to be understood and blessed by God and
experienced as a God-given task or mission. People in the groups
invariably recall such times, and occasionally someone is led to a
specific action as a result. A prominent black leader told about an
occasion when his daughter was refused a ride on a roller coaster
controlled by whites. It was as if God tapped him on the shoulder and
said, "Do something about this." He went on to devote his life to
building understanding between people of different races.

The first awareness of God's call may occur in a moment of inspiration. Sometimes the initial experience comes as a surprise. Seemingly,
we have nothing to do with it. We feel visited or approached by God in
ways we did not expect or earn. But as we seek greater clarity, we find
that our own effort and decision come into play. Sometimes it is not easy
to create that place of silence and solitude where we can have further
dialogue with God. Dolores Leckey recalls how, as a busy young mother
of four youngsters, she began to find the time to be alone with God in
silence:

A household full of small children, telephones, community and
church responsibilities does not readily lend itself to silence.
Yet my journey into books, my discussions with spiritual friends,
my innermost instincts were all pointing to the need to be in touch
with the experience of silence—quiet prayer. Hadn't God spoken
to Elijah in a close-to-silent whisper? How would I learn to listen?

I looked at the shape of a typical day and noticed some space.
There was *nap time*, usually grasped at as an opportunity to accom-

plish tasks I couldn't get to when the children were awake. Shift, reverse. Instead of stuffing the space of nap time with various good deeds, I stopped. I did nothing . . . or so it seemed. No radio, no telephone, just silence. . . .

I entered this mid-day Sabbath, sometimes with Scripture, sometimes with other writings; often with restlessness and anxiety; sometimes with eager anticipation and frequently with fatigue. My time alone often ended in sleep, just like the children. "I give sleep to my beloved," sings the psalmist. One thing became clearer and clearer: The less articulate the experience, the greater certitude I had of its importance.[3]

As we have seen, one thing Moses did in his silence was to bring all his complaints and objections to God. In our groups, we encourage people to think about a call they may feel from God or an area in which they would like to have a sense of calling. Next they are invited to address to God their resistances, reservations, or problems with that call and then to imagine the kind of reply that God would make to each of their difficulties. It is surprising what breakthroughs can happen when such a dialogue develops.

But before people can get started on such a dialogue, they need to deal with their initial questions.

- What does a call feel like?
- How do I know if I am really called by God, or if it is a figment of my imagination?
- What about the things I'm already doing—my job, my marriage, my family? What if I entered into them without a consciousness of God's call? Can they become a call?
- Does being called by God always mean leaving what you're doing for something else?
- What if God calls me to do something I can't do or don't want to do? It's a scary idea. Is God going to require a kind of giving or sacrifice I'm too small to make?
- Can I have more than one call? Or does my call change as my life develops?
- Is God's call a general one, such as being obedient in everything, or loving God and neighbor, or does it involve a particular work for me?

• Do I have to be at a certain level of spiritual development to hear God's call?

These are some of the questions that come up when we introduce the idea that God calls each one personally. Of course, a clear answer does not come for each of these questions at once. Clarity of call is an evolving thing and takes much time. Certainty or conviction about call seems to come and go. In Morris West's *The Clowns of God,* the former pope, Jean Marie Barette, experienced a call from God that was crystal clear; but listen to how he felt as he tried to live it out each day:

> Sometimes I am in a darkness so deep, so threatening, that it seems I have been stripped of all human form and damned to an eternal solitude. At other times I am bathed in a luminous calm, totally at peace, yet harmoniously active, like an instrument in the hands of a great master. . . . I cannot read the score; I have no urge to interpret it, only a serene confidence that the dream of the composer is realized in me at every moment . . . the problem is . . . that the terror and the calm both take me unaware. They go as suddenly as they come, and they leave my days as full of holes as a Swiss cheese.[4]

We need to be cautioned against taking too rigid an idea of call. If we learn anything from the biblical record, it is that call is experienced in countless ways. But several common threads run through these experiences. It does seem that those who feel called by God have at one time or another said yes in a definite and wholehearted way, however much they may have doubted later. Also, these people continually position themselves to listen to God and nurture this sense of calling by making space for time alone with God daily and for longer periods of retreat. They are intent on attuning themselves to how God is working today through contemporary reading, taking account of historical trends, participating in growth events, and talking with people who have a sense of call.

For some, call is always quite general: "I do not feel I am called to a specific task. I believe I am being called to find and follow God," said one group member recently. For others, it becomes more specific. "Welcome all people into my church" was one man's call as he worked with this material. Some have a lifelong call. For others, it changes as life conditions change. One central call comes to some people, whereas others may feel twin vocations to family and work, for example. One of our participants gave a firm yes to God and found she was called to move from a cherished home in one city where she was known and loved to a new city where she knew no one. Eight years ago as a newcomer to our area, she joined one of our groups and said, "I know I have a call, but I don't know what it is. I just know I want to find out." Over the years, she thought and prayed and talked with people and investigated possibilities. Recently she told a group of us that she felt settled and happy as the director of a new center for the elderly poor in the inner city. Not only was she called away from Philadelphia to Washington, but from the suburbs to the inner city. In contrast, another participant said, "It wasn't that I felt called to do something different after I dealt with Moses. Rather, I felt called to do what I was already doing but in a different way."

As for waiting to achieve a feeling of adequacy or spiritual maturity, the Bible reminds us that doubting Abraham, barren Sarah, and resistant Moses were not perfect. They had limitations and handicaps like the rest of us. But they were open to act in a new way and to respond to God's inviting love.

So we encourage people to cultivate a similar openness, to plunge in and start thinking about God's calling. In each course we return to the idea of vocation, knowing that responding to God's call is a lifelong challenge.

Group Design

Purpose: To learn more about one another, reflect on a time of closeness with God, and discuss our feelings and thoughts about being called by God.

A. Gathering Time   (15 minutes)   Large Group
This is a way to connect with one another on the basis of points of origin. Using roughly one minute for each person, share your name and hometown. Then tell one good thing and one bad thing about your hometown. For example, "My name is Ben Davis, and my hometown is

Washington, D.C. A good thing about it is the stimulation of living in the nation's capital. A bad thing about it is that many people are here for only a short time, so friends move away and leave us behind."

B. Sharing Groups   (20 minutes)
The art of sharing what you did with the individual work reinforces your learnings, enhances your perspective through exposure to other people's experience, and is a way of being accountable to the group for what you were able to do. Each in turn, share what you did with the individual work. Tell one insight that occurred, a feeling you had, and a difficulty. Also report how it felt to hold your group members and their expectations in prayer. Remember to keep your sharing brief and pertinent to what happened this week as you did the work. After each person has had a turn, use the rest of the time to respond to one another. Try to be open with both your positive and your negative feelings and reactions. Only in that way can you assess where you are and proceed from there.
    Note: This is a time to check in briefly with one another rather than to share fully. Our experience is that such brief times can inspire more exploration and growth.

C. Check-in Time on the Reading   (35 minutes)   Large Group
See if everyone read the chapter. If necessary, summarize the main points as a review. Then discuss the material objectively—i.e., what the session text said and what your reactions were. You might use these questions:
• What do you think of the statement that each of us is called to companionship and collaboration with God?
• Where am I in my response? Do I believe God is calling me? Do I want to hear that call? Do I want to respond? What are my hopes and fears as I consider my response?
• Regarding the questions on page 27 of the text, can we illustrate them through personal experience, either our own or that of someone we know?

D. Meditation and Sharing on a Holy Moment   (40 minutes)   Large Group
This is a way to open ourselves to God's presence and to consider its meaning for today.
    1. Get settled comfortably with paper and pen for a time of quiet

meditation. Be together in a few minutes of relaxed silence.

2. Someone read aloud, slowly, the story of Moses' encounter with God in the burning bush (Exodus 3:1-6).

3. Silently recall a time of closeness with God, a time when you sensed God's presence. It might be long ago or recently; it could be vivid and easy to recall, or more dim and difficult to remember. Be silent now and remember. When something comes to mind, get back into that experience; relive it. As you do this, describe the experience in writing. Where were you? What were you doing? In what way was God real to you? What awareness came to you? What was your response?

Note: Some people will write very readily and at length. Others will write very little. Perhaps some will not be able to recall such a memory or have not had such an experience. This is all right. Simply rest in the silence, noticing the thoughts that come. The learning for today may be that you have not had such an experience.

4. After everyone has finished, divide into groups of two or three, preferably with people not in your sharing group. Share what you have written, either reading or telling about the experience. Again be brief. Give each person a turn before you open your session to general response. Feel free to pass if you do not wish to share.

E. Closing   (10 minutes)   Large Group
Choose one or two of the following as appropriate for your group: evaluation of session, song, details of next session, prayer of thanks for those times God has been revealed to you and to others.

Individual Work

Purpose: To examine our sense of calling, our problems with it, and ways God might help us.

1. Read Exodus chapters 3 and 4:1-17. Examine the call of Moses, his various objections to it, and God's response to each of his problems.

2. Reflect on an area in which you might feel called or would like to hear a call from God.

3. Like Moses, be honest about your objections or resistances to this call. Write them down.

4. In response to each objection, try to imagine and record what God's response might be. Remember that you are dealing with a loving, compassionate God who wants to offer illumination and help, not an angry God who wants to belittle or discourage you.

5. To prepare for the next session, write a brief summary of your personal work with this assignment as mentioned in Session 1, Individual Work, number 6.

Notes

1. For an extended treatment of this theme of blessing, see Matthew Fox, *Original Blessing* (Santa Fe: Bear & Company, 1983), especially pp. 42-57.
2. *Markings* (New York: Alfred A. Knopf, 1964), p. 205.
3. "A Personal Pilgrimage: Experiences of Common Contemplatives," in *The Wind Is Rising,* William R. Callahan, S.J., and Francine Cardman, eds. (Hyattsville, Md.: Quixote Center, 1978), p. 27.
4. (New York: Bantam Books, 1981), pp. 118-119.

Session 3

Deliverer

For centuries the story of Moses leading the Israelites out of Egypt has been pivotal for Hebrew people. Over and over again they hearken back to this story. It speaks to them of one colossal truth: God is our deliverer!

But this story makes the point in a strange way. In Egypt, the Hebrew people lived in oppression and slavery under the rule of the Pharaoh, who governed with a cruel and firm hand. Along came Moses. Although a Hebrew, he had been brought up by the Pharoah's daughter among the Egyptians. Subsequently Moses returned to his own people with this message: Yahweh wanted to free the Hebrews from slavery, adopt them as his own people, and bring them to the land he had sworn to give to Abraham and Sarah.

Moses then went to Pharaoh with these words of Yahweh: "Let my people go, that they may celebrate a feast to me in the desert." Pharaoh refused. "I know nothing of Yahweh, and I will not let Israel go" (Ex. 5:2, JB). His response was to increase the workload of the slaves so they would not have time to listen to the glib speeches of Moses.

About this time, a series of calamities, commonly known as the ten plagues, fell upon Egypt: infestations of locusts, mosquitoes, gnats, and frogs, distressing disease in cattle and humans, and fearful thunder and sandstorms. The severity and rapidity of these events caused both the Pharaoh and the Israelites to reverse their positions. Pharaoh believed this death and destruction was caused by the angry god of the Israelites. Summoning Moses and Aaron in the middle of the night, he told them to be off quickly, to worship God as they had asked. The Hebrews concluded that Moses was indeed a messenger from God and a worthy leader to follow. Leaving their homes for the desert, they celebrated a feast with unleavened bread to commemorate their safe deliverance.

But they soon found themselves pursued by the Egyptians, who had had a change of heart. The Israelites berated Moses for having dragged them into the wilderness. "Far better for us to be the slaves of the Egyptians than to die in the desert," they cried (Ex. 14:12, NAB). Somehow Moses calmed their fears and convinced them that God would indeed come to their rescue. Then he led his people safely across a shallow place in the Sea of Reeds just before the wind rose. As the tide returned, it overwhelmed the Egyptian forces.

This wholly unexpected destruction of their pursuers filled the Israelites with wonder and thanks. The writer concludes the story by saying the people "put their faith in Yahweh and in Moses" (Ex. 14:31, JB). With the prophetess Miriam leading, they exulted that Yahweh was their strength and song (Ex. 15:1-2).

They knew their deliverance was due to no merit of their own. They were at the end of their resources and could do nothing to help themselves. To them their deliverance was miraculous: God had used the wind, the tide, and the panic of the Egyptians to save them. Over and over again they returned to these events in song, history, and prophecy and saw them as reminders that God cares for people and acts on their behalf. They believed that in a special way God had selected the Hebrew people, a tiny, weak, often cowardly and ungrateful nation, to be a vehicle for divine revelation. In dark nights of fear and oppression, God could indeed bring freedom and song.

What about today? What about us? Can we, do we, see and experience God as deliverer? It is clear that many people in the midst of various kinds of political, psychological, or spiritual oppression do experience freedom and the ability to sing a new song. Bruce Laingen, American hostage returned from Iran, told his home congregation that there was no hostage he knew of who failed to draw on religious strength during the long ordeal. He admitted that at times some felt that "God must be sitting this one out." Yet in solitary confinement during "nightly dialogues with my God," Mr. Laingen was able not only to repeat but to believe powerful faith statements in the psalms. A favorite was the great 118th Easter psalm containing the same lines as in the song of Moses and his people:

"Yahweh is my strength and my song."

(Ps. 118:14, JB)

Sometimes our deliverances can be personal and private. One man approached faith from a skeptic's viewpoint, poking fun at the faith of others, seeing where he could trip them up. He did this good-naturedly with wit and finesse, but then he came to see how unproductive and destructive that was. "I feel free to move to a different place. I'm not yet a believing person, but now I want to approach the faith of others with respect and interest, rather than with an angry skepticism. I'm excited by this new attitude."

Down the ages, the Exodus story has inspired many oppressed peoples around the world. "Go Down Moses" was the well-known rallying song for black slaves; by it they signaled to one another the freedom of their spirits and their willingness to help escaped slaves use the underground railway. Similarly, Bishop Desmond Tutu, a leader in the struggle against apartheid in South Africa, says, "You whites brought us the Bible; now we blacks are taking it seriously. We are involved with God to set us free from all that enslaves us and makes us less than what he intended us to be." For oppressed people in Poland, Latin America, and other areas, the Exodus is a powerful story motivating them and their friends in their struggle together for freedom.

It is important to note another point in the Exodus story. One would think that if this were a story about deliverance, it would begin with a description of danger and end with a picture of safety. Yet the reverse is true. The Israelites in Egypt were not free, but they had a familiar way of life that at least provided meals and a roof over their heads. They were freed from that to spend forty years in the wilderness, with no knowledge of how they would procure food and shelter, and with no social structure to which they could belong. Why would God free them and then send them to such a desolate place as a desert or wilderness? The answer seemed to be that deeper experiences of deliverance were in store for them there—ones that they could experience only away from the familiar material and social supports.

Hunger pangs fueled angry complaints from the Hebrew community against their leaders. Moses again took the complaints directly to God, who provided quail for meat each evening and a strange bread each morning. Enough quail and manna were provided for each day, but no more—a lesson in total dependence on God's goodness.

The people also told Moses they were dying of thirst. Again they felt delivered. God told Moses to strike the rock at Horeb and "water will flow from it for the people to drink." And that is exactly what happened. The place was then named Massah and Meribah or "trial and contention" because that was where the people put God to the test by asking again, "Is Yahweh with us, or not?" (Ex. 17:7, JB).

In a third story, the Israelites were attacked by a tribe called the Amalekites. The battle leader for the Israelites was Joshua. Moses promised to go up on the heights with his special staff (see Ex. 4:1-5 and 7:8-13) and to raise his arms in prayerful support for the duration of the engagement. As long as Moses was able to keep his arms raised, the Israelites were successful; but when he became tired and let them fall, the advantage went to the enemy. Moses' companions, Aaron and Hur, gave the tired leader a stone on which to sit and then held his arms up themselves. With this cooperative support, the Israelites were victorious.

It was in events like these that the Israelites continued to experience their God as deliverer. One psalmist wrote:

Give thanks to Yahweh. . . .
Some had lost their way in the wilds and the desert,
not knowing how to reach an inhabited town;
they were hungry and desperately thirsty,
their courage was running low.

Then they called to Yahweh in their trouble
and he rescued them from their sufferings.

                                        (Ps. 107:1,4,5,6, JB)

This is the psalm that Pastor John Robinson prayed in 1620 with his little congregation before sending some of them off on the *Mayflower* to start life in the New World. It expressed his conviction that as these loved ones went from safety to the unknown dangers of a new existence, they would somehow, in unexpected ways, experience support, nourishment, and an inner freedom in the midst of struggle.

This must be something of what Rose Elizabeth Bird, Chief Justice of California, experienced in her bouts with recurring cancer. In an address to a community forum on breast cancer she spoke of the devastation and desolation she felt when her disease flared up again and when she found that her own physician had died of cancer. "As a direct result of these two circumstances, I went through a type of catharsis," she said. She read all she could on the subject and seriously considered the possibility that she might have only a few years left to live:

> When you face the fact of your own mortality, you must also face the facts about what you have done with your life. In a peculiar way, death can teach you what life is all about. It is a painful lesson and a difficult journey, but I am personally grateful that I was made to travel this path at a relatively early age. For I have learned much about myself, much about what I want out of life and much about how precious life and people are. It is our relationships with others, especially those whom we love, that give the fullest meaning to life. I don't think I ever really knew that, emotionally or intellectually, until my second bout with cancer.[1]

In her personal desert, Rose Elizabeth Bird found in a new way the support of loved ones, the nourishment of hard knowledge, and a kind of inner liberation despite the statistics on breast cancer and mortality rates. She concludes with this word of encouragement:

> For those who are facing this disease and for those of you who may one day face it, let me say to you . . . [h]ave courage, face the facts, and you will find that when you have faced your fears and stood your ground there occurs a kind of liberation. It is not an easy journey. It can be quite painful and lonely. But it is a journey that must be made.
>
> [I]t is not a hopeless situation. It is neither too painful nor too fearful to face. Most importantly, it is an opportunity to find out about life. And isn't that really why each of us has been placed here?[2]

To relate to this material and to discover God's message in it for us, during our group sessions on this theme we share Karl Olsson's method called relational Bible study from *Find Yourself in the Bible*. Very simply, there are four steps:

1. Make the story my story.
2. Identify with a character or element in the story.
3. Find the good news in the story.

4. Name the story.[3]

As a demonstration, we suggest doing a group study on the story of the Exodus. Principal elements of the story are put on newsprint, and then the group suggests words and phrases to describe these elements. This is what resulted in one session:

• Egypt: place of bondage, oppression.
• Red Sea: a boundary that needs to be crossed, an obstacle to be overcome.
• God: opting for freedom; practical, offers help in specific ways.
• Moses: persistent, tuned to a new vision, not stuck in the old way.
• Israelites: complaining, kicking and screaming, moving but not happily.
• Egyptians: opponents of freedom, plowing ahead despite destructive possibilities.
• Desert: unknown, place of no support.

People in the group identified with different elements. One, engaged in developing a literacy program that was moving along slowly, felt like a resistant Israelite until the board, with a Moses-type vision, offered to help her overcome resistance to fund raising and thereby enabled her to expand the scope of the work. Another person admitted to feeling that he was his own Red Sea by allowing his inner attitudes to become obstacles to his creativity.

The good news that people perceived was that often in situations where we feel bound or stuck, tangible help is available even though we sometimes don't recognize it.

Groups and individuals who go through these steps for relational Bible study and then name the story can have some humorous and profound insights. One group, for instance, called the story of the manna and quail "Don't Wail, There's Quail!" Although approached with a playful attitude, even this final step of relational Bible study can heighten people's consciousness of God's deliverance in their own lives.

Individuals and oppressed peoples may see or experience God's deliverance in tangible ways, but what about great events, natural disasters, wars, and unthinkable acts of brutality like the Holocaust? It goes without saying that in certain circumstances we cannot recognize God as deliverer. It is an inappropriate or implausible image. In retrospect, we can sometimes see the true meaning of this image: that in all circumstances God is for us, caring deeply about our well-being. Sometimes, however, we cannot see even that. We are left with pain, mystery, and questions for which there are no ready answers. The absence as well as the presence of God is a part of the biblical story and our story as well, and it can be seen most powerfully in Isaiah's image of the Suffering Servant, which will be described in the fifth session.

Nevertheless, one persistent biblical message is that in the midst of suffering, when people feel most hopeless and helpless, new life and promise can and do break through.

Group Design

Purpose: To strengthen the sense of community among group members, to review some of the major biblical examples of God's delivering action, and to learn a method of relating biblical material to our lives.
Materials: Bibles, newsprint sheets, marking pens.

A. Gathering Time   (15 minutes)   Large Group
This is a way of strengthening the sense of community and caring. Standing in a circle, all share briefly what they left behind as they came to this session—e.g., dirty dishes, some unmade phone calls, an important conversation. Then turn to the person on your right and give him or her a shoulder or back rub; you will be forming a connecting chain to do this. After a couple of minutes, turn around and rub the back of the person who just did yours. Then face inward and begin with informal prayer for the session.

B. Sharing Groups   (20 minutes)
Each one share briefly the work you did with the assignment and how the prayer for one another went. Remember the basic suggestions for effective sharing: Make it brief, personal, to the point. If you prefer not to share, say that simply. No excuses or justifications are necessary. Be honest, and describe what happened this week with the assignment. Give everyone a chance to speak before offering responses or encouragements.

C. Check-in Time on the Reading   (15 minutes)   Large Group
If necessary, summarize the main biblical and contemporary stories mentioned in the reading, and the major points they are meant to illustrate.

D. Relational Bible Study on Deliverance   (60 minutes)   Small Groups, then Large Group

If you have not already done so, briefly review the instructions for relational Bible study in the text. Now divide into three groups different from your regular sharing groups. Each group will do a relational Bible study on a different scripture, choosing from these three: Exodus 16:1-21 (the story of the manna and the quail); Exodus 17:1-7 (the water from the rock); Exodus 17:8-13 (the battle against the Amalekites).

1. Each group move into different parts of the room, or if possible different rooms, for privacy. One person in each group read the passage aloud.

2. List the principal characters or elements in the story, with descriptive words beside them.

3. Each one share the element or character with which he or she identifies and why.

4. Share what seems to be good news in this story for you.

5. Brainstorm on names for the story, and select one or two favorites.

6. Work out a way to present the story, the good news, and the name to the whole group. Consider doing a skit, a drawing, or some other way to get the story across.

Pointers: Use about 20 minutes for the above. You will be working quickly. Go with first impressions. The mood can be light and fun even though you are dealing with profound material.

When all the groups are finished, present your stories for one another. As time permits, allow a few moments for discussion of the material or the method.

E. Closing   (10 minutes)   Large Group

Choose one or two of the following suggestions as appropriate for your group: evaluation of session, song, details of next session, prayer of thanks for times when God's deliverance has been real to you.

Individual Work

Purpose: To look at areas in our lives where we need God's deliverance.

1. We suggest the terms *Egypt* and *desert* be used to mean the following: Egypt—areas of bondage, oppression, or satisfaction with the status quo; dependence on things that prevent new growth (in self-understand-

ing, social responsibility, etc.); desert—where God can confront or test me and be revealed in a new way. During the week meditate and journal on how these images apply to your own life. Feel free to let them carry you where they will. The following questions might be useful:

• What is an Egypt for you?
• What is a desert for you?
• Do you have motivation to leave Egypt? What is it?
• Do you need help to leave Egypt? What kind?
• What is happening to you in the desert? How do you react?
• What do you think God is trying to do?

2. To be ready for the next session: Write a brief summary of your personal work with this assignment.

Note: These images strike people in many different ways. For some they explain a great deal of what is happening to them. For others they may not seem relevant at this time. But our experience is that it is helpful for all group members to try the exercises. Experiential learning of this kind has great staying power. If you go through the work now, it will be yours to draw on when it may be more pertinent to your life situation.

Notes

1. An address to the First Annual Community Forum on Breast Cancer, Los Angeles, May 3, 1980. Reprinted with permission.
2. Ibid.
3. Karl A. Olsson, *Find Yourself in the Bible* (Minneapolis: Augsburg Publishing House, 1974), pp. 37-43.

Session 4

Covenant-Maker

We have seen that Old Testament people experienced God as Creator, as one who could bring form out of chaos. They found that there was something good and harmonious about the whole creation, that men and women were invited and called to companionship and collaboration with the Creator. What was needed was a definite yes on their part, although they frequently offered a no or an evasion. Going with Yahweh, following that divine lead, was no guarantee against trouble. Old Testament people were convinced, however, that even in their trouble, God would act as Deliverer. For the Israelites, following Yahweh meant leaving the familiar situation of Egypt for the unknown terrors of the desert, finally arriving at the mountain where Moses had originally heard the call from God. However this time a new revelation was given at the mountain, one that showed the people that God's love for them was tangible and real.

From Mt. Sinai, God called to Moses and gave him this message for the people:

> You have seen for yourselves how I treated the Egyptians and how I bore you up on eagle wings and brought you here to myself. Therefore, if you hearken to my voice and keep my covenant, you shall be my special possession, dearer to me than all other people, though all the earth is mine. You shall be to me a kingdom of priests, a holy nation.
>
> (Ex. 19:4-6, NAB)

This covenant between Yahweh and the Israelites was the groundwork for a flourishing, fruitful relationship. One commentator describes the terms:

> On the divine side the terms were never stated. But it was assumed that Yahweh would be all that God can be to His people. The

42

absence of specific obligations on God's side also suggests that man cannot presume to maneuver God or hold Him accountable. On the human side the obligations were later set down in two sets of commandments rather different from each other.[1]

The familiar Ten Commandments (or Ethical Dialogue) are in Exodus 20. The ceremonial version is in Exodus 34.

Five religious responsibilities (loyalty to God alone, intolerance of idolatry and profanity, public worship, respect for parents) and five social obligations (protection of human life, of marriage, property, and reputation, and restriction upon greed) provided the basis for forming the desert clans into a confederation under God. These commandments were summarized in words inscribed in stone and then housed in an ornamental box called the Ark, which was carried about as the people moved, and which occupied a place of honor in the encampments. Yahweh was thought to reside in the Ark but was not confined to it.

This desert covenant between God and the Israelite confederation was sealed in a public ceremony involving sacrifice. Blood was sprinkled on the altar and on the people to signify solemn bonding. Then a sacrificial meal was celebrated.

As the tribes became more settled, the ramifications of the Covenant were spelled out in greater and greater detail until finally there was danger that the original intent of a love pact would be buried under the weight of rules and regulations. It was against this type of development that the prophets spoke out in later years. In the dying days of the Kingdom of Judah, Jeremiah in particular articulated the idea of the Covenant in new and compelling terms. How could the Hebrews make sense of God's covenant with their nation when that nation was falling apart? Jeremiah voices these words of Yahweh:

> This is the covenant I will make with the House of Israel when those days arrive—it is Yahweh who speaks. Deep within them I will plant my Law, writing it on their hearts. Then I will be their God and they shall be my people.
>
> (Jer. 31:33, JB)

For Jeremiah, the covenant was operative between God and the faithful remnant, not with the entire nation, whose population largely turned aside from that love.

The prophet Isaiah articulated a poignant description of God's reaching to each person's heart:

> "Can a woman forget her sucking child,
>   that she should have no compassion on the fruit of her womb?
> Even these may forget,
>   yet I will not forget you.
> Behold, I have graven you on the palms of my hands."
>
> (Is. 49:15,16)[2]

All through the Bible there are references to the Covenant. To Noah, God said,

> "See, I am now establishing my covenant with you and your descendants after you. . . . that never again shall all bodily creatures be destroyed by the waters of a flood; there shall not be another flood to devastate the earth."
>
> (Gen. 9:8,11, NAB)

The sign of the Covenant for Noah was the rainbow. Ancient writers told the story of Abraham in terms of covenant:

> "I will make you most fruitful. I will make you into nations. . . . I will establish my covenant between myself and you, and your descendants after you. . . . I will be your God."
>
> (Gen. 17:6-8, JB)

The psalms and the prophets make countless references to the Covenant. In the New Testament, Christ is seen as an embodiment of God's covenant love for us, and the Eucharist is the expression of that love.

Why all this emphasis on the Covenant? What does it mean for those who wrote about it and for us today? Though the wording and understanding of the Covenant change and develop in scripture, one meaning remains constant. The unseen God yearns to love us in visible, tangible ways—ways we can see and touch and feel. The terms or elements of that loving relationship God wants with us are clear, written down, and restated often throughout scripture in order to open us to the Covenant's present reality over and over again.

When one begins to get a glimmer of the real meaning and impact of God's covenant love for us, it is as telling and as life-changing as the time when lover reaches to beloved with a proposal for marriage, or when a religious order says, "Yes, we accept you, we want you to be a part of us forever."

All the biblical signs, understandings, and rituals are attempts to express the inexpressible—that our God is not a remote, distant deity who waits to be discovered and worshiped. Yahweh reaches out to humankind, cares deeply, goes after the lost, is faithful even in the face of an unfaithful response.

We who have the privilege of knowing the story of this faithful love as recorded in scripture—how do we respond? Certainly many people see their marriage covenant as a tangible way of relating to God's covenant love. For others, adult baptism or confirmation are ways to mark a desire to begin to live in that covenant love. They see faithful reception of word and sacrament as ongoing nourishment for that relationship. However, these expressions of covenant can go stale and be taken for granted. That is why marriage and faith renewal efforts are so important.

For many people the true impact of God's covenant love for them does not come alive until they approach it in a totally fresh way. This is what we encourage in our groups. We offer an opportunity to respond explicitly by suggesting that participants write a response to these questions:

• Can you consider the possibility of a covenant relationship with God at this time?
• Can you write a statement expressing such a covenant with God? (Include not only what you wish that relationship to be but what you wish to do to bring it about.)

This can be challenging. It not only offers people an opportunity to respond to God explicitly; it asks them to ponder concrete ways to live out that response every day.

When presented with this challenge, people have all sorts of reactions. Some are delighted and feel privileged to articulate their response tangibly. One of these people is Ruth Powell, the widowed mother of a friend of ours. In a beautiful book of quotations and photos entitled *The Widow,* her daughter, Mary Clare, has portrayed Ruth's life in the period of adjustment after the death of her husband. Though she never uses the term *covenant,* Ruth did indeed determine a way of living in covenant love for a whole year. This is how she did it, told in her own words:

> Very quickly, I drew a circle. In the center I wrote R and G—that stood for Ruth and God, meaning that I wasn't in this alone. Then I made pieces of a pie. This was what I wanted my life to be about at this present time.
>
> My physical life—food, clothing, and shelter. Food—I wanted to learn a few new things to cook. Things that were simple and healthful. Clothing—"Well, Ruth, you need to spruce up a little bit," I said, so I put a little emphasis on appearance and so on. Shelter—I knew that my house was to be part of a rehabilitation program any time now, and I would have to spend some of my efforts on that.
>
> A small slice was a little project that I was going to think up—doing something for somebody else. My little mission. I did think of a volunteer activity that I could offer at the North End School. So I initiated that, which I felt very good about.
>
> The next piece was the art of socializing—I put "Fun and Games" in parentheses. I had needs there. I knew I needed more fun. I needed some friends. I needed some social activities.
>
> The last piece was the spiritual side of my life. I listed all the things I did that related to spirituality—worship on Sunday morning, the support group, the disciplines of the church, journaling, prayer, meditating on scriptures.
>
> I shared my pie with my support group, and it was my work for the whole year. It was really nice because it was something very concrete you could look at and keep in mind. It was nice the way I had what was important drawn big—it helped keep me on the track.[3]

Unlike Ruth Powell, some people resist putting things in black and white and asking others to help them live out their part of the Covenant. For them, Covenant can seem heavy. When that feeling comes, it seems helpful to try to think of Covenant in very down-to-earth, everyday terms. A teenager, Rachel, keen on becoming a cheerleader, tried out for the team. To her delight, she made it. As the year went on, her joy ripened into deep commitment and real appreciation for the opportunity.

Good things happened. For the first time, she really belonged in the school. She had an identity with a group that had a purpose and was geared for action and disciplined for growth. She loved the challenge. She grew, reached out, shared her gift with others, catalyzed school spirit. The agreement was clear: Come to every practice; work hard; if you don't want the commitment, there are many who would be glad to replace you. In this arrangement, she thrived!

Covenant with God is like that—a challenge, yes. A terror, no! God is one who loves us profoundly and wants the very best for us. Responding in concrete terms does not open the door for God to do something terrible or beyond us, but to do something wonderful with us. Surely challenges may come our way, but then if Hosea is to be believed, it is not great accomplishment that God looks for but simple faithfulness.

Several women and men in our church formed what we are calling "a covenant life group." We have been meeting regularly for about two years. If we were asked what we have accomplished or what we do in the way of activities, our answer might not seem significant. We share something of how our lives have been since last being together, and we always close with a circle of prayer. We may also study a book together, share some poetry, do a little amateur art work, or watch a TV program together. We could never claim great accomplishment in our group, but we do offer one another faithfulness. Always we meet, except in emergencies, and we listen to one another and care. Like Rachel and her cheerleading, we have a deep sense of belonging to one another, are growing in unexpected and often unprogrammed ways, and leave the group each time empowered to be more caring and compassionate in other settings.

All of us are invited to respond to God's covenant love in specific terms. When we do, important things can happen within us and through us. As we design a "rule of life" or a regular program for spiritual growth, we experience a deepening of our life in God. As groups of people support each other in specific covenants, there is a collective impact for good. They become what Arnold Toynbee described in 1935: a creative minority "turning to the inner world of the psyche," able to summon the vision of a new way of life for our troubled civilization.

God renews the invitation to covenant love again and again in countless ways. How will we respond?

Group Design

Purpose: To evaluate how the group is progressing thus far, to renew our vision of the God who desires a covenant with us, and to examine the difference a covenant makes in our lives.
Materials: Newsprint, a marking pen.

A. Gathering Time   (10 minutes)   Large Group

As you think over your life this past week, share one thing that has been important—e.g., a project at work, a concern about a family member, a book. Collect these concerns in a prayer, offering them to God and asking God's presence with you during this session.

B. Sharing Groups   (20 minutes)

Share briefly what you did with the suggestions for individual work and what this meant to you. Give each person a chance to speak before responding or entering into general discussion.

C. Taking Stock   (20 minutes)

Since we are halfway through this course, it is a good time to take stock of how things are going. Do this first in pairs and then in the large group.

1. In pairs: Choose a person who is not in your sharing group. Speak about what is helpful in the course experience, and what causes difficulty. Take about three minutes per person. Be frank. One recurring comment we get in our evaluations is how important it is to be able to express both negative and positive thoughts and feelings about the course.

2. In large group: Toss into the circle at random the thoughts and feelings that seemed most important in your sharing in pairs. In this type of growth, negative feelings can be both helpful to those who express them and catalytic for the group. For example, someone might say, "We're following the plan of the course in a wooden fashion. We're not touching the deeper places in our lives. It seems superficial." This frankness could trigger some beneficial thinking in the group about how to do things differently. It is best to let several comments surface before responding.

Note: We are suggesting only fifteen minutes for this large group sharing. It is not important to solve all problems at this time, but it *is* important to encourage an atmosphere of honest reflection on the content and process of the course and receptiveness to suggestions for improvement.

D. Sharing a Significant Relationship   (20 minutes)
1. In pairs: In the same pairs as in C above, tell briefly about a person with whom you have had or now have a significant relationship of caring and support. It may be a family member, teacher, friend, or work colleague. Give a few details about the person, the relationship, and why you feel good about it.

2. In large group: In spontaneous fashion, address yourselves to this question: What are the characteristics that make this person special to you? Consider writing these characteristics on newsprint so all can see. Then think and talk a bit about a most astounding fact: God's love for us has these same characteristics! That is the kind of God with whom we are dealing. Help that important fact to sink in.

E. Covenant Today   (30 minutes)   Large Group
In a free-flowing discussion, talk about the difference covenant makes in our lives today. You might like to share some examples from everyday life like the story of Rachel in the text. What has happened when you have entered into a covenant (agreement) with another or with God, having a definite understanding of how it can be carried out? Remember that in the time allowed you will not be able to finish this discussion. The really deep consideration of God's covenant love is a lifetime affair.

F. Closing   (10 minutes)   Large Group
Choose one or two of the following suggestions as appropriate for your group: evaluation of session, song, details of next session, prayer of thanks for God's covenant love in history and today.

Individual Work

Purpose: To examine and make our own response to God's covenant love.

A common response to covenant is "It's wonderful that God wants to make a covenant with us—but I'm not worthy to enter such a covenant."

The book of Ruth is a wonderful response to that problem. By the standards of the day, Ruth had several reasons to feel worthless. She was a woman in a man's world; a foreigner among a very nationalistic people; a woman without a husband in a society that related woman's worth to marriage. This beautiful story shows how the love that God wants for us overcomes all barriers we erect. It depicts bonding (covenanting) between God and humankind, male and female, alien and native, daughter-in-law and mother-in-law. We see covenant described in intensely human and poetic terms. At one point Ruth herself expresses her covenant love with Naomi in the words resembling God's covenant promises to humankind. She says: "Your people shall be my people, and your God my God" (Ruth 1:16, NAB).

Read this short book as background for reflection on the following questions:

In what ways does Ruth's story illuminate your own openness or resistance to commitment with God and others?

How do you personally want to respond to the covenant love being extended to you by God? Do you wish to accept such a relationship? Try writing a statement expressing your covenant with God. Include not only what you wish that relationship to be but what you wish to do to bring it about. It may be helpful to complete the following statements:

• The biggest hope I have in living out my covenant with God is. . . .

• The biggest fear I have is. . . .

• In order to be more faithful to my covenant with God, I need. . . .

To prepare for the next session, write a brief summary of your personal work with this assignment.

Notes

1. James Anderson et al., *An Introduction to the Study of the Bible* (Ann Arbor: Edwards Brothers, Inc., 1951), p. 5.

2 Inclusive Language Lectionary Committee, *An Inclusive Language Lectionary* (Philadelphia: Westminster Press, 1983), Epiphany 8.

3. Mary Clare Powell, *The Widow* (Washington, D.C.: Anaconda Press, 1981), pp. 58, 59. (Limited supply of books available from Ruth Powell, 49F, Ridge Road, Greenbelt, Md. 20770.)

Session 5

Suffering Servant

It is one thing to see God as Creator out of chaos, calling people to assist
in completing creation, delivering them from the bondages that thwart
new life, and covenanting with them to solidify and strengthen that
creative relationship. But what happens when all tangible evidence of
creativity is missing, when things are falling apart, when collapse rather
than deliverance is the reality? What then?

This is the problem that the writer of Second Isaiah tackled. What
kind of god can allow all we hold dear to disintegrate? A response to this
important question is given in one of the most compelling poems in the
history of language—Isaiah 53, in which Isaiah paints a picture of a
strange figure, the Suffering Servant. What is Isaiah talking about? To
gain insight into the mystery of this passage, one can, like the writer,
take a look backward at what had happened to the Hebrew people.

The Hebrew people were conscious of being chosen to embody God's
love and justice. The framework for this chosenness and this mission was
their covenant with God. Though their understanding of the Covenant
changed and grew, the idea that their relationship to God was special and
had been sealed with a covenant never left them.

These people felt led by God through their chosen leaders. Through
Abraham, God led them to their own land and promised them newness
and fruitfulness. Because of a famine, they later left that land for Egypt,
where they eventually were oppressed by the Egyptian rulers. God
delivered them out of Egypt, into the desert, and again into the land of
promise.

The ensuing history of the Hebrew people in the "new land" was full of
ups and downs. At times they were united under strong kings, notably
David, but under weaker monarchs they resorted to civil war. In their more
successful periods they held the land intact, but in their weaker periods they
were worn down and finally destroyed by hostile neighboring nations.

Sometimes loyal to the covenanting God of Abraham and Sarah, they at other times took on the religious practices of their conquering neighbors.

Finally, the religious center and political capital of Jerusalem fell to Babylonian aggression, the nation was destroyed, and the people were exiled to Babylon. At first the exiles were crushed by this turn of events. It was in this mood that the psalmist wrote:

> Beside the streams of Babylon
> we sat and wept
> at the memory of Zion. . . .
>
> How could we sing
> one of Yahweh's hymns
> in a pagan country?
> Jerusalem, if I forget you,
> may my right hand wither!
>
> (Ps. 137:1,4,5, JB)

Some perceptive souls, however, could see light in the new situation. One of these was Jeremiah, who saw the Exile as a necessary discipline to purge the people of their misconceptions about the true nature of God's purpose for them. Thus he foretold the new Covenant that Yahweh would make in the hearts of all faithful persons no matter where or in what situation they were.

Another who saw some hope in the apparently desperate situation was the prophet known as Second Isaiah. Imagine his problem as he tried to reconcile several recurring historical happenings: the chosenness felt by the Hebrew people, the realization that Yahweh was the God of all nations, the tragic defeat of the Hebrew nation, their consistent faithlessness to the Covenant. How could they hope? Was there a way out? If God would not bring redemption through a strong political nation, or through a consistently faithful and moral people, how would Yahweh express love to the world? How would God save the people?

In wrestling with these questions Isaiah received an image of one of the most remarkable and mysterious figures in religious history, that of the Suffering Servant. Four poems of great beauty reveal the profound insights that came to him (see Is. 42:1-9; 49:1-6; 50:4-11; 52:13—53:12).

Who is the Suffering Servant? Interpretations vary. Some believe the

Servant is Isaiah; others, the restored nation of Israel; or the remnant of faithful people; or a messiah. Christians have always felt that these passages are perfect descriptions of Jesus. Surely Jesus read and knew them. The incredible thing is that scholars generally agree that the Old Testament prophets were endowed with unusually deep insight into the history and current events with which they were familiar, but that they had no supernatural ability to predict future events. When one realizes that this profound concept came to Isaiah as he contemplated the puzzling and seemingly unexplainable events of his past and present, one can begin to glimpse its unusual character.

The meaning of the Suffering Servant is really inexhaustible, but we have hints and glimpses. The Servant embodies a radical new way of redemption, achieved not through political success or righteous purity, but through suffering, humiliation, and defeat. The Servant takes on the suffering of the world, bears it, and is crushed by it; but somehow in that apparent defeat, humankind is saved. By voluntarily accepting the tragedy of life and entering into the pain of human estrangement, the Servant is the agent of healing. Silence is his most eloquent expression of caring. However, he is rejected and misunderstood by those who interpret his suffering as the result of his own sin, and his silence as inability or unwillingness to protect himself. Although the suffering of the Servant seems unbearable and at certain moments even meaningless, his behavior is truly great, motivating, and redemptive to others.

Isaiah was calling the exiles to embrace the way of the Suffering Servant and thus fulfill their historic vocation of being "a light to the nations, that my salvation may reach to the ends of the earth" (Is. 49:6, NAB).

The Suffering Servant passages not only illumined the present and past of the Hebrew people but, as has been noted, were also part of Jesus' formation and surely are part of our understanding of who Jesus is.

Moreover, these passages depict the saving love of God in such a gripping way that people down through the ages have been able through them to receive this love in their own lives. Overwhelmed by the magnitude of that love, they have been fired to respond with such deep compassion for others that their lives have begun to resemble that of the Suffering Servant to whom they feel so indebted themselves. Such is the experience of some of the noblest people in history: Martin Luther King,

Jr., Simone Weil, Mother Teresa of Calcutta, St. Francis of Assisi, Archbishop Oscar Romero, and Elizabeth Fry, among many. Less famous but no less noteworthy are the rare and wonderful people within our own families and circles who, though unknown and unsung, reflect this believing, redemptive love.

Like all profound spiritual realities, this idea of the Suffering Servant is open to abuse. When misguided souls mistakenly try to take on the role of the Suffering Servant, a dangerous self-righteousness or false martyrdom can result. Their point of departure is to earn love through taking on suffering. In the process they become insufferable and make the recipients of their efforts feel guilty. But persons like the ones just mentioned are afire with the compelling love of God. Their responses to that unwarranted and surprising gift produce the kind of lives that can truly be called saintly. Their very presence inspires those around them.

As we attempt to fathom the meaning of the Suffering Servant for ourselves, it is helpful to look at contemporary experiences that illustrate its meaning.

Recently we attended a celebration in our community: the dedication of the inpatient facility for the Hospice of Northern Virginia. The dedication was a joyful day. It was clear that dozens of people were proud and happy to be a part of this effort—people who had donated needed items, families who had been served by Hospice, community persons who had lent support in countless ways. The purpose of this new health agency is stated in the dedicatory brochure:

> to provide comprehensive services both at home and in an inpatient setting to help terminally ill patients and their families face the physical, emotional, social, and spiritual aspects of their lives together in an atmosphere of support and acceptance.[1]

More than 150 committed volunteers plus staff enter into the suffering of dying persons and their families and give their time and ability to make this passage as peaceful and redeeming as possible. One person could not do it all, but together the group can achieve important things. Each person involved contributes particular skills: decorating, organizing, gardening, counseling, typing, mopping, painting. A team mobilizes service toward the patient and family. Doctor, nurse, social worker, volunteer, supplemented by clergy and other community care-givers, all backed by the hospice organization, work together to relieve suffering.

A closer look at this experience can give us clues about the meaning the Suffering Servant can have for us. First, the people involved in Hospice are motivated by a profound caring and concern for others. They want to do this work. They are expressing something deep within themselves. For some it is a way to share with others their learnings from a death they have experienced. For others it is a channel for putting talent to work in a truly needed effort. Though they might not say so, these people are offering a love that they have received and that is now overflowing.

It is easy to glamorize this type of giving and not see it for the mix it really is. These people are not only entering into the suffering of the patient and family; they are also taking on all the hardships involved in creating a new institution: the missed deadlines, the disagreements and disappointments, the countless difficulties and conflicts that are also a part of it. The willingness to remain committed, to suffer through the process of creating something new, to rise above feelings of rejection and lack of appreciation—all this might cause many to smile wryly at the biblical verse "harshly dealt with, he bore it humbly."

In looking at such a humane and successful experience as Hospice, it is also easy to forget that there are limits to how completely one person can enter into the suffering of another. This limit is not unhealthy or wrong. One can empathize with another, alleviate some of the pain, be alongside the other, but never *fully* identify with where that person really is. Only God can do that. This, it seems, is one of the really important meanings of God as Suffering Servant. *God* is the Suffering Servant. We are blessed by God's self-giving love, are grateful for it; and when we feel the tug that seems to be of God, we enter into the suffering of another as reflectors of that love. Yet the source of that love is God.

Not only are there limits to how fully one person can enter into another's suffering; there are also obvious limits to how much one person can do. Mother Teresa is often pointed to as one who embodies the spirit of the Suffering Servant today. Recent comments, however, have pointed out that although she offers ministry to the most unfortunate in society, she does little to confront or redeem the societal structures and systems that produce such suffering. That perhaps is for others who feel called to that sort of work.

Walter Brueggemann has written a book in which he attempts to illuminate the role of the prophet in biblical times as well as today.[2] He sees a threefold role for the prophet: to grieve over an existing situation of oppression or suffering; to voice an alternative consciousness (i.e., that it could be another way); and to embody this alternative in a different structure through which people can live out the new way.

Several years ago a group of people grieved over the plight of some homeless children in our city. These were youngsters who were housed in a huge public receiving home that had been condemned in several studies as offering inadequate care for the children. Those who were really upset felt there had to be a better way. They formed themselves into a group called FLOC (For Love of Children) to find that better way. Gradually they have evolved alternative structures that are more humane and effective: several smaller group homes, an advocacy center that proposes new legislation, a learning center to educate problem children in the schools, and a Wilderness School for those who cannot succeed in any ordinary school setting.

FLOC people carry a triple stress: the suffering that occurs in the lives of the families and children they serve; the conflict involved in managing a complex organization composed of special interest groups; and the challenge of working with the structures and individuals in the larger municipal welfare system. They must create ways to enable honest sharing between affluent and poor; to form and re-form themselves as an alternative to existing institutions but in productive relationship with them; and to challenge the established institutions without alienating them, continuing a dialogue even when they do not fully agree with them. These are the hard problems faced by members of FLOC who share the spirit of the Suffering Servant. Certainly there are high moments when a family is reunited or a student returned to school, or when those in need and those who can give truly embrace in common feelings of love and acceptance. But there are hard moments too: when one shrinks from visiting the establishment persons with their belittling responses, when one discovers that the needy recipient has misspent the rent money or filled the cupboard with junk food.

If the Suffering Servant has anything to say, it is that this kind of persistent, faithful, self-giving love even in the face of apparent failure will make real what Isaiah saw in vision:

Lo, I am about to create new heavens
    and a new earth;
The things of the past shall not be remembered
    or come to mind.
Instead, there shall always be rejoicing and happiness
    in what I create. . . .

(Is. 65:17-18, NAB)

Group Design

Purpose: To reflect on the meaning of God as Suffering Servant for the Hebrew people and for us.
Materials: 8½ x 11 paper, marking pens, Bibles.

A. Gathering Time   (20 minutes)   Large Group
Feel free to gather the group informally through sharing and prayer in whatever way is appropriate to your group. A suggestion is to share one thing that draws you to the group and its purpose of deeper growth and one thing that deflects you from it. Then gather these thoughts and feelings into a prayer of offering for each one and for the work of this session.

B. Sharing Groups   (20 minutes)
Share briefly what you did with the suggestions for individual work and what this meant to you. Give each person a chance to speak before responding or entering into discussion. Remember, this is a profound subject that does not lend itself to easy interpretation or application. The purpose of this time is to touch base with one another about what you did with the suggestions and not necessarily to resolve all the questions and issues involved. These latter are something to ponder over time.

C. Suffering Servant Then   (40 minutes)   Large Group
If necessary, someone should first summarize the session material on the Suffering Servant. Second, follow this procedure or one of your own devising to look at the poem and reflect on its meaning:
    1. Make sure everyone has a blank sheet of 8½ x 11 paper and some marking pens at hand. You can put your collection of markers in the

center of the room and people can choose what they need. Then everyone settle into silent receptivity.

2. Each one open a Bible to Isaiah 52:12-15—53:1-12. One person read the entire poem aloud slowly and reflectively.

3. In the silence, each person reflect on these questions: According to the writer of this poem, when all is lost, how does love come through? What is the new dimension of love that is being lifted up? What new way of being is described?

4. As you reflect, journal on your scrap paper with marking pens, portraying in lines, colors, words, or shapes what this poem tells you about God's love.

5. When all are finished, place your papers on the floor in the middle of the group. Then whoever wishes may share what you drew and why. You may have some light moments as each person tries to figure out what others drew, but also some important insights.

D. Suffering Servant Now   (30 minutes)   Pairs and Large Group
1. Choose someone with whom you have not as yet shared.

2. Take a few minutes of silence to think of someone you know or have heard of who exemplifies the spirit of the Suffering Servant. Has there been a time when God or a person reached out to you and you experienced in your own life the self-giving love that Isaiah was describing?

3. Return to the large group and discuss the meaning of the Suffering Servant today for you.

E. Closing   (10 minutes)   Large Group
Choose one or two of the following suggestions as appropriate for your group: evaluation of session, song, details of next session, prayer of thanks for God's love as shown to us by Isaiah.

Individual Work

Purpose: To attempt to fathom the meaning of the Suffering Servant for our own lives. In the session text we examined the meaning of the biblical figure of the Suffering Servant and examples of how that meaning is embodied in human lives. During the session, we tried to absorb some of the meaning in one Song of the Suffering Servant. Now we attempt to experience personally God's servant love.

1. Writing in the first person as if you were God sending a message to you, describe the love God has for you and for all people as portrayed in the Suffering Servant idea. In other words, write yourself a message of God's love as you find it expressed through the Suffering Servant. Take off from the text, be free wheeling, make it personal. (For example, "Dear Bill: My love for you is like that of a person who gives everything for someone he loves.")

2. This week, in your periods of quiet, concentrate on receiving this aspect of God's love in a difficult area of your life. Bask in it.

3. To prepare for next session: Write a brief summary of your personal work with this assignment.

Notes

1. Hospice of Northern Virginia, Dedicatory Brochure.
2. *The Prophetic Imagination* (Philadelphia: Fortress Press, 1978).

Session 6

A New Song

When the Hebrew people looked back at their history, they often broke into song or poetry. Sometimes it was a song of praise for the "wonderful works of Yahweh"; at other times, a plea for deliverance from "the miry pit."

One hundred and fifty of these poems and songs comprise the Book of Psalms, a remarkable collection of writings that span eight hundred years from the Exodus wanderings in the desert (c. 1290 B.C.) to the Post-Exilic period (when the Temple was restored, 520 B.C.). Written by different authors during this long period, they reflect themes and religious ideas appropriate to the times in which they were composed. An angry god spouting fire and smoke, pictured in Psalm 17, represents early conceptions of Yahweh. A later, more universal tone is heard in Psalm 117 (JB): "Praise Yahweh, all nations!

John Calvin wrote in his *Commentary on the Psalms*:

> I may truly call this book an anatomy of all parts of the soul, for no one can feel a movement of the Spirit which is not reflected in this mirror.[1]

In the psalms, we can find the range of human feelings that any one of us would experience in a lifetime—sorrow, joy, gratitude, anger, pain, despair, praise.

The name of this collection is taken from the Greek word *psalmós*, which means a song sung to the plucking of strings. Some of the songs, though not all, were used in temple worship, particularly for important feasts such as Passover (the commemoration of the deliverance), Pentecost or the Feast of Weeks (the beginning of harvest), and Succoth or Gathering-in (a week-long celebration like our Thanksgiving). They were sung or chanted to the accompaniment of musical instruments that emphasized rhythm, with melody probably quite subordinate. The best-known instrument was the harp, which in its various forms probably resembled our lute or zither. The timbrel was much like our tambourine. Cymbals, horns, trumpets, and reed pipes were also used.

An understanding of the different types of psalms can enhance their meaning for us today. Mary Ellen Chase in *The Psalms for the Common Reader* offers a helpful classification:[2]

1. "Hymns" (Psalms 8, 95, 97, 103, 107, 117, 146-150)—composed and arranged for the public praise of God in temple worship; generally objective in character.

2. "Thanksgivings" (Psalms 30, 34, 40, 116, 118, 139)—expressions of personal gratitude for the gifts and mercies of God in one's own life.

3. "Laments" (National Laments—Psalms 10, 44, 79; Personal Laments—Psalms 6, 22, 42, 43, 102, 130)—national reflections of bewilderment and impatient endurance as well as personal calls for help and descriptions of complaints, often ending with an expression of hope and confidence in God's mercy.

4. "Historical Psalms" (Psalms 46, 78, 105, 114, 136, 137, 145)—written to express the Hebrew conviction that God chose Israel to be the people through whom he revealed his purposes for humankind and to relate the events and acts through which God is revealed.

5. "Psalms about Nature" (Psalms 19, 29, 104)—praise of God as Creator of the universe and its many wonders.

6. "Pilgrim Songs" (Psalms 84, 121, 122, 125, 126)—sung by people who had traveled from their homes, sometimes great distances, to Jerusalem in order to participate in the great festivals of the year.

7. "Psalms of Personal Meditation and Reflection" (Psalms 23, 27, 90, 91)—written to be read rather than sung, and thus free from the devices needed for choral singing; expressions of the nature and purpose of God and reflections on life as understood by the psalmist.

The psalms are still used by believers for both private and public worship. In most churches, psalms are either read by the people or celebrant or are sung in hymns and anthems. The psalms have been prayed throughout the day by believers from earliest times; eventually they were compiled in the Breviary or the Liturgy of the Hours, which includes psalms for seven periods of the day, seven days a week.

Perhaps most striking for the modern reader is the fact that the psalms were the prayerbook of Jesus. There are twenty-one references to them in the Gospel of Matthew. Study of these passages reveals that the psalms were in Jesus' mind at nearly every important juncture of his life—at his baptism, in the desert temptations, as he was teaching, in the encounter with the money-changers, in his confrontation with the priests and elders over authority, and on the cross. It seems clear from these and other references that Jesus knew the psalms well; he meditated on them and used their words in prayer.

Dietrich Bonhoeffer suggests that if we, like the disciples, want Jesus to teach us to pray, we would do well to pray with him the prayers he used.[3] There are many ways to do this. Some people use all or parts of the Liturgy of the Hours either regularly or whenever they can. In this way, they feel tied to the ongoing prayer of those who are committed to praying it daily. One of our class members, knowing that busy people might have a hard time with this, suggested that we use Psalm 95 as our opening morning prayer; it is the opening prayer of Matins, the first Hour of the Liturgy. This is a wonderful way to start the day:

> Come, let us praise Yahweh joyfully,
> acclaiming the Rock of our safety. . . .
>
> (Ps. 95:1, JB)

The psalms are enhanced for us when we know how other people have used them. The reading of Psalm 130, which sings of God's forgiving love, prapared John Wesley for his great conversion out of which the meaning and mission of his life evolved.[4] The sister of David Livingstone, the missionary to Africa, wrote of the importance of the psalms to David as he left the family for his new work:

> I remember my father and him talking over the prospects of
> Christian missions. They said that the time would come when rich
> and great men would think it an honour to support whole stations of

missionaries, instead of spending their money on hounds and horses. On the morning of 17th November, 1840, we got up at five o'clock. David read the 121st and the 135th Psalms and prayed. My father and he walked to Glasgow to catch the Liverpool steamer.[5]

Henry Pitney Van Dusen discovered in his study of Dag Hammarskjöld that the Secretary General referred to the psalms with great frequency, particularly during moments of crisis and decision.[6] A striking example is the second-to-last entry in his journal, *Markings:* "And they remembered that God was their strength—Psalm 78:35."[7]

Also, although lists and classifications of the psalms are available, some people find it useful to do their own indexing so that they can readily find the psalms that are most helpful to them in times of joy or sorrow, for consolation, anchoring, or empowering. Some will have favorites for certain times of day. In addition to Psalm 95, the first lines of Psalm 108 are a beautiful way to start the day. At nighttime, Psalms 63 or 131 are appropriate. Psalm 121 is particularly reassuring when contemplating the death of a loved one.

Some people find different translations of the psalms enlightening and helpful. Praying and dwelling on one or two familiar lines is also helpful, rather than trying to meditate on long passages. Changing the words can help make God's presence more real. For example, instead of praying, "The Lord is my shepherd," stop and try to hear God's words: "I am your shepherd. You will not want, because I will lead you beside still waters and restore your soul." When we hear God speaking to us in this way, the familiar words take on a new freshness and depth of meaning.

In our sessions we point out that the Hebrew people often remembered an event in history when God's presence was obvious and then related a current personal situation to it. If they could recall and believe that God had delivered their ancestors from Egypt, then they could believe that somehow Yahweh would aid them in their present trouble. These historical revelations of God's goodness are important rocks on which to build faith. Contemplating them can enable us to sing our own new song.

As a way of concluding this course we invite participants to review the content, to remember God's actions as Creator, Caller, Deliverer, Covenant-maker, and Suffering Servant. Together we remember that God creates out of chaos, calls us to companionship and collaboration, delivers us from our bondages as we try to become free and whole people fostering love and justice, and finally that God enters into our suffering to bring about new life. Then we suggest that session participants try composing their own song to God, using perhaps the parallel style so familiar in the psalms. The first line can describe what God has done in history, and the second, our personal response today.

Nearly everyone rises to this challenge, puts pen to paper, and produces a new song, a statement of what has happened during this time together pondering God in the Hebrew scriptures. Here is one written by a young person struggling with important decisions:

> Out of my chaos
> You spoke your name
> and took me through
> to a pact with You
> O Lord how you suffered
> Thanks Lord, hear this song.[8]

Group Design

Purpose: To summarize the meaning of the course and to share next steps.

A. Gathering Time   (10 minutes)   Large Group
Gather the group informally through sharing and prayer. A suggestion would be to describe one time this week when God's love was apparent or one time when it seemed absent or hard to recognize. Then gather your thoughts and feelings into a prayer of offering for each one and for the work of this session.

B. Sharing Groups   (20 minutes)
Go around the group and describe what you did with the home assignment (feelings, learnings, difficulties). Then if time permits have some free discussion.

C. Group Psalm Writing: A Way to Sing a New Song to God

(40 minutes)

1. If necessary, one person summarize the material in the text about the psalms. End with a quick review of the entire course material. (See the second-to-the-last paragraph in the text.)

2. Then, following the suggestion in the text, each one write his or her own new song to God relating to the material in the course. One way to do this is to compose a first line relating to what God did in history as Creator, and a companion line on your response today. Then write the next two lines on God as Caller in history and your response. Feel free to depart from this form and create your own. A way to begin might be to do a little free journaling on these questions: What newness has happened to you in the course? Does a next step suggest itself to you at this point?

3. When all have finished writing, those who wish to may share their new songs in the large group. If you prefer, you might want to share in pairs and then have a few share in the large group. Remember that anyone is free not to share.

D. Celebrating Newness and Sharing Next Steps (30 minutes) Large Group

1. Take a few minutes of silence to look over your notes and finish any journaling you may have begun on newness and next steps.

2. Spontaneously share your learnings, feelings, and ideas for next steps. Give everyone a chance to speak before opening up for general response and discussion. You might like to describe one place you want to move toward, one step to begin, and one obstacle that might stand in your way.

E. Closing Celebration (10 minutes) Large Group

In prayer and song or in any other ways your group might devise, express thanks to one another and to God for this time together.

Notes

1. Quoted by Mary Ellen Chase in *Psalms for the Common Reader* (New York: W. W. Norton & Co., Inc., 1962), p. 25.
2. Ibid. (This material summarizes content in Chase's pp. 37-69 and 121-159.)
3. *Psalms: The Prayer Book of the Bible* (Minneapolis: Augsburg Publishing

House, 1970), pp. 13-16.
4. John Ker, *The Psalms in History and Biography* (Edinburgh: Andrew Elliot, 1886), p. 162.
5. Ibid., p. 149.
6. Henry Pitney Van Dusen, *Dag Hammarskjöld: The Man and His Faith* (New York: Harper & Row, 1967), p. 191.
7. Dag Hammarskjöld, *Markings* (New York: Alfred A. Knopf, 1964), p. 217.
8. Vicki Garno, unpublished poem. Used with permission of the author.

Two

Meeting Jesus in the New Testament

Two thousand years ago one person lived a life so striking in its compassion, healing, and liberation that many thought he reflected the nature of God more fully and clearly than anyone else had ever done. Indeed, many felt he was God in a unique way.

Today the life of every individual and of the planet itself is threatened. More than ever we need to find ways to implement God's vision of wholeness and peace for ourselves and for the whole created order.

Can this person, Jesus, help us? His life, teachings, empowering of others—are they relevant to the challenges of our personal and global existence today? These are questions no one can answer for another. We can, however, support one another as we look at the experience of Jesus and his disciples and allow ourselves to be guided, changed, and even transformed by this contact.

This course provides a setting in which to do this. In Jesus' day many people had relatively brief contacts with him, and yet often those contacts had lifelong consequences. When we designed this material our challenge was: How can we help adults engage with Jesus in ways that are decisive and life-changing?

Our approach is to look at key events and passages in the scriptures in order to see who Jesus was to the people he knew and loved in his earthly lifetime and then to present some opportunities to reflect and decide on who he is for us today.

The many names people have given Jesus are attempts to capture their experience of him. We chose six pairs that have had major impact on our lives and those of others: *Immanuel/God with Us, Healer/Liberator, Friend/Mystery, Teacher/Guide, Savior/Prophet, and Spirit/Presence.*

In some ways this material is more like a retreat than a course. That is, it does not tell us anything new, but it reminds us of events and themes we already know in the life of Jesus and his disciples. It presents them in a logical progression with some cognitive material, but it is in no way a complete summary of the life and teachings of Jesus. The material provides opportunities to meditate on and to appropriate for ourselves various faith experiences that were important to Jesus and his companions. Participants are invited to approach this course with an attitude of open-minded inquiry combined with a willingness to experience and reflect on the material.

It is important to note that some contemporary thinkers raise a number of issues regarding the theological understandings that have developed regarding Jesus. For example, people of other living faiths question claims that salvation can be found only through Jesus. They see him as one among a number of important religious leaders. Some feminists, such as Rosemary Radford Ruether, ask, "Can a male savior save women?"[1] They reject using Jesus' maleness as the basis for perpetuating male-dominated theologies and structures, but experience grace in his consistent compassion for the poor and marginalized who frequently were women.

Others question seeing Jesus as the champion of our culture and way of life. They stress the importance of his place at the forefront of change, drawing us out of our self-preoccupation and toward the forgotten or emerging parts of society.[2]

Titles given to Jesus raise further questions. Contemporary critics question using monarchical or hierarchical titles such as *king* or *lord,* claiming they foster imperial understandings of religion. They prefer using terms such as *brother and friend* to stress the community of equals that Jesus fostered.[3]

These questions are challenging and important. We are mindful of them as we present the aspects of Jesus that in the midst of all these questions have continuing relevance for us today.

Notes

1. Rosemary Radford Ruether, *Sexism and God-Talk* (Boston: Beacon Press, 1983), p. 116.
2. For an important discussion of these issues, see Tom F. Driver, *Christ in a Changing World* (New York: The Crossroad Publishing Company, 1981).

3. Inclusive Language Lectionary Committee, *An Inclusive Language Lectionary* (Philadelphia: The Westminster Press, 1983), Appendix.

Session 1

Immanuel/God with Us

The faith community of early Christians took pains in their writing and oral traditions to introduce Jesus first as a helpless baby, born to a poor couple in an obscure village in an occupied country.

In the nativity narratives, the mixed responses to the baby are presented in starkly contrasting images and pictures. Mary and Joseph welcomed, held, loved, and provided for the child. The presence of the animals symbolized the natural world as an important part of God's revelation. Dropping their ordinary work and concerns, and guided by a vision of angels, the shepherds came to adore the newborn baby. Three wisemen, representing the three races of humankind—European, Asiatic, and African—came bearing symbolic gifts: gold as a tribute to Christ the royal person, frankincense in homage to the divinity Christ represented, and myrrh, foretelling Jesus' suffering and death.

All of this care, adoration, and giving was threatened by the jealousy and brutality of Herod. As a ruler, he could stand no other claims to leadership and therefore vented his rage in one of the cruelest acts in history, the slaughter of the firstborn sons. This unspeakable anger and hate forced the family of Jesus into a refugee existence in Egypt and tightened the Roman oppression of the people of Israel.

The nativity story is retold around the world each year. Its theological implications have been explained in various ways. But it seems important to begin our course by attempting simply to relate to Jesus as a baby. The life, teachings, and passion of the adult Jesus are obviously significant, but why consider his birth?

In order to understand the significance of Jesus' coming to us first as a baby, we must look at what people were expecting. John Bright describes the longing of the Hebrew people for the coming establishment of the Reign of God. This hope was expressed in different ways. The Zealots, the nationalist party within Judaism, hoped for the "political

70

restoration of independence from Rome through military action led by the Messiah."[1] The Pharisees, members of a formalist sect that believed in rigid observance of the written and oral law, held to the ideal of a Holy Commonwealth that would come through God's action combined with the people's strict adherence to the law. The apocalypticists yearned for the catastrophic intervention of God, when the heavens would open to reveal a divine one descending on clouds to earth (Dan. 7:13).

Political independence, military victory, and religious purity concerned various groups of Hebrew people. They yearned for a strong military leader, a righteous king, or a supernatural figure to intervene and bring greatness to their nation.

Yet the expected one appears first as a baby, shattering lofty expectations and requiring the response not of the powerful but of the tenderhearted.

This response of the heart to Jesus as a baby comes alive each year at the Christmas Eve family service in our church. Most of the year, our congregation would be characterized by its intellectual sophistication and its concern for social and political action. But during this service we express quite another side of ourselves. The mother, father, and newest baby in the congregation are asked to form a living crêche in our chancel. At a certain point in the service, as Christmas carols are sung, all are invited into the chancel to be with "the holy family." The new baby evokes marvelous responses: smiles, cooing, sometimes tears, and a general nonverbal communication that for a few moments makes us feel at one with the family, one another, and with God in a delightful circle of love. In terms of the new brain research that has elucidated the difference between the logical, analytical left side of the brain and the right hemisphere, which is at home with fantasy, dreams, and intuitions, it is as if for one moment the world stands still and we as a congregation are capable of whole-brain knowing, the true wedding of heart and mind. We receive in our hearts that evening what all year long we struggle to understand in our minds: that at the center of the universe is a love of the most ingenuous kind that has the capacity to call forth a similar love from each person in every age and place.

It is as if God, like a Zen master, had struck the earth with a wholly unexpected illumination. God came to us in the form of a baby. Along with being transcendent, God is revealed as personal, approachable, vulnerable, needing and wanting our response of love—first heart to heart, and gradually mind to mind.

This response of the heart to Jesus as baby does not come readily or easily for most of us. We often have other ideas about Jesus' meaning for us. In the first group design we include a time to share our expectations of Jesus for this period of our lives. The course can provide an opportunity for something to happen between Jesus and ourselves. What do we hope for? Some people believe that a close examination of Jesus will help them make sense of the universe so that they will have a clearer purpose for life. Others yearn for a deeper sense of belonging to the family of God and hope that relating in a personal way to Jesus can help them find that. Still others see Jesus as a liberator of the oppressed and look for empowerment in the work of social justice. Is it that we all come to Jesus wanting or looking for something when in reality God is trying to show us through the Baby the importance of simply being with Jesus at first, allowing the wonder of the Baby to penetrate our beings? Perhaps, like his parents, we are invited to hold the Baby and the reality he represents. Maybe that will call forth the giving of ourselves and our gifts as it did for the wisemen.

But do we know how to do that—to allow ourselves simply to be with Jesus? Perhaps in our producer-consumer society many have lost that ability. Tilden Edwards, in his writing and teaching, is one person who is trying to help us recover the ability simply to be. Discussing the concepts in his *Sabbath Time,* he points out different ways of seeing rest and work time:

> We *have* to move back and forth between rest and work, but *how* we do that, it seems to me, has gotten pretty crazy in our society, and the Church has tended to accommodate itself to society's way of doing it, so that we've lost touch with the fundamental rhythm . . . between Sabbath and ministry time, as a contrast to what's increasingly the cultural norm: moving between a kind of driven work time and a very narrow escapist rest time which often isn't very restful.[2]

He suggests that we find a Sabbath time when we can cultivate the appreciation of life as a gift rather than as "a curse or something that has to be made over all the time."[3] During this Sabbath time we can worship with a great deal of space and very little "stuff," i.e., words, action, or reading. We can create a Sabbath time for a few moments every day or several times a day as well as setting aside longer times for this purpose.

Many of the saints seemed to find and use Sabbath time well. They were given to much listening, pondering, and absorbing, and often to few words. Two of the words St. Ignatius used most frequently in prayer were *Mira! Mira!* or "Look! Look!" That was the way he contemplated the mystery of Christ.[4] The prayer of Francis for nights on end was simply: "Who are you, O God? And who am I?"[5]

In our introduction we suggested that perhaps it is best to approach this course like a retreat. As we look at the Nativity or any of the other events or experiences in the New Testament, we must first try to absorb the mystery, not analyze it. A friend once shared the secret of his appreciation of great paintings. He would spend his first moments in a gallery taking in the sweep of the exhibit. Then he would choose a favorite painting, find a comfortable place before it, and spend an hour simply absorbing the great work, letting it speak to him. Approaching Christ in that spirit of contemplation, we will see with Evelyn Underhill that Christianity is not primarily an argument but a person.

When we allow ourselves quiet and disengagement from the busyness of our world, we realize that the characters in the nativity story not only belong in the scene two thousand years ago; they reside in us as well. The same mixed reaction to the divine gift exists inside as well as outside ourselves. Part of us is willing to look for the Light right in our neighborhood and home, and part of us is threatened by it. We want to offer the gifts of our own intellect, love, and suffering to Jesus, but we keep a running account of what we are getting out of it. And if the experience of Jesus beckons us to shabby places or great distances, we often prefer to stay home by the fire and read the paper.

Nevertheless, the welcome mat is out. God invites us to receive something special, divine love in human form, and first in that most lovable of forms, a baby.

Group Design

Purpose: To develop our relationships with one another, share our expectations of Jesus for this period of our lives, and experience the wonder of God's coming to us as a human infant.

Materials: Baby photos (preferably large), Christmas carols (see Closing).

A. Gathering Time   (20 minutes)   Large Group
As a way of getting acquainted and beginning to think about the birth of Jesus, share your name and a remembrance of a birthday, either yours or that of someone else. Use about a minute per person.

For example, "My name is Carlos Diaz, and I remember a recent birthday when my friend, who knew that I loved a certain author, arranged for a private showing of a movie about that person at the public library. Then we had a good time watching it together."

B. Sharing Groups   (30 minutes)   Groups of Four
Move into groups of four so that you are with people you do not know well. Share names and phone numbers, and write them in a notebook for ready reference. Then briefly share what you hope will happen personally as a result of your contact with Jesus through this course. This is not an easy topic, so take a few minutes of silence to think about it, perhaps jotting down thoughts in your notebook. Then briefly share these hopes. You may want to write down key hopes next to people's names so you can hold these in your thoughts or prayer. For example, "Jim hopes to grow beyond his childhood image of Jesus as meek and mild."

Note on sharing: Remember to share what is personal and relevant to the question. If you cannot articulate a response or prefer not to share one, feel free to "pass." Remind one another of these ground rules for sharing as needed.

C. Experiencing Jesus as a Baby   (60 minutes)   Large Group
Meditation
1. *Focal point:* In order to help people get in the mood for meditating on Jesus as a baby, you might wish to gather and display in the center of your circle some baby pictures of family or friends. Larger pictures are easier to see. Enjoy looking at them for a few minutes. The idea is to create an atmosphere of tenderness toward the Infant. Then settle into a comfortable position for meditation, with pen and paper in hand. The leader will read the meditation, and when you hear "Respond," allow your thoughts and feelings to do just that. Jot down what comes to your mind or heart. In this type of meditation, some people have a lot to write; for

others, a word or two is sufficient.

2. *Meditation read by one person in a slow and relaxed fashion:* "In order to move into our meditation, let's take a few minutes to relax, settle down in a comfortable position. (Pause.) Now let's focus a bit on relaxing different parts of our body from our head down to our toes. (Pause.) Let's take a few slow deep breaths. (Pause.) And let's feel silence deepen among us, being aware of the noises around us, yet letting go of them, and letting a silent, caring atmosphere envelop us. (Pause.)

"The procedure for our meditation is this. I'll read a short paragraph, and then say 'Respond.' At that time let your mind and heart respond as freely as possible, and then write down your response in your notebook. It may be anything from 'Yes, I want to be open' to 'I'm having trouble concentrating.' Even though you may be tired and have other things on your mind, try to bring yourself before God as you are, and be ready to hear something within yourself that is valuable. Now I'll begin."

Infancy Meditation

. . . I have come, am born, of an unknown girl in an obscure town. . . . I come at inconvenient times, in inappropriate places. While they are journeying far from home, I arrive. My mother wraps me in cloths and lays me in a manger. She and Joseph warm me with their love, give themselves to caring for me. Can I come to you like that: unexpectedly? inconveniently? Respond. (Reader pause for several minutes, allowing time for others to jot down thoughts.)

. . . My angel appears to men on a hillside, . . . says "Don't worry, I have great news. . . . He has come." Those rough, simple, tired men leave their valuable flocks. They trust, believe, . . . hurry to my side. I send my messengers to you also. Do you recognize them? Respond. (Reader pause as above.)

. . . Not everyone is happy that I have come. Although I am a helpless, tiny babe, a king is threatened by my birth. He plots against me. Human nature is many-sided. Does a part of you feel threatened too? Does it seek ways to avoid me? Respond. (Reader pause as above.)

. . . Wise men, men of science, of wealth, come seeking me. They live comfortable lives, are intelligent, educated, used to stimulating conversation. They have left all this to search for me over rough, lonely roads. You, too, have comfort, material well-being. Are you willing to seek me over difficult paths? Respond. (Reader pause as above.)

3. *Sharing:*
    a. In the same group of four you were in before, go around the circle and share briefly what happened in this meditation as you thought about Jesus as baby. Let each person have a turn; refrain from commenting. Focus on what did or did not happen during this meditation, not on opinions or questions out of the past. If you prefer not to share, say "Pass."
    b. Large group—You may want to finish in this group with any insights or experiences that seemed particularly helpful in the small group. This can also be a time for those who had trouble getting into the meditation to ask for some suggestions.

D. Closing   (10 minutes)   Large Group
Choose one or two of the following suggestions as appropriate for your group:
    1. Evaluate this session. (In a few words, what was helpful? What was not helpful?)
    2. Sing (Christmas carols such as "What Child Is This?" or "O Little Town of Bethlehem").
    3. Pray.
    4. Discuss details of next session if necessary (time, place, leadership responsibility).

Individual Work

Purpose: To establish a time to be alone with God, to meditate on the beginning of Jesus' life and work, and to use some of the processes he went through to reflect on where we are and what we want to be about in our own lives.

Note: This individual work forms a bridge between our contemplation of Jesus' infancy and his public life.
    1. *Read:* "The Beginning of Jesus' Public Ministry" (pp. 77-80).

2. *Meditate:* This week we invite you to meditate on the initial steps of Jesus' public life and work as described in "The Beginning of Jesus' Public Ministry." The baptism account is in Mt. 3:13-17; the rest of the incidents referred to are described in Lk. 3:21-23, Lk. 4, and Lk. 5:1-11. As you read these passages, spend some time gaining a deeper sense of what happened and an understanding of these strange and surprising events. Be there with Jesus, in his shoes (sandals!). Try to share his thoughts and feelings.

3. *Write:* Ponder and then write your answers to the questions on these topics taken from "The Beginning of Jesus' Public Ministry." You may wish to concentrate on one or two topics that seem most relevant to you.

a. Baptism: For Jesus, it was a time of showing publicly that he was dedicated to embodying God's love and justice. How would you describe yourself at this point in your life? To what are you dedicated? Would it be important to say something aloud about this to someone?

b. Temptation: What throws you off course from the way you feel that God and your own deep energy call you to go?

c. Articulation: Can you articulate the purpose of your life and work? Is there a passage of scripture that helps you describe it?

d. Reactions: How do you deal with the reactions of others as you try to discern and be true to God's direction?

e. The Call for Company: What kind of companionship do you want or need as you seek to deepen your journey with God?

As we can see, for Jesus launching the new way had different elements, each of which was important. So the launching or re-launching of God's way in us may require different steps. No two people are in precisely the same spot. As you ponder the steps mentioned above, be conscious of which seem most important at this time in your life.

4. *Summarize:* At the end of the week, summarize in writing what you did with this assignment. Be brief, honest, and to the point. This will help you consolidate your feelings and learnings and prepare you for the next session.

The Beginning
of Jesus' Public Ministry

Name: Jesus
Age: 30
Home Address: Nazareth

Occupation: Carpenter
Education: Scripture study in home and synagogue; on-the-job
    training in carpentry with father

Not a very impressive resumé, but this is all we know of the person who
was about to begin a second career that changed the world forever.
Before we contemplate the content and the outcome of that career, it is
important to look at the various elements that went into launching it and
try to see their meaning not only for Jesus but for us. He left the security
of a known family, a recognized address, and an easy-to-understand
occupation to be with unknown types whose only affinity was that they
said yes to his call. Led by the Spirit, he ventured out, with no sure place
to lay his head, and began a life and work whose depth and meaning have
never been exhausted in 2,000 years of analysis. The thirtieth year of his
life, as he moved from a private to a public existence, was a turning
point.

What was the nature of this turning point? How did he get started?
What were his first moves? Did he know what to do readily, or did he
have to struggle to figure it out? The Gospel writers supply us with some
details, the meaning and implications of which are well worth
pondering.

Baptism. Jesus' first public move was to be baptized by John. Why?
Jesus had a sense of destiny, a special background of blessing by parents
and insightful religious people, and an awareness of being called to a life
of love and service. He submitted to the ministry of a lesser person, one
who saw himself as the usher of a new way but as having only a piece of
the vision of what it was all about. Moreover, John was using baptism to
signify that one had turned away from sin and toward a new relationship
with God. Did Jesus need that? Even John was puzzled by Jesus' request,
but Jesus asked him to "give in for now."

While we do not know why Jesus took this step, we can make certain
observations. It did show that Jesus affirmed John's insistence that
recognizing and turning away from whatever keeps us from God is a
condition for entering a fuller, fruitful life of love and justice. It did, in
fact, usher in a new life for Jesus. Moreover, it was a conscious,
witnessed declaration of his intent, a time when he came into a new

identity and expressed it publicly. As Jesus emerged from the river, two important ratifications of this step occurred. Scripture reports that a voice from heaven assured him he was beloved by God, and a dove appeared, which he took as a sign of God's blessing of that moment.

Temptations. One would think that with that auspicious start, Jesus would have plunged into his public career. But the opposite is true. He went off by himself to the desert to think through everything. What happened there? The scripture says, "He was tempted by the devil." Right on the heels of a sublime feeling of blessing at baptism, he is tempted to misuse his power, love, and insight. Which of the many messianic expectations of his people would he emphasize and try to fulfill? Political strength and dominance, economic or material assurances, spectacular or dramatic indications of God's presence—all of these were options to consider, but he rejected them to focus on the simple, uncompromising love of God that gives all to empower (not coerce or demand) us to embody that love as well.

Articulation of the Mission. What, then, in the deprivation of the wilderness was the path he decided to take? Both there and later in the synagogue, he went to scripture for insight and direction. He countered each temptation with a powerful and positive scriptural expression of the direction in which he felt led by the Spirit. Then, in the synagogue, he had the opportunity for an initial public expression of that mission and ministry. To do it, he used the words of a song of the Suffering Servant (Is. 61:1,2).

The Reaction of the People. One might think that with all the thought and prayer that went into this statement of purpose and with all the blessing upon the one who spoke, the reaction of the people would be one of unanimous approval. But again we are surprised. The reactions are terribly mixed: They run the gamut from adulation to rejection, from welcome to resistance, from wonder to fright. If Jesus needed or planned to take his cues from people's reactions, he would have been thrown into total confusion. But this was not the case. He was able, as the scripture puts it, "to walk through the crowd and go on his way."

The Call of the Disciples. The strength that came from wrestling with all the alternatives, from spending long periods in prayer and discernment, and finally from declaring who he was and what he was about made it possible for Jesus to stand alone. He could teach with authority and effectiveness, heal people's spiritual and physical problems, and bring good news to the many he touched. He could go it alone. But he chose not to do that. Very quickly he selected companions and proceeded to share his ministry with them through an intensive living/learning experience. He had no desire to be the whole show. These persons, whom he called friends, were not at first his friends. They apparently had no special qualities that fitted them for this work. Their only qualification seemed to be that they responded to his call, his invitation, to be "fishers of men." He accepted that response without question and gave himself to forming them into bearers of good news.

Notes

1. John Bright, *The Kingdom of God* (New York: Abingdon Press, 1953), p. 191.
2. Celia Hahn, "Keeping the Sabbath: A Conversation with Tilden Edwards," *Action Information* 7 (Nov.-Dec. 1981):1.
3. Ibid., pp. 1, 2.
4. Quoted by Evelyn Underhill, *The Light of Christ* (London: Longmans, Green and Co., 1944), p. 32.
5. Richard Rohr, "A Life Pure and Simple," *Sojourners,* vol. 10, no. 12 (Dec. 1981):13.
6. Evelyn Underhill, *The Light of Christ,* p. 30.

Session 2

Healer/Liberator

Jesus made his first public appearance in Nazareth, his own hometown, following his solitary time in the desert. In the synagogue where he regularly worshiped he did something so shocking to some of the townsfolk that they dragged him out of the city and threatened to throw him over a cliff.

What caused such a violent reaction? Taking one of the most sacred of Old Testament scriptures, a Song of the Servant, he interpreted it in such a way that people were infuriated by what they saw as arrogance, and refused to believe him. He claimed that the Spirit of God was upon him, anointing him

> to preach good news to the poor. . . .
> to proclaim release to the captives
> and recovering of sight to the blind,
> to set at liberty those who are oppressed,
> to proclaim that acceptable year of the Lord.
>
> (Lk. 4:18-19, RSV)

In our discussion of the Suffering Servant in the Old Testament we saw that the concept of the redemptive value of voluntary suffering was lifted up in a new and radical way, that the identity of the Servant was composite, and therefore ambiguous and confusing. It stood variously for the sufferings of the whole nation, of a faithful remnant, or of committed individuals.

Jesus offered a new understanding of the Servant in one sweeping statement: "Today this Scripture passage is fulfilled in your hearing" (Lk. 4:21, NAB). Jesus used the passage to describe his own mission and subsequently invited others to join him in it. How arrogant for a hometown boy to stand up in front of everyone and declare that he was indeed called by God to be that special servant!

Hebrew people believed that God was their king, but since evil and suffering always abounded, they believed God's reign would come in the future. Jesus had the audacity to declare that it was experientially available to all right then, on that day when he first declared their common purpose to be that of the Servant.

Further, the Hebrew scriptures emphasized Israel as the focus of God's reign and action in history. In his commentary on the Isaiah passage, Jesus stressed that the Gentiles are equally welcome in the realm of God. He pointed out that Elijah was sent to a *foreign* widow, and Elisha to heal a *foreign* leper.

The central message of the Song he quoted had great power to upset people then and has the same power today. Why should the poor receive the good news? Do they not deserve their poverty? Why should captives be released? Criminals and challengers of the prevailing political system are best kept under lock and key. And whoever heard of the blind receiving sight? Isn't most blindness permanent? Why should the oppressed be set free? After all, their own laziness caused them to be underdogs.

A disturbing and provocative way to begin a public ministry! No wonder people wanted to get rid of him. But Jesus not only had a well articulated and strikingly unconventional purpose; he also had a plan of action for himself and others who were drawn to participate.

After years of work in his father's carpentry shop and his lonely pondering in the desert, there was an urgency and immediacy in his preaching that was confronting and compelling. "The reign of God is at hand"—now, today, in your midst—was how the Gospel writers conveyed his first preaching. "Repent and believe the good news." There are two things to do: Make a complete turnaround in your thinking and actions, and believe and participate in the new order of compassion, forgiveness, and justice for all. The new order for the world involves people who have experienced within themselves a new birth of these gospel values.

Jesus sought companionship in carrying out his mission. Those who said no to their old ways and yes to the new reign of God that Jesus proclaimed joined him in preaching, teaching, healing, and challenging the status quo.

They began their mission by emphasizing the healing of individuals. Luke records:

> Now when the sun was setting, all those who had any that were sick with various diseases brought them to him; and he laid his hands on every one of them and healed them.
>
> (Lk. 4:40, RSV)

Healings of all sorts are recorded in the early part of Jesus' public ministry. People had various reactions: joy, relief, surprise, confusion. The good news was that many were emotionally or physically healed and liberated from sin or oppression.

What has become of Jesus' ministry? How is it embodied today? We turn to contemporary expressions of Jesus' servant mission and his initial emphasis on liberation and healing.

Jean Donovan, one of the four women missionaries killed in 1979 in El Salvador, felt a call to the poor in Latin America. She left a comfortable suburban existence in Cleveland and gave her life to serve people who are still captives of poverty and oppression. Home on a brief furlough, she knew it was dangerous to go back. Yet more than anything in the world she wanted to bring healing to a suffering people, and so she returned.[1]

Black people in America have often been oppressed captives of white systems and individuals. Martin Luther King, Jr., was one person who experienced the liberation of God: He was freed both from hatred and from feelings of racial inferiority. Later he became a freedom leader for his people and indeed for all Americans. "Free at last, free at last" were his words shortly before his death. His willingness to embody and live out that liberation enabled many people of all races to do the same.[2]

Lech Walesa, the first leader of the Solidarity movement in Poland, was placed under house arrest. Just before this happened, he participated in an interview. Asked if he was afraid, he replied that he was afraid of no one but God. Even though the threat to himself and Solidarity was increasing, the rightness of his goal gave him a sense of freedom. He said:

> Someone could say that because Christ was crucified, it means

He lost. He lost because He was crucified. But He's winning for 2,000 years. The fact that I lose today because someone breaks my jaw, or hangs me, does not mean I lost. It only means I lost physically, as a man. But the idea, whatever happens later, may prove to be a greater victory. I can say that our victory is certain.[3]

People like that are impressive, inspiring, and challenging. Yet sometimes their courage and commitment are so strong that we feel discouraged by our seeming weakness. How can ordinary people like us participate in the good news, healing, and liberation Jesus talked about? Perhaps one of the healing stories of Jesus can help us. Mark has a vivid account of the disciples' failed attempt to heal the boy with epilepsy. Everyone is crowded around, arguing heatedly. At that point Jesus comes along and asks what is happening. The boy's father tells him the disciples cannot cast out the evil spirit. As the boy is brought before Jesus, he has another frightening convulsion. The father pleads with Jesus, "If you can do anything, have pity on us and help us." Jesus replies, "If you can! All things are possible to him who believes." The father cries out in response, "I believe. Help my unbelief" (Mk. 9:14-24, RSV).

It is not hard to see ourselves in this story. Many of us have had faith in Jesus, in the church, or in individual Christians, only to be disappointed. Jesus is not present and alive for us; the church seems weak and ineffective; Christians appear no different from anyone else. Or, like the disciples, we ourselves have tried to offer help and healing to another, but with no apparent results. Many have the combination of belief and doubt that the father expressed. And like the boy, nearly all of us, at one time or another, have felt totally incapacitated—unable to love or relate to others, to ourselves, or to God. The interesting thing about this story is that the father, despite his mixture of faith and doubt, acts on his belief and brings the boy directly to Jesus. It is much like the well-known advice given to those who would like to believe in God but do not know how to get started: Give as much of yourself to as much of God as you can. This is what the father does.

In our sessions we provide an opportunity to experience this story together and ask God for any healing or liberating we need. Release from oppression and restoration to wholeness is easier to imagine today than it was even twenty years ago. In addition to the evidence of healings within religious circles, science and medicine are now moving toward a holistic concept of healing. Cancer researchers are experimenting with guided imagery as an aid to healing their patients. Norman Cousins describes his use of humor in a self-healing process that cured him of a degenerative disease.[4] Brain research of all types is emphasizing the importance of the body/mind connection. Acting as if we believe in healing and visualizing or imagining that happening is coming to be recognized as efficacious by people in many fields other than religion. Yet these understandings do not explain everything. There is an element of mystery in healing that no amount of human understanding can fathom.

There are plenty of blocks to our believing in the healing power of Jesus' love. Stories of ill people prayed for who continued to suffer, tragic instances of brutality and cruelty, our own past and present physical/emotional hurts and damage all conspire to prevent us from reaching out for the possible healing, freedom, and newness Jesus describes. We are tempted to act on our skepticism and unbelief.

But if Jesus is to be believed, God is not passively waiting for us but is reaching out to us, stirring up our yearnings for liberation and healing, and offering us fullness of life through Jesus. The invitation is to come and see and experience.

Blind faith on our part is not required. Rather, what is necessary is an attitude of openness—both to our blind spots and to the healing and restoration that closer contact with God can bring.

Healing does not always happen in the way or time we expect or through the means we might choose. But aligning ourselves with the healing power within us, and with the expressions of God's healing that are around us, can be one of the most important things we do for ourselves, for our family and friends, and for the world.

Attending to our own needs for healing—whether physical, emotional, or spiritual—brings us back full circle to where we began this chapter. Jesus saw the Reign of God as a new order for persons and for society. Studies of the student reformers of the '60s show that as their plans for world reform were not realized, they suffered burnout. Numbers of them are now stating that they had nothing within to

sustain them and that they now realize that the road to social transformation must include personal transformation. There seems to be an
ageless wisdom in Jesus' starting his plan for universal re-formation
with the healing of individuals.

Group Design

Purpose: To share what we did with the individual work, to discuss
the personal relevance of Jesus' work of liberation and healing, and to
open ourselves to the Spirit's healing within.
Materials: Bibles, candle, oil, cross, small tables, record of meditative music.

A. Gathering Time   (10 minutes)   Large Group
Begin in a way that brings everyone (including any newcomers) on
board. This might be a prayer or a brief sharing of an important
moment in your week.

B. Sharing Groups   (20 minutes)   Groups of Four
This is the time to describe briefly what you did with the suggestions
for individual work and how they affected you personally: your
insights, feelings, difficulties. Give each person a chance to speak
without interruption, comment, or discussion before opening up for
free conversation. Remember, you are free to pass if you prefer.

C. Discussion of the Session Text   (35 minutes)   Large Group
Read Lk. 4:18-19 and consider these questions for discussion:
• Where do you see God's liberating action at work today?
• How are you personally participating or failing to participate in
  liberation?
• What in your own experience causes you to be open to seeking
  healing from God?
• What factors block your belief in God's healing power today?

D. Experience of Healing   (45 minutes)   Large Group
Preparation: Place a lighted candle in the center of the circle as a
focus. Perhaps you could add an object or two that symbolizes God's

healing (for example, a small container of oil, a cross, a Bible). Play some meditative music for a few minutes to help you relax. Sit in a comfortable position with notebook and pen at hand. (A member reads Mk. 9:14-29 slowly, then reads the following meditation.)

Meditation on the Boy Who Was Healed

"Now I will help bring the story to life with a few questions. After each I will pause. This is the time we can use for meditation and, if we wish, for recording some of our thoughts and feelings in our journals.

"First, imagine you are in the crowd arguing with the scribes. You see Jesus coming, and you run excitedly toward him. You hear the father's complaint and see his son. You hear Jesus' strong assurance that, of course, he can help the boy. Then you hear Jesus command the deaf and dumb spirit to come out of the boy and never go into him again. You see the boy collapse and then witness Jesus lifting him up. The boy stands on his own two feet and finally walks off. How do you feel? (Pause.)

"Now imagine you are the boy . . . incapacitated in some way. Think of your life today. Where are you incapacitated in loving God or yourself or another? Where do you need healing in your life? (Pause.)

"Now think of the father. Like him, you have belief and unbelief in God's ability to heal you today. In what ways do you believe God could heal this area or this situation in your life? And in what ways do you doubt that healing can happen? (Pause.)

"Again, like the father, how can you act on your belief and bring your hurt to God for healing? (Pause.)

"At this moment imagine that a father or a friend is bringing you, like the incapacitated boy, to Jesus for healing. Visualize Jesus healing you now, ordering the destructive spirits out of you, calming and restoring you, then lifting you up and setting you on your own feet. Take time to let this happen, and move into that experience with Jesus in any way that is helpful. (Pause—a little longer this time.)

"Slowly, when you are ready, open your eyes and return your awareness to the room. If you want to make an entry in your journal, take time to do so."

E. Closing   (10 minutes)   Large Group
Choose one or two of the following suggestions as appropriate for
your group: evaluation of the session, song, details of next session,
prayer in pairs, perhaps including, "Jesus wants you whole, and I do
too," or something similar.

Individual Work

Purpose: To continue to be open to the healing and liberating work of
Jesus in our own lives, in our relationships with others, and in the
healing of the world.

1. Read the story of the healing of the paralytic in Lk. 5:17-26. Notice
that for Jesus, bodily healing and forgiveness of sins are intimately
connected. List areas of your life where you feel you need forgiveness
or healing, where you feel broken, hurt, unfree, stuck, or paralyzed.

2. Jesus taught that freedom and healing come when we take on his
outlook and activity, i.e., when we are instrumental in healing and
freeing others. "Forgive us the wrong we have done as we forgive
those who wrong us" (Mt. 6:12, NAB). List as many people or
situations as you can in which you sense there is something wrong in
your relationship: estrangement, distance, feeling offended, hurt.

3. The proclamation of "the acceptable year of the Lord" in Jesus'
mission statement referred to the Year of the Jubilee (mentioned in
Lev. 25:8-55), a time when "the liberation of all the inhabitants of the
land" was to be proclaimed and realized. Consider proclaiming your
own Jubilee Year by forgiving all the people you have just listed,
letting them off the hook completely. It may help to picture them as
doing the best they could to enter into a good relationship with you.

4. Reflect on how this free act of forgiveness affects your own areas
of paralysis and unfreedom mentioned in response to the first
question.

5. Continue the reflection begun in the session on how your own
transformation and your concern for social transformation are inter-
woven in your life. Are there changes you want to make?

Note: The theme of healing and cleansing is given further consideration in the third course, Tools for Christian Growth, Session 4.

6. To prepare for the next session: Write a brief summary of your personal work with the assignment.

Notes

1. Claire Safran, "Unforgettable Jean Donovan," *Readers Digest,* vol. 119, no. 713 (Sept. 1981):103-106.
2. Coretta King, *My Life with Martin Luther King, Jr.* (New York: Avon Books, 1969), p. 334.
3. Ania and Dysia Bittenek, "We Are Our Greatest Threat," *The Washington Post,* January 10, 1982, Outlook, p. 1 (excerpted from an interview in *Playboy,* February, 1982).
4. *Anatomy of an Illness* (New York: W. W. Norton & Co., 1979).

Session 3

Friend/Mystery

As we offer this course over and over we notice that people want to get to the heart of the matter, to find out who Jesus really is, and then more personally, what that means to them.

Years ago a woman we know began asking the same questions. She knew that Christianity was a rich system of belief. It had good intellectual structure and some vital ethical principles. But she was looking for something more personal. Some people talked about having a relationship with Jesus, but she could not figure out how anyone could have such a relationship with someone who lived 2,000 years ago. Also, she was wary of people who spoke too glibly of "having a personal relationship" with Jesus. That sounded somewhat fanatical, and they seemed to be too familiar with a God of mystery and transcendence. Yet significant persons whom she loved and admired talked about relating to God personally through Jesus and about prayer as a source of vital spiritual nourishment.

She knew that scripture was important, but the Jesus she found there seemed rather stilted, matter-of-fact, and not all that appealing.

Then one lonely year in Scotland she ran across a book that changed all that for her. This book made Jesus come alive and portrayed one so compassionate and committed to justice that she wanted to allow him more access to her life. She began to experiment with talking and listening to God and imagining herself relating to Jesus as portrayed in the Gospels. At one point she came to realize the wonderful gift he wants to give us all: the gift of himself and his love and the invitation to allow that love to live in us. In the preceding session we saw the mission and plan of action he had for his life and for those who wanted to follow him. It was the gift of his presence as companion and guide that enabled his friends and followers to commit themselves to this purpose and plan. Jesus was there to interpret the plan, live it with them, and pick them up when they failed. This is what made the difference.

The word *gift* is used in scripture to name the life of love to which Jesus calls us. We can accept this gift with gratitude or, of course, ignore or refuse it. But we cannot earn it. Yet most of us continue to feel that if we try harder, believe differently, or imitate Jesus or outstanding Christians more perfectly we will earn God's acceptance and love. The good news is that a free gift is offered, one with no strings attached. The gift is a relationship of love with one who accepts us as we are but empowers us to be more, and whose love endures within and beyond the mystery of death.

God's love given freely and to all challenges us to embrace others with compassion, particularly the needy and oppressed. "I was hungry and you gave me no food, I was thirsty and you gave me no drink. I was away from home and you gave me no welcome . . ." (Mt. 25:42-43, NAB). These words are demanding and confronting, yet when understood in the context of the friendship and love of Jesus, they take on new light. Most of us have a loved one for whom we would do "anything," give our time, our energy, our very selves. "He's not heavy, he's my brother," reads the poster showing a young man carrying an injured friend. Love gives us energy and purpose with which to perform the difficult, the unappealing. That seems to be what St. Paul experienced in his demanding life when he said, "The very spring of my actions is the love of Christ" (2 Cor. 5:14, Phillips). How do we experience this love? There are different ways, depending on temperament, circumstances, and background.

Some experience this love by relating to God as friend, lover, companion, or parent. For them, prayer is like being with a loved one—talking, listening, being silent, or engaging in work or play.

Others find this sort of intimacy at odds with their concept of God as mystery. For them, prayer is real and effective but may take the form of a walk in the woods, listening to music, or reading poetry. Ralph Keifer writes that the vocation of those who experience God in this way "is to live before God as mystery, not as friend; or, more accurately perhaps, they are called to befriend the mystery that haunts them . . . ."[1] He says:

> Part of the experience of this spirituality of mystery is an intense intuition of there being something elusive, haunting, indirect, yet utterly compelling about which life relentlessly revolves. There is a

sense of being drawn or pursued by something that is never quite
tangible, that never quite allows any sense of a face-to-face
meeting.[2]

Those who approach God this way have a sense of God's being positively
involved in their lives and in the world, sustaining them but remaining
intangible and mysterious. They acknowledge God's being as ultimately
loving, supportive, calling them forth into deeper involvement with God
and the world.

For those who relate to God in more personal terms, the sense of Jesus
or God as personal friend may be steady for long periods of life or may
come and go. Also, certain temperaments tend toward one approach
rather than the other. And finally, early childhood training and experience with religious traditions and expressions will affect the way one
responds to God.

Acknowledging that there are different ways of experiencing God's
love, how can we enter into that love and allow it to ignite our own
capacity for caring? How does it become real to us today? Several
elements are involved. First, it seems necessary to recognize and name
our hungers, whether for meaning, purpose, compassion, or empowerment. Spiritually hungry people recognize and take advantage of spiritual nourishment when they find it. Those who are satisfied with their
present existence usually are not interested. Once I asked a wise person
what types of people he thought would respond to our courses. He said,
"Your courses attempt to present the basics—no frills—the essence of
Christian faith. Those who would respond would probably be those who
are very needy and hungry, or those who are already committed to a
serious Christian vocation and who need help and support."

Second, God's invitation requires a response, a conscious decision to
accept God's gift of love. Jesus asked some people to follow him. They
had to say yes or no. Was that an intellectually sound thing to do if they
did not have all the facts? And what about us? We too are faced with this
challenge. If we say yes, we open ourselves to another level of knowing,
one based on experience rather than on observation from the outside.
The image used by Evelyn Underhill illustrates this way of knowing. It is
like a cathedral with stained glass windows, she says. From the outside,
the windows are just there—nothing special. But from the inside, with

the light streaming through, the most wonderful scenes come alive. So it is crucial at some point for persons who wish to experience the new life Jesus offers to step inside and begin practicing, testing, experimenting, experiencing.

Third, the imagination can play an important part. Teresa of Avila taught a method of prayer that engages the imagination in using scripture passages for reflection. First, read through the passage in order to see its sweep. Next, read it slowly and imagine the setting, the people involved, and the action. Try to enter into the scene, relate to the story in a personal way, and hear the words of Jesus spoken to you. Finally, ponder the significance of the scripture for your own life. Many Christians throughout history have used some form of this method in developing a deep awareness of the presence of Christ in their lives. (One such method is Karl Olsson's relational Bible study introduced in Session 3 of Course 1.)

Finally, God's love becomes real as we live out Jesus' teaching in Mt. 25:40: "Truly, I say to you, as you did it to one of the least of these my sisters and brothers, you did it to me."[3] This can be seen in the experience of Frank Laubach, a pioneer in teaching illiterate adults to read. Dr. Laubach spent some years as a missionary in the Philippines. At first he was very much alone there, learning the language of the Moros, a primitive people among whom he felt called to minister. During that period he resolved to be as open to God and to the needs of the people as possible. In his diary, later published under the title *Letters by a Modern Mystic,* Dr. Laubach describes the year as "a succession of marvelous experiences of the friendship of God." How does this friendship develop? "Precisely as any friendship is achieved. By doing things together. The depth and intensity of the friendship will depend upon the variety and extent of the things we do and enjoy together." He goes on to describe how God's friendship becomes a reality:

All I have said is mere words, until one sets out helping God right wrongs, helping God help the helpless, loving and talking it over with God. Then there comes a great sense of the close-up, warm, intimate heart of reality. God simply creeps in and you *know* he is here in your heart. He has become your friend by working along with you.

So if anybody were to ask me how to find God I should say at once, hunt out the deepest need you can find and forget all about your own comfort while you try to meet that need. Talk to God about it, and—he will be there. You will know it.[4]

In terms of what we have said in this book thus far, then, to say yes to the love and justice we see in Jesus means to align ourselves with his purpose, to avail ourselves of a spiritual power that activates our own, and to be open to a presence—whether of mystery or friend—that we can come to know and love more deeply by reaching out to those in real need.

Group Design

Purpose: To open ourselves to a more intimate relationship with Jesus as friend and as mystery.

A. Gathering Time   (10 minutes)   Large Group
Begin in a way that brings everyone on board, including any who were absent. Use a song, moment of silence, or perhaps sharing in a word how you are feeling as you come to this session. (For example, "I'm feeling uneasy because I have a new babysitter with my children tonight.")

B. Sharing Groups   (20 minutes)
Describe briefly one or two concrete ways you dealt with this assignment and in what ways you are open to the healing and liberating work of Jesus in your own life and with others.

C. Discussion of the Session Text   (35 minutes)
1. As you read the descriptions of those who relate to God most readily as friend or as mystery, with which description do you identify? Or are there other ways you would describe your response to God's love as expressed through Jesus?
2. The way that others perceive and respond to God's love can expand our own relationship with God. As you share with those who respond differently from you, can you consider expanding your response? How? Give examples.

D. Experiencing Jesus as Friend/Mystery   (45 minutes)

In the session text, four ways of becoming more intimately related to Jesus as friend or as mystery are mentioned. They are:
• recognizing and naming our spiritual hunger;
• consciously deciding to be more open to the love of God in our lives;
• imaging or visualizing God's loving involvement in our own lives and those of others;
• extending ourselves to others and thus embodying the love of God in tangible ways.

Take about 15 minutes to write your reflections on the following questions:

1. Am I open to a deeper relationship with Jesus as friend or mystery?

2. Which of the steps mentioned above have I taken?

3. Are there steps (mentioned or others) I should take in order to deepen this relationship?

After you finish writing, pair up with another and share your reflections as you wish. Writing and then speaking our clarities or confusions can often move us to a new place. Respond to one another with encouragement and/or prayer (15 minutes).

Use the remainder of your time (15 minutes) for a group reflection on the insights that may have occurred or on the difficulties encountered through your journaling and sharing.

E. Closing   (10 minutes)   Large Group

Choose one or two of the following suggestions as appropriate for your group: evaluation of the session, song, details of next session, prayer. Here is one prayer suggestion. Perhaps the oldest Christian prayer is one word, *maranatha,* the Aramaic phrase in Jesus' language that means "Come, Lord!" (Rev. 22:2). Many people around the world use this as a mantra (a sacred word or phrase repeated in meditation).[5] Your group might like to use this mantra, either in English or Aramaic, each one simply repeating it around the circle.

Individual Work

Purpose: To gain a biblical overview of Jesus as friend, to open ourselves to God's befriending of us in our needy areas, and to consider how we extend God's love to others.

1. Read the Gospel of Mark, the earliest and shortest account of Jesus' life and work, taking note of how you see Jesus embodying God as friend. Make a special note of any newness you discover or any insights that evoke a fresh response to God's love in you. (*Note:* If possible, read through Mark at one sitting, much as you would read a novel. Choose a readable translation. Then in other periods, during the week, review and ponder the reading you did. This seems like a demanding suggestion, but most of our participants are glad to have been challenged to do this.)

2. The psychiatrist C. G. Jung felt that the key to healing the world and making it a place of compassion was to identify those parts of our inner world that we most reject and then to befriend those parts and allow God to love those parts as well. Our groups have found the following passage from Jung helpful:

> If the doctor wishes to help a human being he must be able to accept him as he is. And he can do this in reality only when he has already seen and accepted himself as he is.
>
> Perhaps this sounds very simple, but simple things are always the most difficult. In actual life it requires the greatest discipline to be simple, the acceptance of oneself is the essence of the moral problem and the epitome of a whole outlook upon life. That I feed the hungry, that I forgive an insult, that I love my enemy in the name of Christ—all these are undoubtedly great virtues. What I do unto the least of my brethren, that I do unto Christ. But what if I should discover that the least among them all, the poorest of all the beggars, the most impudent of all the offenders, the very enemy himself—that these are all within me, and that I myself stand in need of the alms of my own kindness—that I myself am the enemy that must be loved—what then? As a rule, the Christian's attitude is then reversed; there is no longer any question of love or long-suffering; we say to the brother within us "Raca," and condemn and rage against ourselves. We hide it from the world; we refuse to admit ever having met this least among the lowly in ourselves. Had it been God himself who drew near to us in this despicable form, we should have denied him a thousand times, before a single cock had crowed.[6]

Identify and practice ways to do what Jung suggests in this passage. Perhaps you can visualize an area of your life or a trait that you find unacceptable. Can you then visualize yourself in Jesus' company befriending this enemy within?

3. Ponder the quote from Frank Laubach in the text: "So if anybody were to ask me how to find God I should say at once, hunt out the deepest need you can find and forget all about your own comfort while you try to meet that need . . . ." Focus on one way you could try that out this week. Record in your journal what you did and how you felt about it.

4. To prepare for the next session: Write a brief summary of your personal work with the assignment.

Notes

1. Ralph Keifer, "A Spirituality of Mystery," *Spirituality Today* 33 (June 1981):107.
2. Ibid., p. 105.
3. Inclusive Language Lectionary Committee, *An Inclusive Language Lectionary* (Philadelphia: The Westminster Press, 1983), last Sunday after Pentecost.
4. (Syracuse, N.Y.: New Readers Press, 1979), p. 46.
5. Lawrence Freeman, *Man of Maranatha, Praying,* no. 1 (Supplement to the *National Catholic Reporter*), pp. 39, 40.
6. C. G. Jung, *Modern Man in Search of a Soul,* trans. Dell and Baynes (London: Routledge and Kegan Paul, 1933), pp. 271-272. Published in the U.S.A. by Harcourt, Brace & Co. (New York: 1933).

Session 4

Teacher/Guide

One of the most universally believed truths about Jesus is that he was a great teacher. Although not formally trained, he was often called "teacher" or "rabbi" in his day. Even today it is not uncommon to hear, "I don't know if he was God, but I do believe he was a great teacher."

Teaching occupied a substantial part of his ministry. As he inaugurated a new order of living and invited people to participate, he offered basic training in a new way.

When a lawyer asked him how to live this new way, he replied:

"You shall love the Lord your God
with all your heart,
with all your soul,
with all your strength,
and with all your mind;
and your neighbor as yourself."

(Lk. 10:27, NAB)

In answer to the lawyer's question, "And who is my neighbor?" Jesus did not give a direct answer, a lecture, or a sermon. He told an unforgettable story that caused the lawyer to do his own thinking. He painted a vivid picture of a man beaten by robbers and ignored by two members of the respected establishment. A third passerby was a Samaritan, a foreigner usually looked down upon by the Jews, who stopped and gave the man tangible help. Jesus then asked the lawyer who he thought acted as neighbor to the man in need. "The one who treated him with compassion," was the reply.

In describing Jesus as a teacher and guide, Matthew Fox points out that he was "a poet, a storyteller, an artist. He was not primarily a priest or a theologian or an academician, but an awakener to the sacrament of the cosmos."[1] Jesus deliberately chose to teach in parables, stories with vivid images that did not give answers so much as they enabled listeners to discover truth for themselves. These compelling stories, according to Fox, "invite the listener to change his or her life, to metanoia, to transformation. And they invite a whole society to let go and start over again, trusting its images and its power for creativity."[2]

Jesus lived what he taught. He himself was a neighbor to all sorts of children, women, and men. It was one thing to hear him tell this pointed story about compassion but quite another to see this compassionate man in action, reaching out to hungry people, the distraught woman in the kitchen, the dying thief on the cross.

Today it is possible to hear Jesus' stories, read collections of his teachings, for example, in the Sermon on the Mount, Matthew 5-7, observe his life, and yet be untouched. The familiar stories and sayings, radical and transforming as they are, can in reality fail to move us whether we like to admit it or not. The Lord's Prayer is an example. Jesus used these words to teach us the art of prayer. Hundreds of words have been written to illuminate its meaning, yet when all is said and done, we know how often we mumble it without recognizing its power.

We need help in discerning truth and direction in the perplexing situations we face today. Jesus as teacher/guide can help us if we move beyond the familiarity to the transforming power of his teaching. We can do this just as he did: Engage in lively conversations with the people and issues of our day, couch the truth we discover in fresh contemporary language, tell stories that illustrate this truth, and live it out in our own lives.

Dorothee Soelle and other liberation theologians are doing just that. They are listening to and speaking with the poor and the powerful, the dispossessed and the affluent in First World and Third World countries. They are using fresh language to describe gospel values. They say that living God's way involves siding with, befriending, and empowering the poor, the marginalized, the oppressed, the hurting. It means placing persons and compassion before profitability. This is how they interpret teachings such as "Blest are you poor; the reign of God is yours" (Lk. 6:20, NAB). They point out that Jesus was not neutral but sided with the poor, the despised, the outcasts, the invisible ones. Soelle suggests that taking up one's cross and following Jesus means:

breaking with neutrality;

making the invisible visible;
sharing a vision.[3]

In our country, one group of people who are invisible are the inner-city poor. How can a group that is not poor break with its neutrality and side with the invisible poor of the city? How can they together envision ways to empower one another to live a full life? The story of Jubilee Housing, Inc., offers one answer.

In 1973 some people in Washington, D.C., formed a group to address the inner-city housing needs of low-income residents. Their vision was that everyone in Washington could have adequate housing, but they began with a realizable goal—to upgrade one city block of a deteriorated neighborhood. If they could begin with one section and create a model, perhaps a method to renovate other blocks would develop. But at first even that was too much. They began by acquiring one house and renovating it with the help of residents. Then they purchased and reno-vated two apartment buildings. Almost one thousand building code violations had to be corrected before the ninety units could pass inspec-tion. More than 50,000 hours of voluntary work was spent on this task.

The group named itself Jubilee Housing, Inc., after the Jubilee Year mentioned in the Book of Leviticus when, according to their anniversary booklet,

> . . . slaves were to be freed; debts were to be forgiven; land was to come back to the original families. The burden of the past was to be removed; the future could beckon with new opportunities. Thus the Jubilee Year was intended to structure *fairness* into the ordering of society. The poor and the weak were to be given the tools necessary to lift themselves out of dependence and poverty. They were to be given the hope of a new beginning.[4]

After ten years, Jubilee Housing is now able to provide 258 housing units for low-income families. In addition, it has created organizations to address the needs of these families such as employment, job-skill train-ing, job creation, health care, education of preschool and damaged children, and emergency assistance.

"Blessed are the peacemakers" is a theme elucidated with fresh language and stories by sociologist Kenneth Boulding in *Stable Peace*, in which he describes concrete and comprehensive proposals for peace in our time. Among his ideas is one related to loving one's enemies. It involves reciprocal acts of good will between potential enemies. According to Boulding, a gradual reduction in tension can begin "by some rather specific, perhaps even dramatic, statement or act directed at a potential enemy."[5] To illustrate, he tells the story of Anwar Sadat's visit to Jerusalem in 1977. Interviews with Sadat revealed that he was well aware of the risk involved and the personal consequences of failure. However, inspired by Gandhi, he was ready to take a risk for peace.

Fresh language and interesting stories of people who take Jesus' teachings seriously can open the transforming power of such language and stories for us. In the end, however, it is when we experience them working that real growth occurs. We two had often read Jesus' words about reconciling with those from whom we are estranged before going to the altar. A few years ago, the two of us found ourselves incapacitated by misunderstandings and negative feelings toward each other arising from our differing interpretation of shared experiences. Finally we decided to tackle our differences directly. Aided by some learnings from the art of conflict resolution, we agreed to identify each hurtful incident, say how it made us feel, and listen to each other with care and respect. Then we attempted to construct a composite picture of what had really happened. We began the process somewhat fearfully, but by the time we were through there was a new desire to work together. A creative flow of ideas came from the shared experience.

There is transforming power in the truths Jesus taught. Why are they not taken seriously more often? They have the potential to unleash enormous creativity and compassion, so needed in our world threatened by destruction. The observation rings true: It is not that Christianity does not work; it has not been tried. How challenging to think that we and others could try the kind of living and loving Jesus describes!

Those of us who have said yes to God's loving presence have access through the Spirit to Jesus' companionship as on-the-spot guide, encourager, and mentor. This is what he has promised:

> "I have said all this while I am still with you. But the one who is coming to stand by you, the Holy Spirit whom the Father will send in my name, will be your teacher and will bring to your minds all

that I have said to you."

(Jn. 14:25-26, Phillips)

As we open ourselves to this Spirit in prayer, we find new life in scriptural events and teachings and know their possibility, power, and relevance to our situation. We also become sensitized to God's action within us and all of creation.

Jesus' teachings are not easy. They are full of paradox: simple and complex; comforting and confronting; compelling and freeing. They are open to endless misinterpretation and abuse. People are tempted to absolutize specifics when he intended to stimulate thought and love. Some confuse the ideal of love with the contemporary wish to "feel good" or to "feel comfortable" about things.

Yet transformation and growth occur when we are open to fresh articulations of his teaching, when we exchange stories that bring his teachings alive, and especially when we try them out in our own lives.

Group Design

Purpose: To reflect on the qualities of a good teacher and to share those teachings of Jesus that have been most transforming for us.
Materials: newsprint, bread, serving tray or plate, Bibles.

A. Gathering Time and Evaluation   (30 minutes)   Large Group
Gather and get started in a way that is appropriate for your group. Then move into a brief period of taking stock of how you and the group are doing. In the first session we shared our hopes about what might happen to us as a result of this course. Take a moment to look in your journal to recall how you stated your hopes. Now make a few notes about how these hopes are or are not being realized. What could you and/or the group do differently to enable you to realize your hopes more fully? When you have finished your individual reflection, go around the circle sharing briefly one thing you appreciate about your experience and one idea for improvement that either you or the group could try.

B. Sharing Groups   (20 minutes)
Consider sharing your reactions to these questions:

1. What new perception of Jesus as friend surfaced for you in your reading of Mark?

2. How did you respond to the quotation from Jung?

3. How did you choose to implement the Laubach quotation?

C. Teacher of the Year   (25 minutes)   In Pairs and Then in Large Group

If you were selecting one person in your life as teacher of the year because she or he encouraged you to discover truths in a helpful way, who would that be? Take a few minutes to think of a person and then turn to someone you have not talked with much and describe briefly why that person was important to you.

Move into the large group and informally share the qualities of the people you talked about. What made them special? Consider recording the qualities on a piece of newsprint for all to see.

When you have finished your group portrait of a good teacher, reflect on how many of these qualities may have been present in Jesus, who was known as an effective teacher. An awareness of his human qualities as teacher may shed light on some of his scriptural teachings.

D. Experiencing Jesus as Teacher/Guide   (30 minutes)

Breaking open the biblical word through sharing, and breaking bread together have been common activities among Christians throughout history. Here is a chance to engage in these activities.

1. *Preparation:* In the center of the circle place some bread that can easily be broken and shared in the group.

2. *Alone:* (15 minutes) Take time to look at the Sermon on the Mount (Mt. 5-7) or other passages if you wish. Select one teaching that has made a difference in your life. That is, think of a time when you found Jesus' words life-giving or illuminating, or a time when you saw Jesus' teachings come alive in the life of another.

3. *Large Group:* (15 minutes) When you are ready, share your example with the group. Then break a piece of bread off the loaf, but leave it on the serving tray. You may have extra time, so feel free to end with informal discussion of how to incorporate Jesus' teachings more fully into your lives.

E. Closing   (15 minutes)   Large Group

Choose one or two of the following suggestions as appropriate for your group: evaluation of the session, song, details of next session, prayer. One suggestion: In the circle around the table, each one take and eat one of the pieces of bread symbolizing Jesus as the bread of life. Those who wish to do so may end the session with informal prayer.

Individual Work

Purpose: To become conscious of persons who embody Jesus' teachings in memorable ways and to focus on practicing one of Jesus' teachings more fully.

1. List a few of the people you have read about or know personally who make some of Jesus' teachings alive and relevant for you. Select one to think about more carefully. Why does this person impress you? What do you find attractive about the person? Are there ways you would like to be like that person? Write your reflections in your journal. (*Note:* Often the people we admire have qualities that are latent within us and could be developed. Becoming conscious of why we admire another can be a step toward finding and nurturing those qualities in ourselves.)

2. Reread Mt. 5-7 and select one teaching you would like to concentrate on this week. Ponder how you can practice this more fully. Make regular entries in your journal about your attempts to embody this teaching.

3. To prepare for the next session: Write a brief summary of your personal work with the assignment.

Notes

1. *Original Blessing* (Santa Fe: Bear & Co., 1983), p. 239.
2. Ibid., p. 240.
3. Dorothee Soelle, *Choosing Life* (Philadelphia: Fortress Press, 1981), p. 55.
4. Jubilee Housing, Inc., *Year of the Jubilee: June 1, 1983 Through May 31, 1984* (10th Anniversary Report, available from Jubilee Housing, Inc., 1750 Columbia Road, N.W., Washington, D.C. 20009). p. 3.

5. Kenneth E. Boulding, *Stable Peace* (Austin & London: University of Texas Press, 1978), p. 112.

Session 5

Savior/Prophet

It is said that at the center of everything lies the cross, the pivot of history, at once the symbol of the failure of Christ's way of love and the beginning of its ultimate triumph.

What do statements like this really mean? How can something that happened 2,000 years ago have a personal effect on people today? An onlooker might say that the cross is a horrible way to die, a disgusting tribute to hatred and cruelty, the resurrection an unbelievable event that flies in the face of 2,000 years of scientific research, and Pentecost a strange happening among distraught people unwilling to accept the death and disappearance of their leader.

A look at the Gospel accounts reveals a deepening storm over the impact of Jesus' life and work. Acceptance of his early teaching and works of healing gradually gave way to a divided response among his disciples, the crowds, and the authorities. Conflict and confrontation increased. Authorities questioned his interpretation of the Law and concluded that his healing power was of the devil. People in the crowd walked away when challenged with the demands of the new order. Bewildered at their lack of power and their leader's increasing unpopularity, the disciples misunderstood and wrangled at times.

Finally, events converged at the cross. This good and loving person who healed the suffering, took little children into his arms, and inspired ordinary people to believe in their value as channels of God's love was put to death as a criminal.

In the desert, Jesus had chosen the power of love as his way. As effective as that had been in healing and transforming individuals, it was subjected to a deadly challenge. The disappointment of the people, the blindness and intransigence of the religious authorities, and the misuse of imperial power all climaxed at Calvary. Jesus was nailed to a cross. Yet he had not been trapped. He had known what was coming and had

106

walked toward his fate with confidence and love while hoping with all his heart that he could be spared.

So the darkness of despair and the light of faith converged in Jesus on the cross. He continued to address God as Father even though feeling utterly abandoned, and he reached out to the dying thief and the torment-ing guards with words of love and forgiveness. Alone, except for Mary and her friends at the foot of the cross, he offered his life in loving commitment to the way that had been given: faithful, personal love for friend and enemy. Yet most of his own friends had fled or turned away.

Gradually Jesus' followers huddled together in prayer and mourning. Imagine their bewilderment when three women burst in with the news that Jesus was not dead but had risen and would meet them in Galilee. The disciples dismissed them with disbelief. However, astonishing things began to happen, things that transformed their doubt. Jesus appeared to them at their meetings and on the road and gently instilled in them the belief that the spirit and power of love that he had embodied was alive and accessible to them at any time. It did not depend on his physical presence. What began as a period described by Mark as one of mourning and weeping (Mk. 16:10) ended with great joy.

In one of his final appearances, Jesus promised his followers that they would be baptized with the Spirit and would be given power.

Luke vividly describes the outpouring of the Spirit in the second chapter of Acts. A mighty sound, flames of fire, and the power to speak the message of God and be understood in different languages were the tangible signs of a new presence and power among the disciples. In one of the most important sermons ever preached, Peter explained what happened by quoting Joel, an Old Testament figure who had prophesied that God would pour the Spirit upon all flesh. Then Peter insisted that it was through belief in Jesus that the Holy Spirit would be conferred. In response to their question as to what to do, he replied:

"You must repent and every one of you must be baptized in the Name of Jesus Christ, so that you may have your sins forgiven and receive the gift of the Holy Spirit."

(Acts 2:38, Phillips)

Luke describes the impressive result:

Then those who welcomed his message were baptized, and on that day alone about three thousand souls were added to the number of the disciples.

(Acts 2:41, Phillips)

Thus begins the story in the Book of Acts of the young church in action. Even a cursory reading of this remarkable book reveals an astounding change of mood and activity among the disciples. Afraid and defeated at the crucifixion, then hopeful but uncertain during the resurrection appearances, they appear in the Book of Acts as confident preachers, effective healers, and power-filled proclaimers and embodiers of the Reign of God. As J. B. Phillips says in his introduction to his translation of Acts,

> It is a matter of sober historical fact that never before has any small body of ordinary people so moved the world that their enemies could say, with tears of rage in their eyes, that these men "have turned the world upside down!"

(Acts 17:6)[1]

As we attempt to absorb the importance of these events and actions in our lives today, we must move from pondering to participation. Pondering can reveal the profundity of these events; participation can open us to their transforming power.

But how can this kind of growth happen in us? In our sessions we look at this through the experience of Peter. As we observe Peter in the four periods of his life with Christ, we notice distinct changes. The pre-crucifixion Peter was eager, impetuous, enthusiastic, sometimes mistaken, but certainly earnest. He left everything to follow Jesus, took part in his liberating mission, was one of the first to recognize Jesus as the expected Christ, but also dismayed Jesus by insisting that the Jerusalem trip was unnecessary.

During the crucifixion it seemed as if everything and everyone he believed in and loved had collapsed. Even though Peter insisted he would stay by Jesus' side, he could not stay awake with him to pray in the garden. And in the courtyard he could not even admit knowing Jesus, whom he had loved so unabashedly only days before. At the crucifixion Peter was hopeless, weak, distraught, afraid.

After the resurrection, the disciples and Peter waited, prayed, and were filled with wonder, new hope, and puzzlement when they recognized the presence of Jesus guiding and empowering them.

At Pentecost, a new energy surged into Peter and the disciples. Suddenly they were catapulted into action. No longer were they waiting. They knew their mission and were eager to accomplish it; they felt challenged by obstacles, were unafraid of opposition, on fire with a message and a ministry. Peter and the others boldly carried on Jesus' ministry of healing, preaching, teaching, and challenging the authorities. They established house churches as alternative communities of caring and nourishment that became bases for ministry. Open to the wider implications of the vision, Peter extended God's love beyond the Jewish community to the Gentiles, those outside the original company of believers.

Many people find that as they open themselves more fully to a relationship with God, they have the variety of experiences we see in Peter.

Pre-crucifixion. When persons consciously affirm the fullness of life embodied by Jesus, they are introduced to a life of commitment and compassion. In this initial response, there may be many ups and downs, times of deep knowing and understanding, and times of failure. Gripped by the needs of others, they often become seriously involved in those needs. However, they can get carried away with an impetuousness not unlike that of Peter, who tried to do everything. Initial enthusiasm can be replaced by weariness and dismay at what they perceive as a lack of support by others.

Crucifixion. A variety of factors can cause a person to be involved and confronted with the crucified Jesus in a personal, profound way. Perhaps certain individuals let one down; the Christian community fails to extend love in a time of need; a loved one dies prematurely in a seemingly cruel or useless way; one can become exhausted and disillusioned by taking on too much without sufficient spiritual resources. In short, the person is disappointed in Christians, in the church, in God, or in self and is tempted to give up the committed life as Peter did. These disappointed Christians sometimes withdraw quietly from their faith communities without saying what is really in their minds and hearts. Often, however, they remain, but as foot-dragging, cynical, hopeless people. They are in a "death place" and can see no hope in others or themselves.

Resurrection. This kind of disappointment may not last; some people move beyond it. A direct experience of God's presence, an undeniable healing, real connections with caring people, or other catalytic experiences can cause persons to believe that God is not dead but alive. They begin to believe that the fullness of life that Jesus embodied really is attainable. Wonder, expectancy, and hope revive. Like the disciples, they know there is more to come and are waiting to see what it is.

Pentecost. Some Christians have a personal encounter with the Holy Spirit. Whether or not they speak about this openly, we sense that for them the Spirit is not a question mark but a personally known guide, comforter, confronter. This experience with the Spirit places them in a whole new realm. Prayer, scripture, commitment, deep caring, and mission are alive and important. A profound sense of joy, trust, and exhilaration in the creative Spirit often occurs, but it is accompanied by a keener participation in the pain of the world. A more mature commitment to the Reign of God increasingly becomes the center of their lives. They become carriers of God's healing, teaching, mercy, and justice.

Each experience described comes into sharper focus and has deeper impact when we consciously respond to its challenge. As we identify with Jesus and his way, we can experience his presence and teaching as vital. By becoming conscious of the pain caused by indifference, hatred, and evil in self and others, we open ourselves to the cleansing and pruning that happens through personal exposure to Jesus. In beginning to recognize Jesus' compassion and justice operative in outside events and within ourselves, we join the disciples in their wonder, joy, and hope. And when we consciously invite the Spirit to dwell within, we find ways of extending and sharing that life with others.

Unfortunately, we sometimes try to live the life appropriate to one of these experiences without ever consciously entering into it. For example, enticed by the example of those who know the Spirit, we try to live that life without inviting the Spirit to live within us.

Another danger is believing that these experiences are like the rungs of a ladder on which we steadily climb to heaven. Actually, they are more like threads that weave in and out of life in unexpected ways. Once a Christian has experienced these aspects of faith in an introductory fashion, he or she is open to their presence throughout life. They do not always happen in the same sequence as Peter's did. Someone already acquainted with the Spirit can come to a place of crucifixion. Or a resurrection person, filled with hope, can become bogged down in duty.

How and in what order these experiences happen defies explanation. Here we have just touched the surface. It can be said, however, that many people find the pre-crucifixion, crucifixion, resurrection, and Pentecost sequence the most helpful model for a life of love that has ever been offered. Moreover, as these events continue throughout history to transform people, their universal effect becomes apparent. It began with the transformation of the disciples, continues in the lives of countless persons, and has the potential to transform the whole world.

Group Design

Purpose: To relive Peter's experience with Jesus and to allow it to touch us personally.
Materials: Bibles.

A. Gathering Time   (15 minutes)   Large Group
Bring everyone on board in a way that seems appropriate for this session.

B. Sharing Group   (25 minutes)
Go around the circle and share the second item in the individual design. Which teaching did you choose, and how did you work with it? If you have extra time, speak about the first item: What did you learn from your reflecting on a person who makes Jesus' teaching alive and relevant for you?

C. Walking in Peter's Shoes   (65 minutes)   Large Group
One of the members of our community, Mildred Allen, made a private silent retreat, taking only her Bible and a notebook. Moved to read the Gospel of Mark, she became fascinated with Peter's experience and found herself writing a journal from the vantage point of Peter as he is portrayed in that Gospel. Putting herself in his shoes was a powerful experience. In this session we join her in this experience by reading excerpts from "Peter's Journal" as she wrote it, then by studying crucial passages involving Peter, and finally by writing our own continuation of

his journal.

1. Ask one person to read aloud the following excerpts from "Peter's Journal," found below. (This takes about 15 minutes.)

2. After listening to "Peter's Journal" divide into four small groups. Assign each group one of the following passages: Peter's denial (Lk. 22:54-62); empty tomb (Lk. 24:1-12); after resurrection (Jn. 21:1-19); after Pentecost (Acts 4:1-22).

a. In your small group choose one person to be a recorder/journalist who will write the continuation of Peter's journal based on the group's discussion. The group does the thinking. The recorder simply records it in the first person as if it were Peter writing.

b. Read the scripture aloud or silently in your group. As you do so, attempt to stand in Peter's shoes, imagining his feelings and responses.

c. Talk about your perception of how Peter thought, felt, and responded.

d. Help the recorder/journalist record your perceptions in journal form. (Use about 30-35 minutes for this read/share/write process.)

3. All come together. Have someone reread aloud the last paragraph of "Peter's Journal." Then have the recorder/journalists read the four journal sections in chronological order. Leave a little silence after each reading for assimilation and pondering. (This should take about 15 minutes.)

D. Closing   (15 minutes)   Large Group

Choose one or two of the following suggestions as appropriate to your group: evaluation of session, song, prayer, discussion of details for next session.

An Imaginary Journal of Peter
Drawn from the Gospel of Mark

I'm Simon. I'm just an ordinary fisherman, but some extraordinary things have begun to happen to me and I want to keep track of them.

The other day I was working with my brother Andrew a bit offshore in our boat, casting nets. Along the beach we saw the Nazarene, Jesus, walking. We waved and he called to us, "Come with me."

Andrew and I looked at each other and, wonder of wonders, without a word we dropped our nets, pulled the boat ashore, forgot about fishing and went with him. We've hardly been home since.

What made me do that? Suddenly, Jesus' authority, his strong, pure beauty, the truth of him took me over. I have a sense that all fulfillment is in following him, and what I've been doing for a living takes a back seat and claims me no more. The "Come with me" of Jesus was a command really, but it was so promising, so loving, without guile, that it seemed powerfully alluring. (Pause.)

The past Sabbath day a number of us got together in the synagogue in Capernaum. Jesus speaks with such authority. I'm awed by it and feel very drawn to him, to find out about him, and to learn what he knows.

He really stunned us all when he spoke to a shrieking man who cried out, "Have you come to destroy us? I know who you are—The Holy One of God." Jesus spoke—as if to something in the man—"Be silent and come out of him!" There was no force stronger than his command. The man went into convulsions and then was quiet and free from this unclean spirit.

We five went to my house after that synagogue episode—my brother, James, John, Jesus, and me. My wife's mother had been sick with a very high fever. I told Jesus about her as we came close to the place. He went right over to her as if he knew her, took her hand, and helped her out of bed. She wasn't sick at all. The fever left her, and she began fixing us things to eat! Really amazing! I'm trying to figure out what's going on. It seems unnatural, but it's good—always good. (Pause.)

Early this morning I woke up to discover that Jesus had left the house. (Pause.)

Later we found him. Strange—he was all by himself in a lonely place, praying. When we told him everybody was looking for him, he said, "Come along. Let's get moving. I must do the same work in other country towns of Galilee. That's what I'm supposed to do." So off we went—a few of us staying with him, committed to it, and lots of curious stragglers, too, walking along.

Jesus says over and over in the synagogues, "The time is now. The Reign of God is at hand—repent—change your life around. Believe the gospel." It's curious. I hear this over and over and I don't know what he means. The way he heals is helping me know there's something available right now that I haven't known about. It's something wonderful and good. (Pause.)

But Jesus isn't particularly careful about the way he puts these ideas across. He irritates the powers that be by keeping "bad company," eating with just anybody, and what's more, doing things on the Sabbath that have been forbidden by the religious laws. It bothers me the way he challenges the Pharisees and the fellows with all the learning. He could get all of us in trouble. (Pause.)

Wonder of wonders, we're up in the hill country and Jesus has made twelve of us feel a terrific fraternity with him. He's appointed us to be his companions. It feels different from that day he said, "Come with me." Now I feel a deep belonging. He says he's going to send us out to "proclaim the gospel," and he's going to "commission" us to drive out devils like he does. I don't feel much more able to do these things than when I started out with him, but he wouldn't expect me to do them if I couldn't. He's given me a new name—calls me Peter instead of Simon. That makes me feel something fresh and new is happening to me. I think he knows me better than I know myself. (Pause.)

How busy life is getting now! I'm away from him a lot. Some of us are exercising more and more the gifts we've been given in being able to cast out unclean spirits and heal the sick. Jesus is sending us by twos, teaching us his style of ministry. We take nothing with us but a walking stick—no food, no pack of clothes or provisions, no money—depending upon households to provide our needs in the villages where we go. (Pause.)

Yesterday Jesus was teaching a huge crowd. They stayed on and on. Some of us suggested that he send them off to nearby villages to buy some food because they'd be weak with hunger. "Give them something to eat yourselves," he said. What! Feed five thousand people? "There are only five loaves of bread and two fishes," somebody reported. "That won't go very far in this situation." But then Jesus told us to get people to sit down on the ground. Before our eyes, Jesus took the bread and fish in his hands, looked up to heaven, said a blessing, proceeded to break up the bread and fish, and give the pieces to us to distribute. Can you believe it? Everybody had enough, more than enough, and we had twelve basketfuls left over. How do you account for that? (Pause.)

We're in a village in Caesarea Philippi. My spirits are so high I can hardly keep my feet on the ground. We've all been telling Jesus the rumors we hear about who people think he is. The general feeling is that he's a resurrected John the Baptist, or Elijah, or some other reborn prophet. Jesus suddenly turned to me and asked, "Who do you say that I am?" To my utter amazement, I fell to my knees before him and replied, "You are the Messiah, the Son of the Living God!" There is no reason for me to have had those words so ready. It was as if something took me over. I could tell that Jesus was very moved by my response. Now I know who he is! And he knows that I know. How can I contain it? (Pause.)

Up so high one minute, down so low the next. This kind of life is impossible to understand. Now, just when we are beginning to feel like an effective group under Jesus' leadership, he's begun to talk about being taken over by the authorities in Jerusalem—rejected, tormented, killed. I just couldn't take his talking like that. I love him and I'm depending on him so much. When he finished talking, I took his arm and said, "Don't talk like that. I can't stand it." He turned to me, looked me in the eye and said, "Away with you, Satan! You think as a human being, not as God thinks!"

That surely shut me up. Yet how can I imagine this man that I love, the one I've watched for over two and a half years doing astonishing works for good, put to death by powers that are afraid of him? How can I bear to let the hope of Israel be overcome by evil schemers?

He says plainly something I almost missed in my burst of temper: Three days after his death he'll rise again. I've seen him bring the dead alive. I've seen it. But why does he have to suffer? It's terrible. It isn't right. (Pause.)

I can scarcely believe what's happened. Yet I was there. Jesus chose me, chose me and James and John, to go with him up a high mountain. We were alone there, we four, and suddenly before our eyes Jesus was transfigured. His clothes became dazzling white, whiter than anyone can imagine. And then two figures appeared. They were Elijah and Moses. Jesus, Elijah, and Moses were talking together. I was so amazed I blurted out, "O Jesus, it's so good to be here! Should we make three shelters—one for you, one for Elijah, and one for Moses?" I was so flabbergasted that I was talking nonsense. I don't even know what I meant by the question. But I was completely silenced by a voice that came from a cloud overshadowing us. "This is my Son, my Beloved; listen to him." And just as suddenly as it had all happened, it all disappeared—and there was Jesus alone with us. He knew we had experienced this and told us we were not to mention it until after he had risen from the dead. There it was again—that forecast. We just can't take it in, and we're afraid to ask any more questions about it. It surely is unsettling, and we wonder what's to become of us. We want to keep on living and working with him and win his favor. About that, he has been saying an astonishing thing: "If anyone wants to be first, he must make himself last of all and servant of all." (Pause.)

What a day! My spirits are high. Jerusalem went wild over Jesus today, shouting and yelling and singing his praises. He confounds me. Of all things, he decided to ride on the colt of an ass to go into the city! We put our coats on the colt to make it look a bit more regal, and people threw flowers in his path all the way to the Temple. It was terribly exciting! He has gathered a lot of followers in these three years we've known him. When we finally reached the Temple, it was late in the day and we were all exhausted. (Pause.)

Another day to remember! We walked to the Temple in the morning—a long walk without breakfast. I guess Jesus had had his fill of that Temple scene the day before, because he went into furious action, driving out all the people who were buying and selling in the Temple. He upset tables and sent money and pigeons flying. He directed everybody away from the Temple who was using it as a thoroughfare, and then spent the whole day teaching from the scriptures and preaching to justify his actions. The priests were so furious they could have done away with him, but they were scared, too, because he is so popular with the crowds. When evening came, we all left the city again. (Pause.)

My brother Andrew and I and James and John had a private time with Jesus up on the Mount of Olives, looking down on the Temple. Our minds are confused about the way things are going and by what Jesus says is going to happen to him. But now I've become completely devoted to Jesus. I'd give my life for him! I'm willing to do anything for him, but I'm frightened about being put to the test. There's a lot I don't understand. Why is he insisting on walking into trouble? I'll stick with him, though. No matter what, I'll stand by him.

Individual Work

Purpose: To use Peter's experiences as stimulus to becoming more conscious of where we are at this point in our own experience with God and what next steps are appropriate in our situation.

1. Reread and ponder "Peter's Journal" and the scripture passages used in the session, noting points that seem particularly relevant to you.

  2. Reflect and do some writing on these questions:
• At what point or in what ways do you identify with Peter? (A consideration of the four periods, pre-crucifixion, crucifixion, resurrection, and Pentecost, may be helpful.)
• Does this reflecting on where you are point to a next step for you?

  3. To prepare for the next session: Write a brief summary of your personal work with the assignment.

Notes

1. J. B. Phillips, *The Young Church in Action: A Translation of The Acts of the Apostles* (New York: The Macmillan Co., 1955), p. viii.

Session 6

Spirit/Presence

An extraordinary promise is recorded by the writer of the Gospel of John. In his last conversation with the disciples, Jesus says,

> "Truly, truly, I say to you, whoever believes in me will also do the works that I do; and greater works than these will the believer do, because I go to God."
>
> (Jn. 14:12, RSV)[1]

In these sessions we have taken a brief look at some of the "works" of Jesus and the life that backed them up. He proclaimed the new order of love and justice, taught its implications, and called other persons to participate. Through vital prayer and close companionship, he and his disciples released people from the bondage of disease, myopic vision, and social and religious oppression.

What would happen when Jesus was not physically present to guide and encourage? Could this ministry of love survive? And could it expand as Jesus had promised? The Book of Acts addresses these questions with engaging detail. It describes how the women and men who loved Jesus and wanted to continue and expand his ministry of love did so without his physical presence.

The outpouring of the Spirit as described in the second chapter of the Book of Acts marks the beginning of a new period for the early Christians. In one of the resurrection appearances, Jesus is described as giving the Spirit to his personal friends and followers gathered together in private:

> . . . he breathed on them, and said to them, "Receive the Holy Spirit. If you forgive the sins of any, they are forgiven; if you retain the sins of any, they are retained."
>
> (Jn. 20:22,23, RSV)

118

At Pentecost, this gift of the Spirit was received in public and affirmed with some striking signs, including the ability to make known in many languages the message and way of liberation. This immediately extended the range of the loving ministry of Jesus. The power of this experience was so compelling that a remarkable number of people wanted to be counted among Jesus' followers: ". . . there were added that day about three thousand souls" (Acts 2:41, RSV).

Similar experiences of people receiving the Spirit are recorded throughout the Book of Acts. This happened to the Samaritans (Acts 8:14-17), to Paul (Acts 9:1-19), and to the gentile Cornelius and his relations and friends (Acts 10). As Jesus' followers tried to understand and interpret what was happening, they began to identify two elements of conversion: being baptized with water in the name of Jesus, and being baptized in the Holy Spirit. There seemed to be no set order to how this happened. What was essential, they realized, was the act of deciding to place faith in Jesus. Those who fully opened themselves to the Spirit experienced an outpouring of power, guidance, inspiration, and joy.

Their lives were marked by three common characteristics. First, people experienced *direct access to God through prayer* and felt guided by God even though Jesus was not physically present. For example, Philip felt led to ride alongside the Ethiopian official whom he had never met and found him hungry for God and open to baptism. In Corinth, Paul was initially discouraged by resistance to his message, but in the night he received these words from the Spirit:

"Do not be afraid, but go on speaking and let no one silence you, for I myself am with you and no man shall lift a finger to harm you. There are many in this city who belong to me."

(Acts 18:9,10, Phillips)

Second, this direct access to God accounted for unusual *power and effectiveness in mission.* They preached boldly (Acts 9:29), healed all who came (Acts 5:15,16), confronted resistance with the wisdom of the Spirit (Acts 6:10) and with unconquerable joy (Acts 5:41).

Third, for *mutual encouragement and support,* the early Christians met in small groups to share resources, break bread, pray, solve problems and differences, and plan for mission. Often they paired in ministry—Paul and Barnabas, Paul and Timothy, Peter and John.

These early Christians received their calling directly from Jesus:

"You shall receive power when the Holy Spirit has come upon you;
and you shall be my witnesses in Jerusalem and in all Judea and
Samaria and to the end of the earth."

(Acts 1:8,9, RSV)

Spreading the word about Jesus "to the end of the earth" would have
been an enormous task for the most competent, experienced people.
How impossible, then, for this uneducated, inexperienced group who
had failed so miserably when Jesus was tried and killed! Yet they were
empowered through a special anointing of the Spirit; they felt called and
sent by God to carry out tasks of utmost importance for establishing
God's reign on earth. This empowerment was nurtured through three
dimensions of life that were present with Jesus and his disciples. Prayer,
support, and mission were combined and produced works of liberation
and healing similar to those of Jesus but also "greater" in that they
extended to more persons and places than was possible with Jesus and
the first band of twelve and then seventy disciples.

Three movements in history highlight these means of fostering and
extending the power of the Spirit and illustrate how the Spirit presence of
Jesus can be more fully operative today: the Society of Friends, the
various religious communities, and the Christian missionary experience. Each of these embodies all three vital dimensions, but we will use
each one to highlight only one of those dimensions.

In 1643 in England, a young man named George Fox began questing
for a fuller life with God. Search as he would for help through the
churches, clergy, and other "professors" of faith, he found that "they did
not possess what they professed." Profoundly disturbed by his own deep
God-hunger and the mediocrity and compromise he found in himself and
others, he was driven deep within himself for insight and guidance. This
came in the form of "openings" as he contemplated the scripture and
communicated with God. The first had to do with the unity of Christians.
He realized that "all Christians are believers, both Protestants and
Papists; and the Lord opened to me that, if all were believers, then they
were all born of God, and passed from death to life, and that none were
true believers but such."[2] All who know God's immediate fellowship are
believers, he said, and thus each person can have direct access to God for

guidance and sustenance.

Examining and critiquing the life of the church, he concluded that what equipped one for ministry was not theological education but rather the experience of this fresh, ongoing, illuminating fellowship with God. God lives in such people. They are the holy temple that Paul referred to in his Second Letter to the Corinthians (6:16). God did not live in church buildings but in people. So one must be weaned away from too heavy a reliance on external church membership, doctrine, or symbols and must go deep into the Home of God within.

How can we do this? Surely by a study of the scriptures, yet not simply by an intellectual examination but rather by a personal one, seeking first to be in touch with the Spirit who inspired the writers of the scriptures and who teaches the reader from within his or her own heart. As Fox wrote in his journal:

I brought them [the people] Scriptures and told them there was an anointing within man to teach him, and that the Lord would teach His people Himself.[3]

When George Fox finally gave up all hope of receiving help from persons outside himself, he gave full assent to the teacher within. Here is how he described it:

When all my hopes in them and in all men were gone, so that I had nothing outward to help, nor could I tell what to do, then, O! then I heard a voice which said, "There is one, even Christ Jesus, that can speak to thy condition." And when I heard it my heart did leap for joy.[4]

Within him there blossomed a power to spread the love of God and a clarity of vision that were to affect England dramatically. Other God-hungry people had similar experiences of the Light of God within; gradually they formed societies that became known as the Society of Friends. Their worship and faith practice were deceptively simple. They waited individually and together in silence for the Spirit to manifest itself, for the soul to clear away the distractions and be receptive to that infilling. From these silent times with God, great things happened. Listen to one description of that time:

A great light and spiritual power blazed out in England, beginning about 1650, which shook thousands of their complacent formalism, which kindled men and women with radiant fires of divine glory and holy joy. It sent them out into the market places and the churches, ablaze with the message of the greatness and the nearness of God, His ready guidance and His enfolding love. The blazing light illuminated the darkness, the shams, the silly externalities of conventional religion. It threw into sharp relief the social injustices, the underpaying of servants, the thoughtless luxuries, the sword as an instrument of social or "Christian" justice.[5]

Today the Society of Friends is small numerically but continues to make a significant impact on prison reform, peacemaking, and efforts to build bridges between people of different races and political persuasions.

Similarly, past and present religious communities point up the powerful impact of the Spirit through groups of people who sustain one another as they do a common work. Wholehearted commitment is a key here. Members bond together through living a common rule designed to foster growth and commitment, and undertake a special work that others cannot or will not do. Founders and members of religious communities seem to hear a call to follow Jesus in a deeper way than is sometimes possible alone or in the more usual settings of work and family. In them, vocation, prayer, and caring support are intertwined and lived out with others.

The Taizé Community in France, founded during World War II by Roger Schutz, is one example. The rule of this small community of Protestant and Roman Catholic men devoted to working for Christian unity and among young people and the dispossessed says, "Have a passion for unity." Taizé ecumenical worship, music, and theological work have enabled many around the world to experience the unity for which Jesus prayed.

The missionary movement has also had an impact far out of proportion to its numbers. Some individuals, through periods of quiet personal searching for God, have felt called or sent by God to do a special work, often among people different from themselves. Alone or sometimes with wives and families, they have set sail for distant lands to spend a lifetime learning language and culture, befriending people, sharing the love of God, and offering practical help in medicine, agriculture, and education.

During a year of internship with the Presbyterian Mission in Taegu, Korea, Jackie and Dave McMakin worked with such a group of missionaries. These people felt called to offer their lives to work with the poor, the ill, and the oppressed in Korean society. They lived a life of commitment, spiritual power, and practical effectiveness whose impact was impressive. In collaboration with Korean sisters and brothers, this handful of people were instrumental in establishing a teaching hospital, college, mobile medical clinic, urban ministry training institute, leprosy treatment center, and several schools.

In summary, as we attempt today to live the life of the Spirit, two things seem necessary. The first is a conscious decision to accept Jesus and the loving justice he embodied and to open ourselves to God's Spirit as did Peter and his companions. The second is to recognize and nurture the threefold aspects of Spirit living: prayer, community, and mission.

The experiences of the Society of Friends, religious communities, and missionary efforts can help us. Like the early Christians and George Fox, we can experience God directly. For many of us, churches, symbols, reading, guides, and friends can all be helpful, but only if they lead us to God and do not obscure the importance of direct access to God through prayer. For some, the lively singing and praise at charismatic meetings will be an avenue to or an expression of that personal communication with God. For others, such as the Society of Friends, being alone in silence is crucial. No one way is best for all.

Like members of religious communities, we can be open to the power that comes from banding together with others to find a way to receive the love of God more fully and share it more effectively.

Like missionaries, we can be attuned to the inner voices of God, self, and experience that point us to a particular vocation. This may involve picking up and moving, either figuratively or literally. Often it means that we quiet down, be still, and listen to the call of God in our own homes, our current work, and our life in the community. An attitude of receptivity and an eagerness to see the vision of God illuminating the tasks of life are what seem to matter.

Openness to these three empowering dimensions of the Christian life can make an enormous difference. Prayer, community, mission—these are realities of Christian living that help keep alive and strengthen the power of the Spirit in us so we can extend the ministry of love that Jesus began and that he entrusted to us to expand.

Group Design

Purpose: To share how relating to Jesus through this course has affected us personally and to consider new ways of growth we might pursue as we leave the course.
Materials: newsprint, marking pen.

A. Gathering Time   (15 minutes)   Large Group
Bring everyone on board in a way that seems appropriate for this last session.

B. Sharing Groups   (30 minutes)
Go around the group and share your responses to the two suggestions for individual work in the last design. Use the time left for discussion and response.

C. Final Experience of Sharing   (45 minutes)   Large Group
1. Place these questions on newsprint so all can see.
• In what ways has contact with Jesus through this course nourished your spirit? What questions and resistances remain for you?
• How did Peter's faith experience affect your own? In a few words, describe where you are at this point in your faith experience.
• Next steps: Are there new ways of growth you want to consider as you move from this course? Can you describe them?
   2. *Journaling:* Use 15 minutes of silence for reflection and writing on these questions.
   3. *Large-group sharing:* For about 30 minutes, have a free time of sharing feelings, insights, questions, perceptions of growth, and appreciations.

D. Closing Celebration   (30 minutes)   Large Group
Devise a way to celebrate the ending of this course with music, prayer, movement, refreshments.

Notes

1. Inclusive Language Lectionary Committee, *An Inclusive Language Lectionary* (Philadelphia: The Westminster Press, 1983), Easter 5.
2. George Fox, quoted by Thomas Kelly, *The Eternal Promise* (New York: Harper & Row, 1966), p. 52.
3. Ibid., p. 56.
4. Ibid., pp. 58, 59.
5. Ibid., p. 47.

Three

Tools for Christian Growth

One of the remarkable developments in recent Christian experience has been the emergence in Latin America of groups known as *Comunidades Eclesiales de Base*—CEBs or Basic Ecclesial Communities. They are explained by one writer in this way:

> The CEBs are . . . groups of people from the same area and same class who come together to discuss concrete problems in the light of the Bible. The overwhelming majority are poor and the initial stimulus for their association is found in the problems which face people on the margins of society. They meet in groups of between 10 and 30, reflect on the Bible for their situations and draw conclusions for action.[1]

Small study-reflection-action groups such as the CEBs have often flourished in Christian history. What is significant in Latin America is that they are multiplying rapidly. For example, it is estimated that in Brazil today there are 70,000 CEBs. They are effecting change in national as well as local policies and are promoting justice at all levels of national life.

The CEBs embody the characteristics of "Spirit living" that we examined in the last session of the New Testament course: that is, direct access to the energy and guidance of God through prayer, genuine caring for one another in practical ways, and banding together to foster social change based on gospel values.

The purpose of our third and fourth courses is to offer tools to incorporate these three aspects of Spirit living into our lives. The third course, "Tools for Christian Growth," focuses on prayer and caring, while the fourth course stresses mission. In the first two courses we introduced many tools for growth: Bible study and pondering, prayer, caring for one another, commitment. In this third course we deal with

126

these tools more thoroughly and offer some new ones. The challenge is to move beyond tasting to incorporating some of these practices more permanently into our lives.

The assumption in these last two courses is that banding together in some kind of communal effort is an important aspect of Spirit living. In this third course the participants experience this banding together as the class develops into a community.

Each session in this course offers a particular tool for growth and a specific aspect of prayer. The first session, "Commitment," presents the tool of individual commitment and accountability to a group, and the prayer of consecration.

In the second session, "Collectedness," we focus on listening to God, ourselves, and others. Like George Fox and the Society of Friends, we consider our capacity to be attentive and aware. The prayer of recollection or quiet is introduced.

If we are indeed created in God's image and are a part of the unfolding of creation, then the story of how that happens in and through us is an important part of revelation for ourselves and others. In our third session, "Recalling My Story," we look back over our lives and reflect on our awareness of God along the way. Then we expand that awareness through writing and then sharing with another. This process is undergirded with prayers of intercession for one another.

Reliving our story heightens our awareness of the light and darkness in our lives. Affirming the light and accepting the dark is an ongoing process for us all and is the subject of the fourth session, "Cleansing and Healing." The special kind of prayer known as "healing of the memories" is introduced here.

If we want to deepen our commitment to the Way, we must allow every aspect of our lives to be evaluated by the confronting love of Jesus (Session 5: "Being Confronted by Gospel Values"). We ask what changes related to time, money, energy, and life-style would liberate us to express God's love more fully. Here the prayer of discernment is helpful—how do we express God's love specifically in our lives?

Finally, in "Charting Our Course" (Session 6), we deal with the tools we want to focus on in the future, and how we will incorporate them into our lives. Which ones need to be strengthened in order to have lasting value for us whether or not we have the support of a group? What will be our program for continued growth once we have completed these courses?

This third course was originally designed when Transcendental Meditation was gaining enormous popularity. It was as if TM had touched a deeper spiritual hunger in people that was not being fed by Christians who seemed to have forgotten the tremendous resources in their own tradition. In this course we try to take advantage of these resources and so address our own God-hunger and find nourishment. Strengthened in this way, banding together in commitment, like the CEBs, we can then be agents of reconciliation and liberation in the estranged and oppressed places to which God calls us.

Notes

1. Thomas C. Bruneu, *The Catholic Church and the Basic Christian Communities: A Case Study from the Brazilian Amazon* (Montreal: Centre for Developing-Area Studies, McGill University, 1983), p. 6.

Session 1

Commitment

If you had the task of describing what God is like, and you wanted to do it in a way everyone could understand and no one could forget, how would you do it?

Faced with this challenge, Jesus told a story of a runaway son who squandered his resources, lived a wild life, and finally decided to return home. The father's reaction? Was he angry, surprised, unaware, or uncaring? No. In one sentence, Luke paints a very different picture:

> But while he [the son] was yet at a distance, his father saw him and
> had compassion, and ran and embraced him and kissed him.
>
> (Lk. 15:20, RSV)

The father longed for the son's return. He rushed out to meet him and showered him with affection.

Thus Jesus describes the core of religious experience: to be found, welcomed, and embraced by God. This is what the prophet Hosea was saying in the Hebrew scriptures. God goes after us even if we are unfaithful and offers us a committed love like that of marriage:

> I will betroth you to myself for ever,
> betroth you with integrity and justice,
> with tenderness and love;
> I will betroth you to myself with faithfulness,
> and you will come to know Yahweh.
>
> (Hos. 2:19-22, JB)

It is another way to picture the covenant love of God, who says: "I will be their God and they shall be my people" (Jer. 31:34, JB).

And what about our response? Does not the fullness of this kind of reaching-out love evoke a wholehearted response in us? For the Jesuit paleontologist Pierre Teilhard de Chardin it did. Listen to his beautiful prayer:

> What can I do to gather up and answer that universal and envelop-
> ing embrace? . . . To the total offer that is made me, I can only
> answer by a total acceptance. I shall therefore react . . . *with the*
> *entire effort of my life*—of my life of today and of my life of
> tomorrow, of my personal life and of my life as linked to all other
> lives.[1]

Surely there is a time in our life for questions, for pondering, for
waiting. But when we grasp something of the depth of God's commitment to us, that is a time for response and decision. We saw in the session
"Caller" (Course 1) that what seemed important in Old Testament
people was not their great talent, intelligence, or moral rectitude, but
rather a yes to God's call to collaboration and companionship.

This is faith. Dorothee Soelle gives a good contemporary definition of
it:

> Arriving at faith means entering into the struggle against the
> prevailing cynicism. It means being more and more free of fear. It
> means affirming the great "Yes." It means renewing and making
> true the old confidence which perhaps shone into our childhood. It
> means loving God with all our hearts and all our souls and all our
> minds, without any reservation, without saying "Yes, if you give
> me this and that," and without saying, "But you once . . ." *It is a*
> *"Yes" without ifs and buts.* It is the great "Yes."[2] (Italics ours.)

What will happen to us if we give this kind of wholehearted response?
Some people are afraid of the consequences. Jesus, however, describes
himself as the good shepherd who wants the best for his sheep—in fact,
abundant life (Jn. 10:10). Forgiveness, the chance to start over with a
clean slate, a sense of direction, belonging to a person and a community,
discovering a new power that enables us to help others more effectively—these are aspects of the abundant life that Jesus wants to give us.

Is it possible for ordinary people to offer God a yes "without ifs and
buts"? Our initial yes, given as freely as possible, can gradually develop
into more wholehearted assent. This is how it happened with the disciples. Jesus' strategy for passing on the love of God was to embody it first
in a small band of committed people who then would be empowered by

that love to extend it to others. First, be together. Second, go forth.

Gradually, the initial yes that the disciples gave to Jesus deepened, was tested, failed and succeeded, and finally, after Pentecost, ripened into wholeheartedness. This was made possible by the ongoing presence of the Spirit, together with the help and encouragement of one another.

How can all of this become real for us today? As with Teilhard de Chardin, it is often helpful to mark our yes with a personal prayer of consecration. Years ago a group of young mothers banded together to support one another in making and deepening their response to God and in doing a good job as wives and mothers. One day a visitor gave them an idea that had lasting impact on them all. She suggested that each one compose a short "life prayer" summing up her aspirations at that point in her life. These women still remember that experience as a turning point in their commitment.

A prayer of consecration or a life prayer need not be lengthy. After denying three times in the courtyard that he even knew Jesus, Peter later, in response to Jesus' questioning, simply says three times "I love you." For Thomas the disciple, after questioning, doubting, and finally touching the wounds of Christ, it was very simply, "My Lord and my God!" (Jn. 20:28, RSV). Another Thomas, after five years in the monastery, was struck by his own self-absorption. He realized that although he claimed to trust God, he was in fact afraid of God and trusted only himself. Thomas Merton then prayed this prayer of consecration:

> Take my life into Your hands, at last, and do whatever You want with it. I give myself to Your love and mean to keep on giving myself to Your love—rejecting neither the hard things nor the pleasant things You have arranged for me. It is enough for me that You have glory. Everything you have planned is good. It is all love.[3]

Responding to God's betrothal as mentioned in Hosea, Dorothee Soelle offers, in less obviously religious language, these words of consecration:

> I betroth myself to real life. I give my life for righteousness and justice. I have chosen life, even if the obvious choice seemed death, and even though the death-wish is strong in me. I am learning the self-surrender of my life.[4]

No matter how profound our experience of formulating and offering our prayer of consecration may be, we must remember it is a beginning step for growth. What is needed is some sort of program to carry it out. To get our bodies in shape and then keep them in first-rate condition, we follow a plan for fitness. The same holds true for the life of faith. A rule of life is a way of referring to a spiritual fitness program. Many people find such a plan an invaluable tool for growth. The experience of others can give us ideas on how to construct our own.

To begin with, it must be achievable. It is demoralizing to set too ambitious a goal, such as spending an hour in prayer each day, and then fail continually. It is much better to start modestly and work up to something more demanding. A five-minute period of prayer, faithfully kept, can bring us much closer to the loving Spirit of God.

A good discipline should touch each aspect of life—body, mind, and spirit, relationships to God, others, and things. So it can include portions like "I will do vigorous physical exercise three times a week" and "I will leave my business at work so as to be freely present to my family at night and will engage in recreative activities." Like effective physical exercise, it should be enjoyable as well as challenging. Music, art, good books, gardening, walks can be included in our plan. Whatever increases our capacity to receive and convey God's love is appropriate.

The more specific the rule of life, the more helpful for growth it will be. Instead of promising "to give generously of my money" it is much better to say, "I will give_____% of my gross income to others."

It is also good to include some way to receive support and critique from others. We easily let things slide if we keep too much to ourselves. Some people check in regularly with a friend or a spiritual guide, go over their rule of life, and give an accounting of what is life-giving, what is unproductive. In addition, they ask for prayerful support and guidance.

It is always good to build in a time for review and recommitment to our way of discipline. This can be done annually. Sometimes a general confession is involved. We go over with another what has happened over the past year: areas of doubt, belief, faithfulness, and unfaithfulness. This can be a time to adjust our spiritual plan, adding or removing something or emphasizing a neglected area.

When groups of people want to live by the same rule of life or plan, it can be good to have a basic, simple rule that is held in common, leaving it up to individuals to add personal practices. This is what our Partners Community does. We are pledged to read and pray daily the readings for the coming Sunday from the lectionary that the Roman Catholic church and many Protestant churches have in common. When we meet, we can use these readings as a basis for common prayer. Individuals then work out the rest of their fitness plan regarding the giving of time and money, additional spiritual nourishment, and prayer.

These, then, are some practical suggestions for constructing a fitness plan. To devise one that works well takes thought and experience. That is why the idea is introduced in the first course and returned to in the third. In the session on "Covenant-Maker," it was suggested that we write a statement expressing our covenant with God and that we begin thinking about what we wish to do to live that covenant. This course gives us experience in several individual and group practices that can strengthen our relationship with God, self, and others. It is in itself a spiritual fitness plan. At its conclusion, we will consider working out a spiritual plan or rule of life for ourselves to enable further growth on our own.

Spiritual growth does not just happen. It needs attention and focus. Expressing our committed response to God through a prayer of consecration is a good step.

Working out a framework for deepening our response through a rule of life is a time-tested way to be specific in our growing and loving. But all of these, in the end, are simply frameworks for something much more important: the daily living encounter between God and ourselves. This will have many surprises, openings, and blind spots. Like any close relationship, at times it will have deep meaning and power and at other times will be quiet or uneventful or even stormy. Some periods will seem nourishing; others will appear dry and empty. The important thing is to place ourselves daily in the presence of God and let God's love work in us.

Group Design

Purpose: To share experiences of growth, our hopes and questions about the course, and to examine the power and freedom that come with

commitment decisions.
Materials: 8 ½ x 11 sheets of paper, marking pens, newsprint.

A. Gathering Time   (35 minutes)   Large Group
In order to prepare for this and our subsequent sharing in small groups,
take a sheet of paper and a marking pen, and in 5 minutes draw a picture
or use a word to symbolize these:
1. a person, book, or event that has spurred your growth in the past;
2. your hopes for this course;
3. a concern, question, or resistance you have regarding this course.

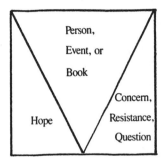

   This is how Dick's sheet of paper looked. His father spurred Dick's
growth by his frequent encouragement and affirmation. He always liked
to hear Dick practice the piano and enjoyed having his friends around.
Dick depicted his father smiling, and with some musical notes in the
background. As for his hopes for the course, he hoped that being with
others, feeling their support, and hearing their experiences would stimulate his own growth. So he drew a group of stick figures supporting one
another. His concern was about time (would he be able to give this the
time it deserves?), so he drew a clock.

When everyone is ready, each one share your name (if it is necessary) and describe the person, event, or book that spurred your growth. For example, here is what Dick said. "My name is Dick Avella, and I drew my father because he was always encouraging me. He especially enjoyed hearing me practice piano—that's why I put the notes there. My hope is that being with others who want to grow will help my growth. My concern is that I may not have the time I'd like to devote to the course."

B. Sharing Groups   (25 minutes)

Move into groups of four so that you are with people you do not know well. Share names and phone numbers, and write them in your notebook for ready reference. Then briefly share hopes and concerns for the course. You might want to jot down key items by people's names so you can hold these in prayer.

C. Stories of Commitment   (45 minutes)

The chapter on commitment describes the importance of these three steps:
• marking your yes to God's love with a prayer of consecration;
• working out a spiritual fitness plan;
• having regular living encounters with God.
The introduction to the course uses the CEBs to illustrate how commitment combined with teamwork makes for growth and impact. The sessions on covenant in the Old Testament course and on healing in the New Testament course include some stories about commitment.

1. Each person take a few minutes to think about a positive experience of commitment in the life of someone you know. What are the details and implications of this commitment? (5 of the 45 minutes)

2. In twos (pairing with the person next to you), share that experience. (10 of the 45 minutes)

3. In the large group, brainstorm: What are the characteristics of commitment, and what happens as a result of commitment? Use only a word or a phrase, and record on a piece of newsprint. (15 of the 45 minutes)

4. Place newsprint description of characteristics of commitment on the floor in the center of the group. Take a few minutes to ponder how they illustrate the importance of commitment. Then ponder another dimension—how they illuminate this important fact: God has this kind of commitment to us and invites us to respond with commitment individually and in company with others. (15 of the 45 minutes)

D. Closing   (15 minutes)   Large Group
Choose one or two of the following suggestions as appropriate for your group:

1. Evaluate this session. (In a few words, what was helpful? What was not helpful?)

2. Sing ("Kumbayah, My Lord").

3. Pray.

4. Discuss details of next session if necessary (time, place, leadership responsibility).

Individual Work

Purpose: To examine our commitment to God; to express this by spending time regularly in God's presence; and to compose a personal prayer of consecration.

1. *Read:* Luke 9:57-62 describes the importance of commitment and reasons people hold back. Romans 12 is a picture of the committed life.

2. *Meditate and Write:* Using scripture for background, ponder and write on these questions:
• What is the importance of commitment to God for me?
• What holds me back?
• How specifically do I want to offer myself to God?

3. *Pray:* Prayer of Consecration. Write your own consecration prayer to be used each day as you awake (keep it on your dresser). *Bring this prayer to the group next session.* Pray for the other members of the group and for your small group. Hold them and yourself in the committed love of God.

4. *Summarize:* At the end of the week, summarize in writing your experiences, successes, failures, doubts, and joys as you worked with this material.

Notes

1. Pierre Teilhard de Chardin, *The Divine Milieu* (New York: Harper & Row, 1960), p. 105.

2. Dorothee Soelle, *Choosing Life* (Philadelphia: Fortress Press, 1981), p. 19.
3. Thomas Merton, *The Sign of Jonah* (Garden City, N.Y.: Harcourt, Brace & Co., 1953), p. 76.
4. Dorothee Soelle, *Choosing Life,* p. 19.

Session 2

Collectedness

> I know you believe you understand what you think I said, but I am
> not sure you realize that what you heard is not what I meant.[1]

In this amusing sentence, Dody Donnelly sums up a dilemma we all
face: giving lip service to the importance of listening but falling short in
practice. Yet what an important tool for growth it is! Three dimensions—
listening to oneself, others, and God—are integrally related to one
another.

Listening is a way of loving, cherishing, and expanding our understanding of ourselves, others, and God. Often the church has stressed an
order for these three. Put God first, others next, and self last is what we
have been taught in a thousand ways, but that is not always how it works
out. Caring about our own God-hunger can often lead us to the love of
God. Cherishing an aspect of another can lead us to valuing that aspect in
ourselves. Seeing how God delights in us can often open the door to
greater self-esteem. For our discussion, we will begin with listening to
ourselves, move to listening to others, and conclude with listening to
God.

"Being in touch with our feelings" has a narcissistic ring to it but truly
is an important way to begin listening to ourselves. Most Christians have
been taught in one way or another that it is permissible to have and share
only "good feelings." "Bad feelings" such as jealousy, anger, and
resentment are considered sinful but can be overcome through grace. So
the "real" Christian is victorious over those feelings and appears to be
happy, reconciled, and at peace.

As absurd as that description is, we know that most of us have been
affected by that type of thinking. In such a view, the church is a
community of successful, helpful people (or at least people who appear
to be that way) but not a place of care for broken, needy persons.

The Bible, however, gives a different picture. Listen to the variety of deeply felt feelings expressed by the psalmists (RSV):

I suffered distress and anguish. (116:3)
I was brought low. (116:6)
. . . my heart is steadfast! I will sing, I will sing and make melody! (108:1)
I am so troubled that I cannot speak. (77:4)
Every night I flood my bed with tears. (6:6)
I seek thee, my soul thirsts for thee. (63:1)
I delight to do thy will, O my God. (40:8)

In his Second Letter to the Corinthians, Paul very frankly shared how he felt about his life and work. At one point he could say,

I wrote you out of much affliction and anguish of heart and with many tears, not to cause you pain but to let you know the abundant love that I have for you.

(2:4, RSV)

These are selections from only two books, but throughout the Bible there is a freedom about admitting and then sharing all kinds of feelings.

Why is it important to return to that freedom? Feelings or passions contain our energy; they are what give life its drive and verve. Just as surely as "love makes the world go round," so jealousy or anger has the power to stop the world, block human interaction, turn promising possibilities into deadly poison. Ideas and intellectual work are important, but it is feelings that give them power. One person can say, "God is love" without feeling, and we are unmoved. Another may pour lifelong feelings into the same words, and we are gripped and motivated.

Unlike the pseudo-Christian teaching that certain feelings are good and others bad, the Bible poses other values. All of Jesus' teachings on hypocrisy show us it is more important to be honest and authentic than right. The tax collector who simply pleaded, "God, be merciful to me a sinner!" (Lk. 18:13, RSV) was honored by God in contrast to the Pharisee who thought he was doing everything right.

Feelings are neutral in moral terms. Bruce Larson makes an important distinction and offers some valuable thoughts on sharing feelings:

Don't deny that you have either negative or positive feelings.

Remember that there are no good or bad feelings, just good and bad acts. One doesn't have to do everything his feelings prompt, but one should never deny the presence of those feelings. All true feelings need some kind of expression. If we seal our feelings too tightly, or deny them, our emotional energy will emerge sideways and obliquely. This is dishonest. This means that a wife may get the anger that her husband does not dare to vent to his boss at work.[2]

People in our courses often find it difficult to share negative feelings. Hearing and reading about the feelings of others has helped them recognize and share their own. Ann Ulanov articulates many of the ambivalent feelings of women today. Her description, for example, of a woman's gift of nurturing others alongside of her desire to achieve on her own enables us to see these dualities in ourselves.[3] Knowing people who are freer than we with their feelings can also be liberating. This is the effect that the women's movement has had on a man in one of our groups who said: "Seeing women share their feelings freely and openly has helped me to do the same. I feel so much more genuine than I did when I denied having or wanting to share my feelings."

Journal keeping is another useful tool in becoming aware of one's feelings, valuing them, and channeling their energy in fruitful ways. But not just any kind of journal keeping. Some people simply use a journal as a release for feelings, jotting them down as they occur, and doing nothing further. As helpful as that might be initially, it does not move one beyond the feelings and sometimes simply reinforces their negative power. Ira Progoff has pioneered a unique way of teaching people to write, organize, and learn from their reflections.[4] Instead of simply jotting down feelings randomly as they occur, one makes an additional effort to keep track of one feeling—anger, for example—and makes an entry every time it occurs. Then one looks back on the entries and tries to understand them more fully. What situations or persons provoked anger? Is there a reason? Is there another way to approach this problem? Does the anger point to a positive energy that might be frustrated or unused but could be tapped in a creative way?

The more conscious we are of our own feelings and the more we see their value, the better we will be able to love and understand others. Nothing another says will shock us, because if we look carefully we will see the same feeling within ourselves, whether actually or potentially.

Listening to ourselves enables us to listen more deeply to others. To give our attention to another person is hard work. The truth is that no matter how beautiful the prayer of St. Francis sounds, "Let me not so much seek to be understood as to understand," most of us long to be understood and truly known. We would much rather tell our own story than listen to another's. Our deeper desire, however, is not simply to be known and understood, but to have a sense of oneness with another person, to have a give-and-take, a mutual sharing. For this, listening is the key, although we are often tempted to think it is more important to make our point clearly and compellingly.

However, if we can set aside these needs and suspend the feelings that another's deep sharing might generate in us, we can better understand what is truly going on within that person. This is a basic step in building effective communication. It opens doors, fills out the picture, so that when it is time for us to share, we can do so in a way that connects with the other person.

An example of this happened to our family at Easter. A young Jewish woman was visiting. We had had some interesting discussions about the Passover celebration at her home and her own growing ambivalence about the meaning and celebration of Passover but also about her pride in being Jewish. When we asked if she would like to attend church with us on Easter, she declined with little explanation. We assumed that it was the strength of her loyalty to the Jewish tradition that influenced her choice. On the way home from church we discussed our feelings about how our friend might have felt had she come. Later, putting aside our assumptions, we listened to more of her feelings. "I'm questioning everything these days," she said. "I was afraid that the new experience of going to church with you might undermine the foundation I'm trying to build. I wasn't ready to deal with that now. I'm too shaky about too many things."

Her honest sharing and our ability to hear her without loading the conversation with our own feelings opened the door to better understanding. We felt closer, and I think each of us felt valued and respected.

In this kind of bridge-building listening, it is important to listen carefully and make sure we have heard the message intended. An easy way to check that is to repeat in our own words what was said. The other person can affirm or correct our impression. A technique like this can sometimes seem artificial, but if used with an honest desire to understand it can clear up misunderstandings before they escalate. It also is a way of caring deeply for what the other is saying. Further, it can check our tendency to rush to the other's aid with advice, opinions, or solutions. All these may have a place, but only when requested. When we listen with care and attention, we allow the person to share the first layer of feelings and then the next and the next. Our job as listeners is to accept others with all their feelings; this enables them to accept them themselves without shame or embarrassment.

What about listening to God? Someone has said, "Prayer is the lifeblood of the Christian." That is a fascinating thought. But is it true? There is a kind of prayer that is wearing and unhelpful. It is one-way communication; we do all the talking, often going over the same problems repeatedly. Perhaps this is what Jesus meant when he said, "Beware of the scribes . . . who make long prayers" (Lk. 20:46-47, RSV).

How can we pray so as to be in real communication with God? One way is to begin, as in any intimate relationship, by presenting our real feelings to God, being honest and open in prayer. Second, as in all listening, we can try to be present, really present, when we want our prayer to be more than routine. This means that we settle down, relax, perhaps jot down our thoughts or distractions for later attention, collect ourselves, and be still. This attitude of collectedness means entering into a place of silent waiting deep within ourselves. Members of the Society of Friends refer to this as the Divine Center or the Light Within. Listen to Thomas Kelly's description of it:

> Deep within us all there is an amazing inner sanctuary of the soul, a holy place, a Divine Center, a speaking Voice, to which we may continuously return. . . . It is a dynamic center, a creative Life that presses to birth within us. It is a Light Within which illumines the face of God and casts new shadows and new glories upon the face of men.[5]

Third, we can strengthen that Center, our soul, with nourishment. This can come from scripture, but not a long passage. This is not the time for scripture study, for mastering a section. Rather, it is the time to savor a small chunk, a phrase or a verse, turning it around, putting our situation or that of others at its side, and letting it trigger new thoughts or feelings or insights. This we could call scripture pondering.

Fourth, we can have a time of actual communication or conversation with God. Sometimes this communication will be wordless, simply a time of resting in God's presence, "abiding in" God, as Jesus put it, or having "lap time" with God, as a friend described it. Sometimes we need a word in addition to God's presence, and we can ask for it. We can simply say, "This is troubling me, God. Speak your word." Then we listen in stillness. Perhaps a word, a feeling, an image, or an insight will come. It might be important to jot that down for further pondering. Sometimes nothing occurs; these things cannot be forced. God seemed to be absent from Jesus on the cross, and that will happen at times. Yet God has a way of getting through eventually if we are truly open and ready to hear. Illumination from God can enlarge our vision, lighten our load, guide us in the way, comfort or challenge us. All these happen to those who make listening to God a part of their lives.

M. Basilea Schlink, a founder of the Sisterhood of Mary, describes the value of listening prayer in her book *Realities*. As she and others in war-torn Darmstadt, Germany, struggled to build a community in the 1940s, they relied on God's daily guidance in tangible and moving ways. Their faithful listening bore fruit beyond their wildest hopes. In the preface her *exuberant* joy breaks forth: "These true stories and incidents from our own time confirm that God still stands by the word He spoke thousands of years ago: He who waits upon God will not be put to shame."[6]

Listening is a way to deepen our life with God, ourselves, and others. Difficult though it is, it is important to cultivate.

Note: For a summary of suggestions on listening, read the additional section "On Listening" (placed after the group design and individual work). This would be good to do before your group session on listening.

Group Design

Purpose: To learn the importance of listening as a tool for growth and to

practice listening to one another.
Materials: Newsprint.

A. Gathering Time   (20 minutes)   Large Group
Open the group in any way you like. If you want to have some fun, try one of the familiar children's listening games such as "Gossip." (Someone whispers a ridiculous and slightly complicated sentence in the ear of the next person, who in turn whispers it to the next one. This is repeated around the circle until the end, when you compare the last version to the first.)

B. Sharing Groups   (20 minutes)
In sharing what you did with the suggestions for individual work it is not necessary to cover every item thoroughly. You may simply touch on some selected points. Remember to review good sharing practice: Speak about what is pertinent, personally important, fresh. Don't dominate the group. Give each person a chance to share briefly. Then if there is time, go back for further discussion. We suggest that in this session you share what was lifegiving and what was unproductive in your experience with the individual work. When that has been done, close, if you wish, by praying the prayers of consecration you wrote.

C. Lab on Listening to One Another   (65 minutes)
What follows is the instructions for an exercise in listening that has been widely used in groups to teach skills in sharing, listening, and observing. *Note to the leader:* It might help to alert at least two individuals to familiarize themselves ahead of time with the details of this lab so they can facilitate setting it up during the session.

1. Briefly mention the value of listening to others, recalling some elements of good listening mentioned in the text. Make a few points tightly, perhaps with the section "On Listening" in hand.

2. Move people into groups of three. Extra people may join a group to make a foursome. The leader can facilitate this to make sure no one is left out.

3. Set up the lab with one sharer, one reflector, and one observer. Read these descriptions of your roles:

Sharer: Briefly share a problem (no more than 5 minutes). Discuss something that really concerns you: unresolved feelings (positive or negative) that are not overwhelming. For example: leftover feelings from the last session, specific concerns about work or career, interpersonal relations, a pressing social issue about which you feel strongly. It should contain sincere personal, unresolved, confusing feelings.

Reflector: Reflects back in own words what he or she has heard.

Sharer: Amplifies, clarifies, corrects wrong impressions.

Reflector: Reflects back again. Do this for three or four rounds.

Observer then observes how each did in relation to learning/sharing suggestions: What was helpful, on target?

4. If time permits, participants may exchange roles and repeat the process.

5. Large-group sharing

a. Informal feedback from observers: What happened?

b. Brief discussion of ways to improve our listening skills.

D. Closing   (15 minutes)   Large Group

Choose one or two of the following suggestions as appropriate for your group: evaluation of the session, discussion of details for next session, song, prayer. Suggestion for prayer: In keeping with the session on listening, be in silence together. Allow silence to come over you as a group. You may notice a deeper resting in silence as you relax into it, listening to the random noises in the room and around it. After a suitable time, someone close by saying "Thank you" or "Amen."

Individual Work

Purpose: To focus on the art of listening to God, self, and others. A number of suggestions are presented. Some may want to deal with them all. Others might concentrate on one or more.

1. Listening to God: Use these three steps to cultivate the art of listening to God.

• Prepare: Collect yourself, become quiet and relaxed. Let silence happen around and within you. Be in touch with a center of stillness within where God may be met. As preparation for listening to God, focus on being present, at rest but alert, and attentive. If you can, devote several

minutes to this quieting that is a form of prayer.
- Read Scripture: Use a bit of scripture as spiritual nourishment. This week we suggest Lk. 8:40-56 and Lk. 18:35-43. Each day be aware of how Jesus listened and was present to the people who approached him.
- Pray: In quiet recollection, picture the listening, caring Jesus with you. Tell him what is on your mind and listen for his response. It may be helpful to record in your journal what occurs.

2. Listening to self: One way to do this is to *describe* in writing a feeling that is of high intensity. Do this as fully and freely as possible. Then stand back and *reflect* in writing on the feeling. What made you feel this way? Why? What can you learn about it? How can its energy be tapped?

3. Listening to others: Read "On Listening" (below) and then focus on the suggestions that are most pertinent, seeking concrete ways to try them out as you listen to others this week.

4. To prepare for the next session: Write a brief summary of your personal work with the assignment.

On Listening

A simple Australian bushman said to Sir Hubert Wilkins (the Arctic explorer) in his pidgin English, "You set down quiet and listen alla time and eyes belong you lookabout see everything. Allabout feel quiet inside when with you."

From this lovely statement we can catch the image of one who has absorbed into his personality the skills of being present and listening so profoundly that he brings peace to those around him. How does this happen? What can we do to attain it?

A few tips for growth in listening have come to our attention through readings and experience. Let's start with the don'ts (which most of us "do"!).

1. *Don't interrupt.* The greatest gift is to offer our ears.

2. *Don't probe.* Our questions should be ones of gentle encouragement rather than ones to satisfy our own curiosity. Some samples: "Have you said all you'd like to say about this?" Other questions can be to gain enough information to have a good understanding of the problem or to

help the other person think more deeply into the situation.

3. *Don't give advice.* We undermine the other when we try to solve his or her problems.

4. *Don't judge.* We all make evaluations through our own experience, but to listen to others we must accept that they are seeing it their way.

5. *Don't sympathize sentimentally.* This is an aspect of judging and stands in the way of listening.

There are positive techniques for listening to add to our don'ts. Just to *be* there with the other is to give affirmation and a positive feedback. A good listener hears more than just the words. There may be body language communicating anger, fear, anxiety, confusion, bewilderment, hopelessness. To relate back to the other what we hear is clarifying— helpful both to avoid misinterpretation and to let the other realize what he or she has said, perhaps to open the door to deeper understanding of his or her situation.

The good listener may add the dimension of prayer, spoken or silent, as the greatest gift of all, recognizing the resource of the loving Spirit of God present in all situations.

Notes

1. Dody Donnelly, *Team* (Ramsey, N.J.: Paulist Press, 1977), p. 78.
2. *Ask Me to Dance* (Waco, Tex.: Word Books, 1972), p. 79.
3. *Receiving Woman* (Philadelphia: The Westminster Press, 1981), p. 58.
4. *At a Journal Workshop* (New York: Dialogue House Library, 1975). This book describes Ira Progoff's basic process.
5. *A Testament of Devotion* (New York: Harper and Brothers, 1941), p. 29.
6. (Grand Rapids: Zondervan, 1966), p. 9.

Session 3

Recalling Our Stories

One of our prominent North American theologians has had a complete turnaround in the second half of his life. In *Creative Dislocation: The Movement of Grace,* Robert McAfee Brown describes the change. Until recently he taught and wrote about theology, starting with systems and applying them to life situations. Now all that has changed. Realizing that he had been reading and interpreting the Bible from his own geographic and cultural roots, he saw how conditioned he was because of his "listening in too few places," namely in those he found congenial.[1]

So he started to listen to different voices in different locations: "the poor, the oppressed, the marginalized, the voiceless, the exploited, the victims, . . . women, blacks, the physically and mentally handicapped, homosexuals, Asians, Latin Americans."[2] He realized how much the Western world had tamed the Bible, using it skillfully to justify Western bourgeois capitalist culture. He saw how Third World (which for him refers to all who are dispossessed and exploited, whether for racist, sexist, or cultural reasons) brothers and sisters are freeing the Bible "once again to communicate its liberating message."[3]

Reflection on the injustice in the world and on the biblical hope of freedom from oppression has begun to produce a new theology that Brown is celebrating and seeking to build. Three special emphases are important to him in this new effort. We will mention the first two briefly, then concentrate on the third for the purposes of this session.

First, he feels that all new theological work must listen intently to the voices of the dispossessed and exploited, particularly those from Third World areas characterized by want and deprivation.

Second, it is imperative to take into account the Holocaust of World War II, an event that revealed the moral bankruptcy of many Christians as they chose to ignore what was happening. For many, the Holocaust was a searing instance of God not delivering his people, a time when the reaching-out love of God seemed totally absent.

Third, the new theology must begin with stories and then move to interpretation: biblical tales told by those who see them as powerful tools for bringing new life into particular situations, and personal stories of how God is acting today in people. After all, our faith was originally told through the personal stories of countless people who saw God's action in their lives—in exciting accounts that had the power to enliven new generations of believers. Gradually those stories gave way to systems of theology and lost their power. Listen to Brown's indictment of that development:

> In losing the story we have lost the power and therefore the glory. Theologians bear a large measure of responsibility for this. *We have committed the unpardonable sin of transforming exciting stories into dull systems.* We have spawned system after system: Augustinian, Anselmian, Thomistic, Calvinistic, Lutheran, Reformed, orthodox, liberal, neoorthodox, neoliberal. Historically they were very different; today *they share in common an inability to grab us where we are and say, "Listen! This is important!"* (Italics ours.)[4]

Brown concludes that an urgent task for theology is to recover the stories of people of faith in all generations, including our own, and then retell them in today's language so that hearers will say, "Aha! That's *my* story too!"[5]

This is what we have been trying to do in these courses: retell some of the biblical stories and experiences of believers in different times and places, and then offer ways for participants to relate personally to these stories.

Now it is time to focus our attention on a very important story, our own. Starting with the accounts of others and seeing ourselves in them can highlight some of the factors that shape the spiritual journeys of all people of faith. Giving attention to our own story can illuminate the uniqueness of our experience of God. Each of our personal stories contains pieces of God's revelation that can point the way to further growth for ourselves and others. When we ponder the stories of our lives, we open the door to a deeper awareness of ourselves and others and of how God deals with us.

Several years ago, Jean Haldane, an Episcopal laywoman in

Washington, D.C., carried out an interesting project related to people's spiritual stories. She asked eighteen laypersons and one priest in a local Episcopal church to talk to her about their life stories and religious pilgrimages. Each person was interviewed for four hours and was free to explore his or her "unique experiences and his or her sense of what they meant."[6]

These conclusions emerged from the project:

1. Everybody had a fascinating spiritual journey to tell—one shaped by his or her personal history and crises. This seemed to refute the common observation that some people are religious and others are not. As each person related his or her story, a great deal of spiritual content emerged even though people had many different ways of expressing it.

2. Everyone found it helpful, life-giving, and exciting to share that journey, even though this was a church where people normally did not "talk about their religion." The myth that many people do not want to talk about their struggles with faith was exploded. In the presence of someone safe, a person who was genuinely interested and encouraging, and away from those who might judge the story or compare it with others, people were deeply grateful for the chance to talk about it.

3. No one had thought of sharing his or her story in church or with anyone connected with that church. It was a place where this was just not done. In what would seem to be the natural place for people to share their spiritual experience, the opportunity to do so never occurred.

4. No one connected with the church had asked any of the participants about their spiritual journey. This was simply not a topic of conversation.

5. Through the process of telling their stories to Jean, the participants were able to reflect on their journey and frequently discover their next steps. This sharing and reflecting with another person produced a clarity of direction that was empowering. Participants did not need to be told what to do. Rather, in the freeing climate of the interview many knew what to do next.

Out of this study and the subsequent discussions of it in the church in which it was done, Jean Haldane came up with some questions churches could ask themselves:

1. Should not a goal of church life be to help people articulate and share their spiritual journeys?

2. When this happens and people become aware of next steps to take,

can the church be available to assist these steps?

3. Should not every church have ways to encourage this companioning of people on their pilgrimages and perhaps train people to facilitate this?

The Church of the Saviour in Washington, D.C., had already been addressing these challenges before Jean did her study. As part of the process of becoming members, persons write a short spiritual auto-biography. Before joining the church at a public ceremony, each new member reads his or her autobiography before the church council. In this way several people involved in the church have an intimate look at the life of the new member. In addition, members have developed the custom of reading one another's autobiography in order to share their lives more widely in the church community.

Knowing the importance of this practice at the Church of the Saviour and experiencing Jean Haldane's work caused us to include oppor-tunities to share parts of our stories with one another in these courses. At this point, we offer the opportunity to write an autobiography and then to share it with one other person in the group. This has been one of the most positive experiences of our work. Again and again Jean Haldane's findings are corroborated. People are grateful for the invitation to write their story, share it with another, and listen to the stories of others. The encouraging climate of valuing everyone's story is greatly appreciated. As a result of the process, people discover deeper meaning and new directions for their lives.

We have concluded that this is an effective way of getting to know one another, of building community in a small group or a church, and of learning about God's action in our own lives and in the lives of people we know.

Some people fear that it might be hard to do, but they often find the words flowing as they put pen to paper. Our guidelines are few. People welcome being reminded that this is their story to be told in their language—there is no right or wrong way to do it. It is not like a school paper, although sometimes people have these old I-hate-to-write memo-ries running through their heads. Grammar, spelling, and handwriting are not important. What matters is that the story is real and belongs to them.

It is helpful to have a way to proceed or an angle or perspective to consider. We suggest doing a time line of one's life as a way of getting

warmed up. This is described in the group design at the end of this
session. One or two of these questions may stimulate your thinking or
help you begin:

- At what times has God been notably present or absent to you?
- At what times have you felt liberated? Felt oppressed or stuck?
- What have been the places of suffering in your life?
- What turning points or decisions have been important?
- What have been significant persons, places, and experiences for you?
- When have you felt on the path you are meant to walk, and when off-base?
- At what times have you been valued? When rejected, ignored, or discounted?
- When has grace broken through?
- What are the failures or the situations that need forgiveness or healing?

These questions are only suggestions. Our invitation to you is to write
your story in your own way and share it with someone. Thus you will
continue the revelation of God's action in his people.

Listen to Robert McAfee Brown's words at the end of his spiritual
autobiography:

> The particular story that I have been telling does not end with a tidy
> conclusion. In fact, it does not end at all. That is the nature of the
> Christian story, too. It goes on. The book is never finished. We
> simply begin a new chapter. That is why the journey is occasionally
> terrifying, sometimes fulfilling, and always exciting.[7]

Group Design

Purpose: To remember and share ingredients of our life stories that have
meaning for us.

Materials: Colored marking pens, newsprint or legal-sized sheets of
paper, words for song (see closing).

A. Gathering Time   (25 minutes)   Large Group

If time allows, you may wish to open your session by having each person
respond to the following questions.

- Where did you live as a child?
- How did you heat your home?
- What was the center of warmth for you (a person, place, pet, etc.)?

B. Sharing Groups   (20 minutes)
Remembering what you did with the individual suggestions, tell one thing that had power and meaning for you and one thing with which you had difficulty.

C. Lab on Remembering Your Story   (35 minutes)
1. *Drawing your lifeline.* For this exercise, it is necessary for each person to have two marking pens of different colors and a piece of newsprint. Each should find a comfortable place where there is room to spread out and write on his or her paper.

Note to the leader: You or someone who volunteers and has prepared ahead of time should read aloud the following instructions:

We're going to do an exercise that will help us listen to our past. Take two marking pens of different colors and a piece of newsprint.

As a first step, take one color and represent your life events by drawing a line on the paper from left to right, moving up and down, using a curved or jagged line. Proceed with drawing the line as I read these instructions and we think together of the events from our beginnings to the present. Use symbols of your own choosing to indicate special events and how they affected you (for example, represent the birth of a sister by a dark cloud, moving to a new house by a sunburst). Or use plus and minus signs or a happy face or frowning face.

Begin your line by making an "x" on the left-hand side of the paper about midway from top to bottom. Draw the line forward slowly to the right, and let it represent the kind of feelings you have about your first *preschool years.* Were you happy, secure? Were there illnesses, traumas? (Pause.)

Then make a mark indicating the *start of school* and a visual reminder of your feelings then—frightened, excited, disappointed, confident. (Pause.)

As you remember your *elementary school years,* think of how active or quiet you were, your friends, your teachers, others who played important roles. Indicate that stage of life on your paper. (Pause.)

Mark your *adolescent period* and remember your feelings about

friends, dating, acceptance, hard adjustments, any deaths in your immediate circle, adventures, accomplishments. Indicate the most important
on your paper. (Pause.)

Mark the time you *left home* for work or school and your feelings then
about independence and your sense of purpose or lack of it. (Pause.)

Then mark important events *after schooling:* marriage—smooth and
rough spots; career changes; travel; economic stress or success; children;
changes in direction—successes, failures. (Pause.)

Now, *as a second step,* take the other marking pen, and with that we'll
draw our life line, with particular attention to our relationship with God.
We'll draw a new line on the same piece of paper, beginning from the
same starting point, to show our spiritual journey in relationship to the
events we have pictured. Again we can use fluctuations in our line or
symbols to indicate the peaks and valleys of our spiritual experience.

Begin with how you felt about God when you were a *child*—any times
you were aware of God's loving care, presence, or absence. Was prayer a
part of your life? Were family religious customs? Was church important
to you? How? (Pause.)

Next, consider *adolescence.* Was that a time of turmoil, dryness,
questioning? Did you have people with whom you could share? (Pause.)

Early adult years. What was important then in your relationship with
God? Did you feel near to, or far from, God? Were your concepts of God
changing? Were you searching for God, or were you occupied with other
things? (Pause.)

Middle years. What is happening now in your relationship to God? Do
you feel greater or less commitment than before? Do you have yearnings
about your relationship with God that you could depict? Where is God
for you as you are aware of aging in yourself and others? (Pause.)

D. Sharing from the Life Line   (25 minutes)

We suggest you do this in pairs, selected if possible from members of
your permanent sharing group since you have built some rapport with
them. If this does not work out for all, simply pair people for this part of
the session. As you settle in your pairs for sharing, each person mark two
or three important happenings from your life line. Circle or check those.
Then in the time allowed, go back and forth in your sharing—each
describing one happening, and then listening to the other person's

description. Share as freely and in as much detail as you wish (i.e., one event in detail or several more briefly), but make sure each has about equal time.

Note: It is very easy for one person to get carried away and take too much of the time as the other person in courtesy allows this to happen. Exercise some discipline about this. You'll both be richer for it.

E. Closing   (15 minutes)   Large Group
Choose one or two of the following suggestions as appropriate for your group: evaluation of the session, discussion of details for next session, prayer, song ("He's Got the Whole World in His Hands").

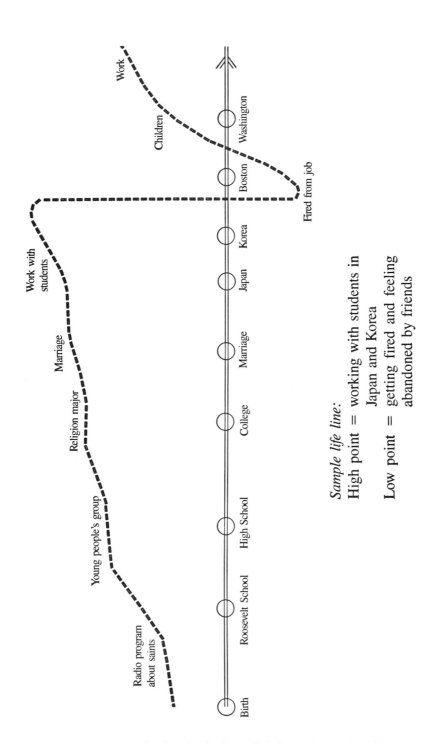

Sample life line:
High point = working with students in
            Japan and Korea
Low point = getting fired and feeling
            abandoned by friends

Individual Work

Purpose: To examine our pilgrimage more deeply through writing our autobiography and to support one another as we do this with intercessory prayer.

1. This week write your *spiritual autobiography.* This autobiography is written for yourself. Trust God (with your cooperation) to give you what to write; then be free to record what comes. Don't worry about grammar, spelling, or "perfect" writing. Just begin at the beginning and let it flow. Content, not style, is important.

Put your autobiography on a paper separate from your journal. After next session we will suggest that those who would like to share their autobiographies (or parts of them) do so with one other person. This is strictly voluntary. The main point for now is to write for yourself in a form that you can refer to throughout life.

Some of the questions given just before the group design may help you get started, but feel free to use your own format.

2. For daily quiet time and for nourishment as you write and reflect on your autobiography, read Psalm 139. During each period of reflection, choose a phrase for meditation and journaling.

3. During the week be a specific intercessor for the person with whom you shared your life line. Pray that God's love may be revealed more clearly in the writing of this autobiography, and that the person be enabled to respond anew.

In John 17:1-26 Jesus intercedes for his disciples in a beautiful prayer just prior to his death. Christians have practiced this form of prayer ever since. How natural to want to support one another with spiritual help as well as physical and emotional help! When we pray for another our openness and sensitivity to that person often increases. It is easy to believe that this can enhance their own openness to God's love and truth. On the other hand, there remains an aspect of mystery in intercessory prayer. Although we can understand partially, faith takes over at some point, and we simply come before God in trust, holding our friend, family member, enemy, or a situation in the light of God's love.

4. To prepare for the next session: Write a brief summary of your personal work with the assignment.

Notes

1. (Nashville: Abingdon, 1980), p. 126.
2. Ibid.
3. Ibid., p. 129.
4. Ibid., p. 131.
5. Ibid.
6. Jean Haldane, "A Study of the Laity . . .," *Action Information* 1 (June 1975):1-4.
7. Robert McAfee Brown, *Creative Dislocation: The Movement of Grace*, p. 144.

Session 4

Cleansing and Healing

When we are tired and dirty at the end of a day, a hot shower does the trick. It feels good to be clean. If a friend comes through an operation successfully and is on the way back to full health, we are delighted. If someone has been feeling estranged from family or loved ones and communication is somehow restored, that is good news. Cleansing, healing, restoration. We feel good about them all.

No wonder the first Christians in the Book of Acts were filled with joy at the privilege of sharing the good news as widely as possible. They were telling everyone that whoever felt soiled by sin could be forgiven and cleansed. Ailing or hurt people could be healed. And estrangement could be transformed into a deep sense of belonging. All of these things were available through believing in Jesus, the forgiver, healer, and restorer.

The ministry of healing and reconciliation was a central and natural part of the life of the early Christians. This passage gives a good picture of the power of the healing ministry:

> Now many signs and wonders were done among the people by the hands of the apostles. . . . And more than ever believers were added to the Lord, multitudes both of men and women, so that they even carried out the sick into the streets, and laid them on beds and pallets, that as Peter came by at least his shadow might fall on some of them. The people also gathered from the towns around Jerusalem, bringing the sick and those afflicted with unclean spirits, and they were all healed.
>
> (Acts 5:12,14-16, RSV)

A major thrust of Paul's sermon at Antioch was to proclaim Jesus as Savior and to spell out the implications of that for his listeners. J. B. Phillips translates the key point in this way:

It is therefore imperative . . . that every one of you should realize
that forgiveness of sins is proclaimed to you through this man.
(Acts 13:38)

Do we still need this ministry today? When we take a searching look at
our past as we do when we write our autobiographies, we notice times of
grace and vitality but also roadblocks to growth. These latter may be
negative feelings, apathy, resentments, destructive acts, attitudes of
unforgiveness, rigidity, or painful experiences that were never healed.
Left unattended, these can thwart further growth and infect our total
well-being. Furthermore this infection will most likely spread beyond us
to our immediate community and the wide world. Surely, then, we still
need the ministry of cleansing, healing, forgiving.

The early church experienced the openness of "walking in the light"
and the naturalness of healing through prayer. Unfortunately those
experiences became obscured by later developments in church life.
Confessing in the privacy of the confessional for Catholics or "to God
alone" for Protestants became common. Healing through prayer became
the province of those on the fringes of church life—certain types of
evangelists or members of small sects.

A number of movements in the so-called mainline churches have
helped many of us return to early Christian practice. An Episcopalian
priest founded the International Order of Saint Luke the Physician in
1953 as an outgrowth of an earlier movement started in 1932. This Order
is open to laity and clergy who want to further the healing ministry of
Christ by establishing healing services in churches, promoting pastoral
and counseling services, circulating literature, and fostering healing
missions in large cities.

Roman Catholics are experiencing new life through the sacraments as
they use the new rite for confession in a face-to-face talk with a priest or
as they support an ill person with prayers and laying on of hands in the
sacrament of the anointing of the sick. Certain people such as Ruth
Carter Stapleton, Francis MacNutt, and Matthew and Dennis Linn have
discovered a call to the ministry of healing and have written helpful
books based on their experiences.[1]

For many years, the Iona Community in Scotland has been a source of
inspiration and innovative ministry for Presbyterians and other Chris-

tians around the world. Their faithful exploration and experience of the ministry of healing through weekly healing services and prayer circles have influenced others to move in this direction.[2] For example, the Christian Fellowship of Healing in Edinburgh, started by Church of Scotland people and supported by members of other church bodies, maintains a ministry of healing, counseling, and prayer through its center and in individual churches that have responded to its example.[3]

We want to single out two persons in this century who have tried to help people in the mainstream of Christian experience recover the healing ministry of Jesus.

The first is Dietrich Bonhoeffer. As Hitler's influence mounted, Bonhoeffer and some colleagues formed an underground seminary to prepare students for both a pastoral and a prophetic role in Nazi Germany. Their aim was to pursue academic studies as well as to forge a life full of Christ's power in that challenging and threatening situation. One aspect of that life was the recovery of the practice of open confession or confessing before a brother or sister. Bonhoeffer chose one of his students, Eberhard Bethge, as his confessor, and described the importance of this practice in his *Life Together*.[4] His idea was that no one person would hear the confession of everyone else in a community, but that each member would be open to hearing a confession and making a confession before a brother or a sister. Thus the whole community bore the darkness of its individual members. Everything was open to the light of honest human interchange and love. This allowed a depth of caring to occur that was impossible when hurts, resentments, and blocks to growth were hidden.

Agnes Sanford, an Episcopalian laywoman, also has helped us understand and recover the healing ministry of Jesus. Her own experience began with her child's earache that did not yield to medical treatment or her own prayers for healing. One day a visiting priest friend casually inquired about the children. When he heard of the baby's illness, he said quite simply that he would pray for him. Going upstairs to the nursery, he laid hands on the baby's ears and prayed:

> Please, Lord Jesus, send your power right now into this baby's ears and take away all germs or infection and make them well. Thank You, Lord, for I believe that You are doing this, and I see these ears

well as You made them to be.[5]

The baby went to sleep and woke up well, but his mother was full of questions:

> Why did God answer the minister's prayers when He had not answered mine? I did not know that I myself blocked my own prayers, because of my lack of faith. Nor did I know that this prayer could not come through me because my mind was clogged with resentment and darkness and unhappiness, as a pipeline can be clogged with roots and dirt.[6]

Subsequently, Agnes Sanford, feeling incapacitated by darkness within, felt an inner urge to ask this priest to pray for her own healing. He talked a bit and then laid hands on her and prayed. She felt immediate relief but within days was again assailed by feelings of depression. This time the priest asked her what she most liked doing. She replied, "I used to like to write, but I can't now because my mind is dead." He replied, "Then you must write. . . . Write two hours every day. These are my orders."[7]

She did begin this regimen and then felt moved to investigate what "Jesus Himself said about faith and about the way of life, and to follow Him and nobody else."[8] Through these very personal explorations she discovered principles of spiritual healing, realized that she had this gift, and since then has devoted herself to this ministry through writing, prayer, and teaching.

One of her contributions is to stress the healing of memories. If Jesus is the same today as yesterday, he can enter into our past experiences and heal them. Our part is to open these memories to him and visualize him present, healing and living right in the painful place.[9]

Open confession of sin before another and prayer for the healing of memories are two tools with which we can deal with the sin and hurt that block our growth and love. There are others, such as interceding for others, laying on of hands, coming together to pray for a critical need, anointing with oil, and cooperating with medical treatment.

As we consider our continuation of the healing ministry of Jesus today, it is easy to get bogged down in intellectual debate, in standing apart and questioning, in finding exceptions rather than instances of healing, and in being cynical. Things change radically when we gain the courage to try some of the available tools, to experience them firsthand, not once but many times, whenever we feel the need. Are we blocked by sin or by hurt? Are we causing our own pain, or was it inflicted by another? Is confession appropriate, or the laying on of hands, or both? The answers to these questions come when we quiet down, set aside our questions and doubts, place ourselves in Jesus' presence, bring the difficulty to him, and simply listen.

It is amazing what happens in a group when we try this. Using a guided meditation such as the one included in the group design, each one goes before Jesus and engages with him uniquely in that situation. Sometimes a person is given a new image. One that occurred to a participant is that of Jesus with his arms around her and the person from whom she felt estranged, both enclosed in his loving arms. In such an experience, one might be given something to do. In our recent session on this subject, one woman felt deeply motivated to write a reconciling letter to her father. Another might feel calmed or released from pain or tension. Someone else may have no immediate experience but may find some benefit later.

Healing and forgiving were central to Jesus' life and ministry, and he taught his disciples how to extend this unique way of loving. The community of faith has preserved tools for healing, restoring, and reconciling. They are available for every believer and believing community. We can read about them and learn about them from others, but only as we try them out ourselves will they become real and vital for us.

Group Design

Purpose: To share points of gratitude in our lives and to experience healing or forgiveness for things that block our growth.
Materials: Candle, oil, small bowls or cups, small table, Bible, record.

A. Gathering Time   (20 minutes)   Large Group
This should be lively since much of what follows is sedentary. Sometimes we sing favorite songs—rousing camp songs from our past—or go through one motion song such as "If You're Happy and You Know It,

Clap Your Hands" or "John Brown's Baby Had a Cold Upon His Chest."

After song and movement, settle down in the large group for some journaling in preparation for your small-group sharing. Think about your life story as you worked with it this week. Jot down in your journal some points of gratitude: people, events, situations for which you are grateful. Then choose one or two items and use a few minutes to expand your thoughts in writing. What made you grateful? Go into some detail. Relive in writing the good feelings associated with that moment. Explore your thankfulness.

B. Sharing Groups   (20 minutes)

1. Report on your experience of writing your autobiography and interceding for your partner.

  2. Each one share a point of gratitude with the group.

  3. End with prayers of thanks for one another's life.

C. Lab on Healing, Cleansing, Forgiving   (45 minutes)

Note to the leader: As part of this lab, we suggest setting up a worship center on a small table in the center of the group. You can do this, or ask for a volunteer to be ready to do it. Have on hand the items you would like to use: perhaps a candle and matches (to be lit as you begin), a small container of oil, and a small cup or bowl for each pair of people in the group, and any other items that symbolize for you Christ's healing, cleansing, or forgiving love.

This lab has three parts, each of which should be led by the leader who will say the following:

  1. *Preparation:* "In this session, we will experience two of the tools for healing suggested in the session text: *imaging* the healing Christ with us in silent prayer and *symbolizing* his healing love with oil as we pray together.

  "For grounding and encouragement, let's silently recall instances when we experienced Christ's healing of ourselves or of others. (Pause.) Let's talk about a few briefly and why they are important to us. . . . (10 minutes for sharing healing stories.)

  "Now let's recall the progress of this course. First, we gave attention to our commitment to growth, then to being present and listening more carefully; next we turned to our own stories. In each of these endeavors, it is likely that we have encountered blocks to our loving and growing. All of us have these blocks; there are different kinds, and they can occur at every level of spiritual awareness. Several were mentioned in the session text: negative feelings; hurts that were never healed; resentments; attitudes of unforgiveness; rigidity; painful experiences we want to forget.

"Our worship center is intended to create an atmosphere of prayer. As we look at the objects before us, let's remember that the lighted candle represents Christ's presence, and the oil his healing love. . . .

"Now let's prepare for our meditative imaging of the healing Christ. First, get comfortable with pen and paper at hand. Relax and become quiet. . . . In this meditation, periods of silence will alternate with time for journaling. We will use our imaginations. The great masters of prayer frequently suggest imaging Christ present as a preparation for prayer."

2. *Guided Silent Meditation:* "Close your eyes and let an *area* come to mind *that needs healing, forgiving, reconciling, cleansing, something more.* It may help to think over your life line or your autobiography to identify a situation, person, attitude, or event with which you feel led to work. (Pause 3 to 4 minutes.)

"Now *imagine you are in a garden*—one you actually know or one created by your imagination. See the colors and forms; hear the sounds; smell the fragrance. Notice the landscaping, natural or well trimmed. Is there a bench? a path? Feel comfortable and at home. See Jesus present with you. (Pause 2 or 3 minutes.)

"Begin to *talk over with Jesus the area* with which you want to work. Say as much about it as you can, turning it over and looking at different sides, listening for Jesus' responses. Listen and then record in your journal. Ask Jesus to help you see the situation through his eyes and the eyes of the others involved. (Pause 7 to 10 minutes.)

"Now ask Jesus for *what you want or need* in this area, what you would like to have happen—e.g., insight, forgiveness. (Pause 2 to 3 minutes.)

"Next, ask Jesus to *show you what is needed*—what he would have you understand, say, or do with regard to another person, your attitude, a situation. (Pause for 2 to 3 minutes.)

"Finally, bring your interaction with Jesus to a close, knowing you can return whenever you wish. Stretch. Stand."

D. Cleansing Liturgy   (20 minutes)

As everyone is standing, perhaps remind people again of the meaning of the symbolic objects you are using. Then be seated in pairs (life-line partners) facing each other.

The leader pours the oil into the small cups and gives each pair a cup with instructions such as these: "Down through the ages, oil has been a symbol of

- healing (Jas. 5:14);
- the Spirit (Is. 61:1);
- cleansing (Lk. 7:36-38; 10:34);
- strength (Ps. 89:20-22);
- joy, celebration (Ps. 45:6-8).

(Read one or more of the suggested scriptures if you like.)

"Now we invite each of you to mention to your partner the area with which you worked. Do this as specifically or as generally as you like, and remember that if you prefer not to say anything, simply say so. (An example: 'I would like healing with a co-worker in the office.') Then we invite the partner to anoint the one who shared by making the sign of the cross, or simply marking your partner's open hand with oil. There is no right or wrong way to do this. Some people mark both hands—some one. Then take your partner's hands in yours and say a word of blessing or encouragement such as 'Let us believe together that Jesus is healing you or giving you the help you need.' Or you might say a brief prayer such as 'We thank you, Jesus, that you helped people long ago and can do so today. Give John the help he needs.' If prayer aloud seems awkward, use a silent prayer."

As these prayers and blessings are going on, you might play as background a suitable song such as "Turn to Me" from the album *Earthen Vessels* (St. Louis Jesuits, North American Liturgy Resources, 2110 W. Peoria Ave., Phoenix, Arizona 85029, 1975).

E. Closing   (15 minutes)   Large Group

Choose one or two of the following suggestions as appropriate for your group: evaluation of the session, discussion of details for next session, prayer, song ("Peace Is Flowing Like a River," from the same album as above).

Individual Work

Purpose: To deepen our reception of healing, cleansing, or forgiveness and to ponder ways of extending that to others.

1. Ponder Lk. 15:11-32 and Lk. 23:32-43 to increase your awareness of the healing and forgiving love of God.

2. Consider receiving a deeper or more extensive healing of your past or present. Become conscious of specific moments or areas of your life that need healing. Envision God's healing power restoring you to wholeness through Jesus.

3. Is there a relationship in your life where you are conscious of causing some hurt, distance, or brokenness? The relationship could be with someone living or dead. (Many people find that although the other person in a relationship has died, there is a continuing possibility for change and growth in their understanding and appreciation of that relationship.) Are there things you can do or ways in which you can restore wholeness to that relationship, either by forgiving yourself or the other within your spirit, by having a talk, making a phone call, or writing a note? Consider taking one such concrete step this week.

4. To prepare for next session: Write a brief summary of your personal work with this assignment.

Notes

1. Ruth Carter Stapleton, *The Gift of Inner Healing* (Waco, Texas: Word Books, 1976); Francis MacNutt, *Healing* (Notre Dame, Ind.: Ave Maria Press, 1974); Dennis Linn and Matthew Linn, *Healing of Memories* (New York: Paulist Press, 1974); Dennis Linn and Matthew Linn, *Healing Life's Hurts* (New York: Paulist Press, 1978).

2. T. Ralph Morton, *What Is the Iona Community?* (Glasgow: The Iona Community Publishing Department, 1957). Obtainable from Community House, 214 Clyde Street, Glasgow G 1 4JZ, Scotland. The Iona Community, *Divine Healing* (Glasgow: The Iona Community Publishing Department, no date given). Obtainable from Community House.

3. Materials available from the Christian Fellowship of Healing, c/o Morningside Congregational Church, 15 Chamberlain Road, Edinburgh EH 10 4DJ, Scotland.

4. (New York: Harper and Row, 1954), pp. 112-113.
5. Agnes Sanford, *Sealed Orders* (Plainfield, N.J.: Logos International, 1972), p. 97.
6. Ibid., p. 98.
7. Ibid., pp. 100, 101.
8. Ibid., p. 102.
9. Agnes Sanford, *The Healing Gifts of the Spirit* (New York: J. B. Lippincott, 1966), pp. 107-141.

Session 5

Being Confronted by Gospel Values

"Actions speak louder than words." We all know that to be true, but most of us long for ways to demonstrate the power of that simple saying. The actions of a Mother Teresa witness to the love of Christ as no words can do. What can we do to demonstrate God's generosity as strongly as she does?

In this complex world, answers are often hard to discover. Unlike Mother Teresa, who has a single commitment to the dying of Calcutta, most of us have multiple commitments—to family, job, and community—and each of them seems to be part of God's plan for us. How can we be faithful to all these commitments and not become hopelessly fragmented? How can we make choices about life-style that truly foster growth in love for ourselves and others?

When we look to the Bible for help, we see two streams of thought. One stresses giving up everything and following Jesus; the other emphasizes our co-creativity with God, cherishing the earth, and participating in its development. This apparent dichotomy can lead to two unfortunate results. On the one hand, we can be tempted to stress one at the expense of the other. On the other hand, we can become so frustrated by the apparent contradiction between detachment and development that we are immobilized. Sidney Callahan described the two attitudes this way:

> I'm always seesawing between two equally attractive ideas, both of which, incidently, have been ably defended in the Christian tradition.
>
> The first is the more ascetic approach. . . . The essence of the message is Don't. Don't spend a penny on anything that is not strictly necessary. . . .
>
> I am also a believer in the opposite ideal. Shall we call it the Chartres principle? It's also our charge to beautify, develop and

order the world. . . .

I envy those people still living in a community where an ordered succession of feasts and family celebrations are still in force. The common expectations must relieve the burden of creating an individual lifestyle. . . .

We (our family) bumble on in completely contradictory fashion. . . . The bed broke and we leave the mattress on the floor but have a lot of expensive new plants. There are never enough blankets, . . . but there's one nice room with a few art splurges on the wall. . . .

It's a mess and mass of inconsistencies, with books, books, everywhere. I can't solve this problem and I can't run away somewhere and start over. The tension and contradictory pulls are always there. But does it have to be this way?[1]

Pierre Teilhard de Chardin in *The Divine Milieu* expresses a more peaceful attitude:

In the general rhythm of Christian life, development and renunciation, attachment and detachment, are not mutually exclusive. On the contrary, they harmonize, like breathing in and out in the movement of our lungs.[2]

In addition to these two streams of thought, the Bible contains some overarching principles that can be helpful in dealing with our questions about life-style.

The amount of cash or material goods that one has seems less important than a spirit of generosity and wholeheartedness that prompts one to use what one has for liberation, not domination, to foster cooperation rather than isolation. Sue was once poor and an invalid. Her situation is now changed. In good health and with enough material resources for herself and her family, she has pondered the question of what the poor really want and what the privileged can really give. She wrote:

My main responsibility from my privileged position is to recognize and utilize the power that is the gift of material things—my education, my health because of medical care and food, my "free" time because I don't have to work. My position on the ladder of wealth is not nearly as important as what I do with it—my mission.[3]

Has she found a key to working with these life-style questions? We believe she has. It has to do with mission and focus. Thomas Kelly in his essay "The Eternal Now and Social Concern" expresses the essence and purpose of what we have said thus far in these courses as he sees it in the Society of Friends. He talks about the interrelatedness of "inward Life and outward Concern."[4] When one is open to God's love, there comes an experience of divine presence that conveys its own joy, tender love, and confident peace that embraces all creation. That forms a background

> of universal concern for all the multitude of good things that need doing. Toward them all we feel kindly, but we are dismissed from active service in most of them. And we have an easy mind in the presence of desperately real needs which are not our direct responsibility.[5]

In the foreground of this general concern for all creation "is the special task, uniquely illuminated, toward which we feel a special yearning and care."[6]

Kelly goes on to emphasize how important it is to be faithful to a few concerns based on guidance from within rather than engaging in "undertakings . . . plastered on from the outside because we cannot turn down a friend."[7] He says, "The concern-oriented life is ordered and organized from within. And we learn to say *No* as well as *Yes* by attending to the guidance of inner responsibility."[8]

Faithfulness to a few concerns and focus on a sense of calling and mission are two aspects of our response to God's love. As these become clarified in a person's life, questions of life-style can be dealt with in terms of how they express each person's central concerns.

For example, a suburban housewife increasingly felt called to work and live in the city. Gradually, she made concrete decisions to foster this calling. She sold her suburban house, moved with her children to a city apartment, enrolled the children in city schools, and found work in an urban parish. Once her central focus became clear, those life-style decisions followed.

One man sees the importance of building both engagement and disengagement into his life. His home is his place of disengagement, a retreat from his demanding job. He invests some time and money in the home and thus makes it a refreshing place for himself and many others who enjoy its atmosphere. Another person's "foreground concern" is housing for the inner-city poor, and so he invests time and energy in renovating and upgrading substandard housing.

In making decisions involving life direction, many have been helped by using some form of discernment in prayer. Much has been written about this recently as Christians have become newly aware of traditional ways to do this. In the sixteenth century, St. Ignatius Loyola developed a process to be used by individuals and communities when making significant decisions. This is still used today, often in the context of a guided retreat. Essentially it involves (1) putting ourselves consciously in the presence of God, (2) examining the elements of the choice to be made as objectively as possible, (3) becoming aware of our areas of unfreedom, (4) making a tentative decision and living with it for a few days, (5) noting our inner state during this time (peaceful or troubled), and (6) proceeding as indicated by these fruits to remain either with that choice or to "try on" an alternative.

Of course, discernment is much broader than a process. It involves growing in consciousness of God's loving way with me and seeking that way with consistency. Over time we learn to detect more surely when we are living in harmony with this Spirit and when we are not.

Life-style questions are challenging. So far we have mentioned only decisions in the private realm. But many touch the wider world as well. Do I use the products of, or invest in, companies with exploitive Third World policies? Does the ease of having my own car make me careless and callous to the need for better public transportation? Does my desire for rest at night or on the weekend prevent me from attending peace rallies that support measures in which I believe?

It is a mistake to think we can settle these questions once and for all. The circumstances of our lives continue to change, as do the needs of the world, and so we have to rethink our ways of dealing with these matters. Some people find a periodic review and reexamination of life-style issues an important way to allow themselves to be newly confronted by changing realities and freshly converted to responses that are loving and just. This can be done in groups or individually. But it is easy to avoid following through on life-style decisions. That is why individuals and groups find it helpful to incorporate decisions regarding time, money, material possessions, home, work, and the wider community into a rule of life that is written down and can be made available for the critique and encouragement of loving friends.

Decisions about life-style can involve changing long-standing habits, which is sometimes a painful process. But they can also free us from attitudes that cripple and prevent us from receiving and offering God's love. Thus they are tools for spiritual growth.

Sometimes a simple word can set us free. This apparently happened to Sue Grant when she read this Native American poem. It seems to summarize what we are trying to be:

You see, I am alive.
You see, I stand in good relation to the earth.
You see, I stand in good relation to the gods.
You see, I stand in good relation to all that is beautiful.
You see, I stand in good relation to you.
You see, I am alive. I am alive.[9]

Group Design

Purpose: To hear some scriptural passages on life-style questions and to share contemporary stories of life-style decisions that have meaning for us.

Materials: Bible, newsprint, marking pens.

A. Gathering Time   (20 minutes)   Large Group
Recently in the newspaper there was a photo of a woman refugee fleeing a troubled area and carrying a huge television set on her head. Was this her most prized possession? If you suddenly were in the same spot, what one item would you want to take with you? Take a few minutes in silence and then each one share what you would take and why.

B. Sharing Groups   (20 minutes)
Give each person a chance to share one point about receiving healing, cleansing, or forgiveness through prayer and one point about extending forgiveness or healing to another. Or share one experience with the individual work that had positive value and one that presented

difficulties.

C. Check-in Time on the Reading   (15 minutes)
Review briefly the main points of the session text and share one way in which you felt challenged by the material.

D. Lab on Life-style Questions   (55 minutes)
1. *What scripture says about life-style questions:*
   a. Read the following scriptures without comment, taking turns around the room:

Lk. 16:13-15	Lk. 14:12-14
Mk. 1:16-20	Mt. 8:19-21
Mt. 19:21-22	Jn. 2:6-10
Mt. 5:40-42	Lk. 6:30
Lk. 12:25	Lk. 6:38
Lk. 11:37-42	Mk. 10:21-25
Lk. 12:33	

   b. Large-group sharing: What do these scriptures say? What general guidelines do they present that can help us with life-style decisions?
   2. *What lives of individuals can tell us* about specific choices:
   a. On large pieces of paper put these categories:

money	time
work	focus
location	simplification
rule of life or spiritual	regular examination of
fitness plan	conscience

   b. Each of these categories refers to ways people have responded to the challenge to live their lives by gospel values, and are mentioned in the session text. Ask the participants to place their initials beside categories that they could illustrate from real life—their own or others'.
   c. Sharing free-for-all: Share as many stories as time permits, recognizing that there may not be time for all of them.

E. Closing   (10 minutes)   Large Group
Choose one or two of the following suggestions as appropriate for your group: evaluation of the session, discussion of details for next session, prayer, song (" 'Tis a Gift To Be Simple").

'Tis a Gift to Be Simple

'Tis a gift to be simple, 'tis a gift to be free,
'Tis a gift to come down where we ought to be.
And when we find ourselves in the place just right
'Twill be in the valley of love and delight.
When true simplicity is gained
To bow and to bend we shan't be ashamed.
To turn, turn will be our delight,
Till by turning, turning, we come down right.

Individual Work

Purpose: To consider decisions about life-style in the light of gospel values.

1. Read Lk. 12:13-48. Jesus talks about seeking first the Reign of God as the focus of a person's life. How does that translate specifically into your life? What is your focus? What is your treasure? Are there areas where you are covetous or excessively anxious? Note your responses to these questions in your journal.

2. Ask God specifically how to relate to the things of your life. Ask what life-style decisions you need to address in order to express more faithfully the focus of your life. Are there changes to make? What are they? Pose these questions and then wait in collectedness and silence for insights and openings that come from within you. Jot these down in your journal.

3. As you reflect on the generosity of God in your life and your central concerns as spoken of by Thomas Kelly, we invite you to experiment with one *concrete change* in your life-style this week. Write down your feelings and reactions. Examples: fast; give time or money; cut something out; take time to be generous with yourself; lighten the load; simplify; allow the replenishing, refreshing, re-creating aspect of God's creation to touch you; slow your pace; express your own creativity.

4. The fourth session in the Old Testament course concerned God's covenant love for us and our response to that love. In the second

suggestion for individual work, we suggested that you write out your covenant with God—what you wish that relationship to be and specific ways to help that happen. Then in the first session in this course, "Commitment," the subject of writing a spiritual fitness plan or rule of life is mentioned, with some specific suggestions.

This week, focus on one aspect of your covenant—your relationship to the material aspects of your life. Try putting that in writing—*your goal in relation to material things and how you intend to reach it.* Example: "Because God is generous, I want to be generous in my gift of time to God, self, and others. Specifically, I want to give away 50% of everything I grow this summer to an inner-city food bank."

5. What do you think about the suggestion made in the session text about periodic examination and review of your life-style? At what intervals do you feel you should make such an examination? Do you feel strongly enough to put it on the calendar?

6. To prepare for next session: Write a brief summary of your personal work with this assignment.

Notes

1. "Seesawing Through a Contradictory Lifestyle," originally published in the *National Catholic Reporter,* June 7, 1974, p. 9.
2. (New York: Harper and Row, 1960), p. 73.
3. "Materialism," unpublished essay circulated at the Church of the Saviour.
4. In *A Testament of Devotion* (New York: Harper and Brothers, 1941), p. 89.
5. Ibid., p. 109.
6. Ibid.
7. Ibid., p. 110.
8. Ibid.
9. "Materialism," unpublished essay.

Session 6

Charting a Course

Several years ago we did some research on burnout among ministering persons engaged in difficult mission. "What are the conditions that seem to lead to periods of burnout?" we asked. Two answers emerged most frequently. The first had to do with spiritual nourishment, the second with companionship or community.

In the challenge of ministry, people often neglected to feed their spirits and thus attempted a high level of mission in a state of chronic spiritual malnutrition. Often an initial period of spiritual inspiration had been the impetus for choosing a life of dedicated ministry, but many people did not know how to sustain that inspiration; they did not know how to create for themselves a spiritually nourishing situation.

In addition, many felt lonely and isolated. They had friends, to be sure, but no friends who uniquely shared their sense of vocation or mission, and thus no one with whom to share the low points of their work and prayer. They were hungry for community, a community of ministering persons like themselves, but they did not know how to find or create this.

The gospel life is hard. It involves transforming individuals and institutions: recognizing and siding with the victim inside and outside of ourselves, making that victim visible, and then constructing alternative visions or ways of being and doing. Spiritual nourishment and companionship are necessary if we are to persevere over a long period, and that is what this course has been about. Together we have studied and practiced several tools for Christian growth: commitment, collectedness, recalling our stories, cleansing, healing, and generosity. These are tools that can be used individually as well as in groups.

The twofold question now is: Which of these practices should I begin to use or strengthen in my life, and how can I develop a life-style formed and fed by them?

As we review each session, more specific questions emerge:
- how to be a person of compassion, *committed to the way embodied by Jesus*;
- how to cultivate the art of *living from the center,* listening deeply and openly to God, ourselves, and others;
- how to interpret *what my journey is saying* about God's love and generosity to me, the gifts, and call that have been given to me;
- how to be a *healed and healing person* in a world of hurt;
- how to *evolve a life-style* that expresses the peace, wholeness, healing, generosity, and compassion of Jesus.

Remembering our different types of prayer, we can ask how we plan to incorporate the various forms we used: consecration, listening, intercession, healing and confession, and discernment.

One way to incorporate these practices is through a spiritual fitness plan (or rule of life) as was suggested in the first session and mentioned again in the fifth session. We can do this as individuals or by participating in a small group that is seeking to live a life based on spiritual nourishment, community, and mission.

There are communities—some old, some relatively new—whose corporate life has been dedicated to a balanced approach and from whom we can learn much. The Sojourners in Washington, D.C., is an example of a relatively new group of men and women, married and single, who have banded together to share resources, to engage in disciplined spiritual growth both as individuals and as a community, and to carry on a vigorous social-justice ministry through their magazine *Sojourners* and through other activities.[1]

While we can learn much from a community like the Sojourners, it is important not to get bogged down by more than we can handle. Many tools are examined in these courses, but when you start on your own it seems best to concentrate on the ones that have particular power for you. Doing one thing well may be a key to getting started. For example, at the end of a recent session, three people realized how much they wanted to do some spiritual reading and so formed a small group to read and reflect together.

Sometimes it is wise to begin simply with yourself and hear what you need now. One person, for instance, formed a rule of life that combined three of the tools presented in this course. He said, "The combination of collectedness, intercession, and commitment seems right for me at this time. First, I listen to God; second, I intercede for those for whom I am concerned; and third, I commit myself to an action related to them. It seems very simple, but it's real, and it works."

Two significant tools for growth not yet mentioned in this course are helpful for carrying on what has begun. Both are enjoying a renaissance in our country.

First is the ancient art of spiritual direction or spiritual guidance. Just as Jesus taught and guided his disciples in the new way, so the spiritual leaders of early Christian monasteries saw themselves as teachers and guides for the people in their charge. Those further along in the way would act as guides for novices and could assist or direct them in spiritual development.

Tilden Edwards, an Episcopal priest who was intrigued by this tradition of spiritual guidance, was also well aware that modern Christians lack competent guides. Immersing himself in the traditions of both Christian spiritual direction and the guidance provided by some Eastern religions, he became convinced of the importance of spiritual guidance and also became willing to offer it himself. Gradually he has developed this ministry and has trained others in it through the Shalem Institute for Spiritual Formation in Washington, D.C.[2]

A spiritual guide is someone to whom people naturally turn for support in spiritual development. Such a person feels called by God to use this gift, to develop it through training and experience, and then to companion people in their spiritual pilgrimages.

Many people, after taking a course like this one, welcome having one person guide, coach, support, and pray with them in their unique situation. Generally, one meets with the spiritual guide monthly for about an hour. The agenda is set by the one coming for direction. This process may go on for months or years as one feels the need. Sometimes appointments are more widely spaced when appropriate.

Where to find a spiritual guide? Sometimes that can be a problem, but if the need is really genuine, it is surprising how one is led to a person who can help. Local spiritual renewal or retreat centers often can recommend people. Certain Catholic religious communities such as the Cenacle Sisters specialize in spiritual direction. And one can call the institutes that train spiritual directors, and ask for recommendations.

For some, the idea of a personal companion in the spiritual life is a great boon. For others, there is an awesomeness or even fear about confiding in another. Sometimes that can be eased by reading some of the fine books and articles that are available on the subject. Thomas Merton's *Spiritual Direction and Meditation,* Tilden Edwards' *Spiritual Friend,* and Kenneth Leech's *Soul Friend* are three excellent resources.[3]

Dorothy Devers has been concerned that there are not enough spiritual guides to fill the need. She and her spiritual friend and partner, Mimi Spillers, worked out ways by which two friends could offer each other spiritual guidance. These exercises, readings, and suggestions were published in a book called *Faithful Friendship.*[4] Small groups and pairs of people find this book a valuable guide to continuing spiritual growth on their own.

The second tool that is becoming better known and used is the experience of retreat. No matter how helpful other people may be, whether personally or through books, we need to cultivate the art of going directly to God. A retreat gives us the opportunity to do this. It is an extended period of quiet prayer away from home and work. In the silence, and with guided leadership, many things begin to fall into place. In such a setting the prayer of collectedness is not just a period of a few minutes at the beginning of one's day; it is a whole milieu in which one lives for the several days away. Moving closer to the center of one's being where God can be found becomes possible as the layers of busyness, conversation, and interaction are gradually removed.

Most people serious about spiritual growth build into their lives regular days or periods of retreat. As they learn to meet God in silence for an extended time, they find it possible to bring quiet prayer back into their busy existence as an oasis to which they can return.

It must be emphasized that what is being described is a silent retreat, not a sharing retreat or a working conference designed to set goals or create community, valuable though these may be. These latter are more commonly available and are often confused with silent retreat. What we are describing is a retreat with large amounts of silence interrupted only by guided meditations offered by a leader. One can experience this in a group or alone. It is true that some people are uneasy with prolonged silence. But once that barrier is overcome, the value of a silent retreat becomes obvious.

Spiritual growth does not happen automatically. It takes practice—faithful practice done with commitment and discipline. Fruits do come. Like dedicated musicians who are eventually able to play a piece of music with real vision and inspiration, we experience grace-filled moments when we know that creation is good and we are part of it. But these moments can evaporate quickly unless there is sustained, committed practice.

All of the tools and practices we have been experiencing have one aim: to help us respond more deeply to God's love and to share it more fully. Paul used a striking metaphor to describe this experience of growth: "If anyone is in Christ, he is a new creation." Jesus described the growth process as being born anew, welcoming the reign of God within. He also prayed that God's reign would come on earth. How we help that happen is the subject to which we now turn.

Group Design

Purpose: To reflect on the tools for growth we have found important in this course, and to plan ways to continue growing in God's love.

A. Gathering Time   (20 minutes)   Large Group
At the end of the session, the importance of practice is mentioned. Think of a time when you had a good experience of practicing an art, sport, craft, or other skill. Briefly describe your experiences. Or begin your session in a way more appropriate to your group.

B. Sharing Groups   (20 minutes)
How did you deal with the questions about your life focus in the first suggestion for individual work? What life-style change did you try this week? Give each person a chance to share briefly on these two questions, and then finish with general discussion of any part of the material of special interest.

C. Check-in Time of the Reading   (20 minutes)
Review the main points and share which had meaning for you. Which concrete suggestions made in the session text would you like to explore

further?

D. Lab   (50 minutes)

1. *Reflection and journaling:* Each person turn to the fifth, sixth, and seventh paragraphs of this session text, beginning with: "The twofold question now is. . . ." Someone read these paragraphs slowly aloud in order to remind everyone of the basic content of the course. Then each person do some writing on these questions:

• Where and how have you grown through this course? Identify areas of growth and what helped them to happen.

• Reviewing all the tools mentioned in the course, which do you want to learn more about?

• Which tools do you wish to incorporate into your life, and how do you hope to do this? Consider writing these down in a spiritual fitness plan.

• What kind of help do you need?

2. *Large-group sharing:* Discuss the questions you just considered. Conclude with any sharing that will bring a sense of conclusion to this group effort. It might be helpful to think of completing these sorts of sentences:

• "I'm grateful for. . . ."
• "I learned. . . ."
• "I feel disappointed. . . ."
• "I wish. . . ."
• "I hope. . . ."

E. Closing Celebration   (10 minutes or more)   Large Group
Devise a way for your group to celebrate the ending of this course. Use music, movement, prayer, refreshments, or other ways you create.

Notes

1. Sojourners, 1029 Vermont Ave., N.W., Washington, D.C. 20005.
2. Shalem Institute for Spiritual Formation, Inc., Mount St. Alban, Washington, D.C. 20016.
3. Tilden Edwards, *Spiritual Friend* (New York/Ramsey: Paulist Press, 1980). Kenneth Leech, *Soul Friend* (London: Sheldon Press, 1977). Thomas Merton, *Spiritual Direction and Meditation* (Collegeville, Minn.: The Liturgical Press, 1960).

4. Dorothy Devers, *Faithful Friendship* (Cincinnati: Forward Movement Publications, 1980). 412 Sycamore Street, Cincinnati, Ohio 45202.

Four

Discovering Your Ministry and Gifts

When we come to know and love God, we want to embody that love in the world. Calls for help come constantly. How to respond? Where to give our time, energy, and commitment?

A way to address these questions was discovered by the ecumenical Church of the Saviour in Washington, D.C. This community was established after World War II by Gordon Cosby, a Baptist minister, and his wife, Mary. They wanted to find a way to address the task of spiritual reconstruction and rehabilitation that confronted our nation after the war. Their inspiration was to create a community that would be grounded in commitment to Jesus and would be free to experiment with fresh ways to express this commitment.

For about fifteen years this community of Christians worshiped together, studied scripture, prayed, and tried to extend Christ's ministry. Although some mission developed out of this devotion, it was not significant. The members felt that genuine Christianity had the power to change the world and really make a difference, but it was not happening. What was wrong?

In scripture, the members had discovered many people who felt called by God and who acted out of that calling. A vision of what God wanted formed the entire activity of these biblical people. The Church of the Saviour decided to follow their example. All the prayer and study groups that had been formed were disbanded. People were given encouragement, instruction, and "friendly open space," as Henri Nouwen puts it, to discern their own calling, and then were encouraged to gather with those who had a similar calling. Each group worked out ways to pray together, to care about one another, and to implement their calling.

The history of what happened is described in several books by Elizabeth O'Connor[1] and one by Gordon Cosby.[2] Mission groups, as they were named, were called into being to minister to neglected children in Washington, to develop low-income housing, to address the problems of war, peace, and disarmament, to provide retreats for rest and reflection, and to carry out other vital ministries. Two of these efforts, For Love of Children and Jubilee Housing, Inc., have already been described in these pages.

The number of people involved at the Church of the Saviour has always been small, one or two hundred, but the impact has been impressive. Each of the members of our Partners Community has in one way or other been touched by that church's life, so it was natural that we would incorporate some of what we learned there into our courses. Nowhere is this more evident than in this one.

We combined what we had learned from the Church of the Saviour and from other experiences and designed a way for people to work with the question of how to respond more fully to God's call. It involves asking six questions and listening for illumination as it comes from within, from God, scripture, friends, and circumstances. The questions, which give both theme and title to the six sessions of this course, are:
1. What are my unique, God-given gifts?
2. How can I be a patron of another's gifts?
3. Which piece of God's vision is mine?
4. What is God calling me to do?
5. Is there a corporate dimension for my vocation?
6. How do my unique gifts and calling tie into the larger body of believers?

Of course, these are not the only questions to ask, but they provide a good start. The order in which they are presented is logical but not necessarily the order in which they occur in each person's life. They should not be dealt with separately but addressed in relationship to one another over and over again. Our course introduces them and presents some of our experience but cannot in the time available cover all the variations that happen as people attempt to discern God's call.

Although we offer working definitions of the terms used in this course, you may find other terms or descriptions more apt in your situation. Try to avoid the temptation to define your experiences too precisely. Use our definitions as a stimulus for your own reflection and build from there.

In addition to presenting this discernment process, we explore ways to incorporate spiritual nourishment, community support, and mission into parish life. These could take many forms, but we focus on one method of organizing that is effective but not often tried today, the servant community.

On our writing desk is a greeting card sent to us by one of our participants. It captures the spirit of this course and the importance we feel it has for us all:

A vision without a task
is a dream.
A task without a vision
is a drudgery.
A vision and a task
is the
hope
of the world.

Notes

1. Books by Elizabeth O'Connor: *Calls to Commitment* (New York: Harper and Row, 1963); *Journey Inward, Journey Outward* (New York: Harper and Row, 1968); *Our Many Selves* (New York: Harper and Row, 1971); *Eighth Day of Creation* (Waco, Tex.: Word Books, 1971); *Search for Silence* (Waco, Tex.: Word Books, 1972); *The New Community* (New York: Harper and Row, 1976); *Letters to Scattered Pilgrims* (New York: Harper and Row, 1979).
2. Book by Gordon Cosby: *Handbook for Mission Groups* (Waco, Tex.: Word Books, 1975).

Session 1

What Are My Unique, God-Given Gifts?

"Through the grace of God we have different gifts."
(Rom. 12:6, Phillips)

The parable of the talents (Mt. 25:14-30, JB) seems cruel. The cautious, careful person who kept one talent buried safely in the ground was given a tongue-lashing ("you wicked and lazy servant"), had the one talent snatched away, and was thrown outside into the darkness, "where there will be weeping and grinding of teeth."

Where is the love of God in this story? Why did Jesus use such harsh terms to make his point? It appears that Jesus was trying to say something important and to drive it home in an unforgettable way.

It was not until we came into contact with the Church of the Saviour and the preaching of Gordon Cosby that we understood the significance of Jesus' teaching in this parable: Our God-given gifts are meant to be used fully, or we and others suffer tremendous loss. The discovery and exercise of gifts is not an optional luxury but are at the core of gospel living. We cannot love others fully until we love who we are and what we are doing—in other words, until we are exercising our own gift, whatever it is.

Doing what we really want or love to do: Doesn't that smack of self-indulgence? Isn't there something sinful in that kind of theology? Matthew Fox addresses this question in the preface to *On Becoming a Musical, Mystical Bear.* He describes the life-denying spiritualities that comprise our heritage and calls for a reaffirmation of the life-affirming spiritualities of the Hebrew prophets and Jesus.

Fox says that the impetus of Jesus and the prophetic tradition in Judaism "is that all of creation, life itself, is a gift—a gift from a life-loving, life-sharing, life-enjoying Creator."[1] That is the way it was seen by the Yahwist author of Genesis, who declared that God surveyed all creation and "found it very good." This is in contrast to life-denying spiritualities that Fox claims have held dominance in Western civilization. They are characterized by "repression, not expression; guilt, not pleasure; heaven, not this life; sentimentality, not justice; mortification, not developing of talents."[2] These spiritualities, he says, can lead to life-denial and deep pessimism. "Yet they have often been the more popular and influential spiritualities in Christianity."[3]

As Paul went about encouraging the early Christians, he wrote about gifts in his letters. He advises young Timothy "to fan into a flame the gift that God gave you when I laid my hands on you" (2 Tim. 1:6, JB). In our groups, we give people the major biblical passages on gifts from Paul's letters and the Gospel of Matthew (Rom. 12:4-8; 1 Cor. 12:1-11; 1 Cor. 12:27-30; Eph. 4:11-16; Mt. 25:14-30). Then we suggest that participants help one another construct their own theology of gifts. One person summarized the message in Ephesians this way:

Every person called by Jesus Christ into his body
is given a gift
to use
on behalf of the whole body!

"In other words," she concluded, "everyone has *charisma*. One aspect of the good news is this: You can be what you were intended to be and do what you were created to do!"

It is important to know what we mean when we use the term *gift*. Karl Olsson differentiates between *gift* and *talent* this way. For him, *talent* refers to our natural powers, "native gifts" given at creation and often used for self-development. Gifts, according to Olsson, are "Spirit powers," given at the time of a Spirit opening or outpouring, and they are used for building up the community or ministering on behalf of it.[4]

In our courses, the working definition we use is that a gift is any skill, task, or role that you and others see as God's gift to the community through you.

The scripture passages already mentioned include examples of gifts that Paul felt were important in the early church such as giving, administration, healing, and loving. Although Paul names specific gifts, the number and variety of gifts God has for us is really endless. You will see this when you begin identifying one another's gifts in the exercises that follow.

What does all this have to do with the church? The Church of the Saviour defines the nature and task of the church in a striking way: It is a gift-evoking and gift-bearing community. The job of the church is to evoke people's gifts, build structures to house them, and then offer them to the world.

Members of this church spend considerable time with newcomers, informally in courses and on retreat, asking questions, giving encouragement, offering helpful readings, enabling them to think, pray, and talk about their gifts, uniqueness, limitations, hopes and dreams for the world. Newcomers are not asked to serve in any way at first. Only when they feel moved to offer a gift or pursue their calling do they join a working group. This "letting a person be" can sometimes feel unnerving to people who need to be needed. But it is important to give people time and space to discover what gifts God has really given them and for what purpose.

The Church of the Saviour is organized around the gifts and vision of its people. Examples of the ministries that develop were mentioned in the introduction. If there is no gifted and called person to lead a certain activity, it is not carried out. For example, people in that community feel it is better not to offer a class than to have one taught by someone who is teaching only out of a sense of "oughtness" or duty. They believe in Paul's assurance to the Corinthians: that each member of the body is in the place God wants it to be (1 Cor. 12:18). This implies that the essential life of the body of Christ will flourish if each member discovers and offers his or her gifts with joy. A look at the creativity and impact of this community bears this out.

How can we be about the work of discovering and using our gifts as well as calling forth the gifts of others? Gordon Cosby provides a response:

> I think all of us had best find out what we really want to do and start doing it with whatever it involves. If you have to give up your responsibility, give it up; if the Church goes to pieces, so be it. But we've got to find what we want to do, *really,* because nothing else is going to help anybody.[5]

In one of his sermons he says:

> The person who is having the time of his life doing what he is doing has a way of calling forth the deeps of another person. Such a person is then himself "good news." You are not saying "good news"; you *are* "good news." You are the embodiment of the freedom of the new humanity. Then the verbal proclamation of the good news becomes

believable.[6]

We can help one another discover what we really want to be and do. Specific ways to do this are included in the following exercises and sessions.

Group Design

Purpose: To reflect on scriptural passages related to gifts and to identify and own some of our individual gifts.
Materials: 8½ x 11 unlined scrap paper.

A. Gathering Time   (20 minutes)   Large Group
Describe either a gift given or received that had importance for you. For example, one person in our groups said: "What comes immediately to my mind was the truckload of manure the kids and I gave my gardener husband one year for his birthday. We borrowed the truck, filled it, and the kids decorated it with clanging cans and streamers and drove down the driveway yelling 'Happy Birthday' at the top of their lungs."

B. Looking at My Gifts   (20 minutes)   Individuals and Pairs
1. Each person take a sheet of paper and draw a picture of yourself complete with head, body, heart, hands, feet, etc. Then add, in a word, what you love doing with each part of yourself. For example, by your feet you might put "hiking and skiing," by your hands, "carpentry work." Then above the figure draw circles representing the places in which you offer yourself— e.g., family, friends, church, self, work, local municipality. Then consider this question: If you had enough time and could do anything, give anything, or be anything in one of these places, what would you like to give, be, or do, and in which place? When you have answered, draw a circle around that item and connect it with a line to the place.
    2. When all have finished, each one choose a person you know least well in the group and share some of what you drew.

C. Sharing Groups   (20 minutes)
Each pair from the previous exercise choose another pair and continue to share drawings. The foursomes you form will then become your sharing groups for subsequent sessions. Before concluding this time, jot down the

names and phone numbers of those in your foursome.

D. Building a Group Theology of Gifts   (50 minutes)   Small Groups
and Large Group
1. Divide the group into six small groups. Give each group one of these
scripture passages for study: 2 Tim. 1:6-7; Rom. 12:4-8; 1 Cor. 12:1-11; 1 Cor.
12:27-30; Eph. 4:11-16; Mt. 25:14-30. Each group move to separate corners
of the room or to separate rooms for study.

2. Each small group read your scripture passage aloud. Spend a few
minutes in silent reflection on what in that scripture seems important to you.
When all are ready, share your insights. Allow about 15 minutes for this.

3. Reconvene in the large group. Informally sum up the passage you
studied and the most important insights that occurred in each group. At the
end of the sharing, one or two people might summarize the total group's
theology of gifts. Use about 25 minutes for this part.

E. Closing   (10 minutes)   Large Group
Choose one or two of the following suggestions as appropriate for your
group:
1. Evaluate this session. (In a few words, what was helpful? What was not
helpful?) Quickly share any ideas for improvement for next session.

2. Sing.

3. Pray (thanks for one gift mentioned for each individual in the group—
e.g., "Thanks for Dick's humor").

4. Discuss details of next session if necessary (time, place, leadership
responsibility).

Individual Work

Purpose: To reflect further on scriptural understandings of gifts and to
continue work on identifying our own gifts.

1. Read and meditate daily on 1 Cor. 12:1-11, an overview of spiritual gifts
with emphasis on their unitive spirit. Other references used during the
session are Mt. 25:14-30; Eph. 4:11-16; Rom. 12:4-8; 2 Tim. 1:6-7; 1 Cor.
12:27-30. Ponder and pray, using any or all of these passages. Note what
comes alive or what seems particularly relevant to your situation.

2. Identifying your gifts: For this we use an exercise devised by Bernard Haldane, an employment consultant. The purpose is to focus on those things you really love to do; this is one way of discerning your gifts.

a. Make a list of "doings" in this way. Divide your life into four quarters (if you are 40, you will have four periods of 10 years each). For each quarter, list five "doings," using this definition of the term:
• something you enjoyed doing;
• something you felt you did well;
• something that made you feel satisfied or proud.

You can list any sort of thing: learning to whistle, building a tree house, creating an event, taking a trip, learning a new skill. Make sure they are things that had meaning for you personally. It is not important that others recognized their value.

Try to have five "doings" listed for each quarter of your life. Don't skip the early years.

Many people groan when they contemplate doing this. We have been taught to be modest and to hide what gives us delight. Some people think they don't have many good things in their lives. Be patient and work on your list in odd moments throughout the week while driving or working around the house. Things will occur to you.

Note: Don't try to do the whole list at one sitting or leave it to the last minute. It takes time.

b. Go over your list and pick out your ten most important "doings." Rank them in order of importance.

c. *Please bring your list to the next session.*

3. At the end of the week, summarize in writing what you did with this session in preparation for the next session.

Notes

1. Matthew Fox, O.P., *On Becoming A Musical, Mystical Bear: Spirituality American Style* (New York/Paramus, N.J.: Paulist Press/Deus Book: 1972), p. xv.
2. Ibid.
3. Ibid.
4. Karl Olsson, "The Giver and the Gifts," *Faith at Work,* March 1976, pp. 24, 25.
5. Gordon Cosby, *Handbook for Mission Groups* (Waco, Tex.: Word Books, 1975),

p. 74.

6. Gordon Cosby, "Christians and the Love of God," unpublished sermons, Church of the Saviour, 2025 Massachusetts Ave., N.W., Washington, D.C. 20036, pp. 14, 15.

Session 2

How Can I Be a Patron of Another's Gifts?

"One more powerful than I is to come after me."
(Mk. 1:7, NAB)

Occasionally a baby is born with no assistance other than from its mother. Usually, however, some kind of help—from a doctor, nurse, midwife, husband, or friend—is not only helpful but necessary.

So it is with our gifts. If they are to be born, develop, mature, and be used, the help of other people is often important and even essential. In writing about these helpers, Elizabeth O'Connor has resurrected the term patron.[1] We are familiar with the patroning work of churches and individuals who *discovered, called forth, affirmed,* and *found outlets* for the gifts of Renaissance artists and Baroque musicians. Indeed, the very survival of some of these artists and musicians depended on the generosity and ingenuity of their patrons. Without their patrons' *sponsorship* and *encouragement,* many of these creative people would have had to quit artistic pursuits for more practical and lucrative work.

If we want to see our own and others' gifts operate and flourish, it is important to give time and attention to the role of patron. Once we are aware of the importance of patroning one another's gifts, we can do it in many ways. The preceding paragraph mentioned some of the things patrons do. We will look at a few more.

A patron is concerned with *understanding and encouraging the uniqueness* of the other person's gifts. For example, in discussing the gift of listening, one of our groups realized there are different types of listening gifts. Some people listen best in situations where a person needs to be supported or encouraged to hang on in a difficult situation. The group described this as a hand-holding kind of listening. Others feel their listening gifts are best used in enabling persons to move and change. The group kiddingly labeled this a "shove-off-the-dock" kind of listening. Clearly, good listening involves both companioning and motivating, but some people are better at one than the other. Perhaps in finding outlets for their gifts, persons who are good at companioning might consider working with the elderly, whereas the persons who are motivators might better counsel people in transition.

One way a patron can help another understand the specific nature of a gift is by *giving it a name that is fitting and evocative.* This happens in our groups when people go over with another a list of things they do well, enjoy doing, and are proud of. The task of the patron is to listen carefully to the person's description of what was delightful, exciting, or motivating and to discover and name the unique gifts of that person, seeing perhaps how they combine.

This happened to one of our participants who is gifted in art and was dividing her time between painting, volunteer work with the elderly, and clerking in a store to earn some money. As she went over her list of enjoyments and achievements, her patron named a way to combine her gifts: art therapy for the elderly. Through this patroning process, our participant gained the encouragement and support she needed to change her life-style and begin training in art therapy.

The work of discovering and using gifts has a delight about it. But it also can create problems. When one person uses gifts well, others may feel threatened, envious, or competitive. Our youth minister in high school had a vivid way of reassuring us as we tried to face these difficulties. "If you don't step on someone's toes once in a while, chances are you're not moving!" No one wants to cause criticism, misunderstanding, or conflict, but these are inevitable aspects of growth in individuals and groups. A patron can *help another live with, learn from, and move through these kinds of negative reactions.*

Often this involves *building a bridge* between the gifted person and those with whom he or she is using these gifts. Barnabas did this kind of bridge building for the newly converted Saul when Saul reached Jerusalem and found the disciples afraid of him. Barnabas took him by the hand and introduced him to the apostles, explaining to them how Paul had encountered the risen Christ on his journey, and had been transformed.

He further explained how Saul had spoken in Damascus with the

utmost boldness in the name of Jesus. After that Saul joined with
them in all their activities in Jerusalem, preaching fearlessly. . . .
                                        (Acts 9:27-28, Phillips)

Barnabas made the disciples aware of gifts in Paul they did not know
about. We can do the same thing for new people who join our group or
community.

Another important function of a patron is expressed by a sculptor
friend. He says that having friends who are *consumers* of his creations—
that is, who use his pieces or find uses for them—is vital to the exercise
of his gift.

Related to this function is the role of *selling*. A patron sometimes is a
salesperson for another, or a *broker*. A person who is beginning to use his
or her gifts in a new way can find it difficult to share them and can use a
promoter. We could do this for each other much more. "John is retiring
as a judge. Why not put him in touch with Legal Aid? I believe he'd love
sharing his expertise with disadvantaged people." "George's construction skills are just what we need for our housing project to aid persons
with low income. Let's ask if he'd like to be involved."

Sometimes gifted people need others to act as their *advocates*. This is
particularly necessary when there is no ready and obvious way to use the
person's creativity in the existing situation. An advocate's job is to help
the system enlarge to incorporate newness and creativity. For example,
in a small community we know, an artist wanted to foster spirituality
through the use of art. One of the members invited her to design a retreat
that would use art as the principal form of meditation. Acting as an
advocate, the member helped the community enlarge its understanding
of retreat, and this enabled the artist to offer her gift.

Occasionally a patron who knows how to offer appropriate help drops
into our lives. But more often we must identify the kind of help we need
and ask for it. No one will know, for instance, that my friend needs
someone to critique his latest piece of writing unless he makes that
known. Frequently, however, we are hesitant to ask for the kind of help
we need. Good patrons know this and seek opportunities to offer encouragement or help without being asked.

In some church communities, and in other groups, the kind of
patroning we have described goes on all the time, and a lively creativity

results. But sometimes the opposite is true. People do not see the necessity for patroning or fail to take the initiative or to give encouragement when a gift or dream is shared. This can cause squelching, discouragement, and resentment that can take years to overcome.

Patroning is not a job description but a life-style and an attitude we can have with everyone. Once we see its importance, we can patron others throughout our lives. There are many simple and effective ways to do this.

In conversation. "You have a marvelous manner on the telephone." A straightforward description of what you perceive to be another's gift is one way to begin. Always be ready for the person's feedback. You can then add a further word of encouragement. The person might reply, "I didn't know that." Then you can elaborate on your perception.

In writing. A short note describing a gift you see in another can be a permanent source of encouragement for that person. This is an excellent way to celebrate birthdays. The eight grandchildren of one grandmother each wrote 9 reasons why they loved Grandma and came up with a total of 72 reasons or 72 descriptions of the gifts they saw in her. They bound them in a little booklet for her 72nd birthday.

Through testing. Various aptitude and personality tests can help you identify gifts. One of the most widely used these days is the Myers-Briggs Type Indicator which helps you identify your personality type according to Jungian psychology.

Through journaling. This has become popular as a tool for self-discovery and awareness of others. You can journal alone or with a small group on the gifts you see in one another and how they contribute to the group. Then compare notes and discuss.

Patroning is something we all need and something we all can do with anyone at any time.

Group Design

Purpose: To practice patroning and being patroned.
Materials: Marking pens; extra name tags or small squares of paper, and straight pins, for use in section C.

A. Gathering Time   (15 minutes)   Large Group
Think of someone who has been a light and encouragement to you (e.g., a teacher, parent, friend, colleague) and a specific way that person gave encouragement. Then, in turn, name the person and describe briefly (about a minute) how that person acted as your patron and encourager. (If you have more than eight people in your group, consider dividing into two groups so as not to exceed the allotted time.)

B. Sharing Groups   (20 minutes)   Groups of Four
Give each person a turn to share learnings from scripture that were alive this week. Then, if there is time, speak about how it went for you as you compiled your list of doings. Don't share specific doings at this point. We will get to that later.

C. The Label Game—Patroning One Another   (60 minutes)   Groups of Four
1. Divide in new groups of four, preferably with people you do not know well. Distribute pens and tags to each group.
    2. Each person write in your notebook three things that fit this description:
• something I love doing
• something I feel I do well
• something that makes me feel proud
These can be either in your work, in an organization to which you belong, in leisure or family activities, or from any other area of your life. Example: "For fun, I love skiing, tennis, and mountain climbing. In the family, I enjoy talking about the development and growth of each family member. At work, I feel proud when I can solve problems and do good staff work."
    3. Then give one person a chance to describe what he or she has written and why. The others help the sharer elaborate on why these three things mean so much. As the person is sharing, the three listeners write on small labels (name tags or paper squares) the gifts they see in the sharer from hearing about the things he or she loves. When the person finishes sharing, each listener reads the gifts that he or she identified and asks the sharer to confirm or modify what was written. For example, "When you say you love doing good staff work and tell us more about that, it makes me think you enjoy carrying out orders." "Well, yes, I do,

but I like to be in charge too." The labeler then might write two labels: "implementer of orders" and "taking charge."

When each listener has read his or her labels and heard feedback from the sharer, stick the labels on the sharer (each labeler may use several labels per person). Go around the group, using the same process for each of the four.

D. Learning About One Another's Gifts   (20 minutes)   Large Group

Regather in the large group. Each person introduce to the whole group a person in his or her small group and share some of the gifts that were discovered. Go around the circle so that all are introduced.

E. Closing   (5 minutes)   Large Group

Choose a way of closing that is appropriate for your group: evaluation of the session, discussion of details for next session, song, prayer. Prayer suggestion: Those who would like to can express gratitude to God for the ways they have been patroned in this course and throughout their lives.

Individual Work

Purpose: To reflect on scriptural passages related to patroning and to experience patroning and being patroned.

1. Meditate on what scripture says about patroning.

  a. Paul's description of the patron (Gal. 4:19).

  b. Experiences of patrons in the Bible: Barnabas (Acts 9:26-28), John the Baptist (Lk. 3:1-20), Jesus (Jn. 14:12-29 and Lk. 22:31-34).

  2. Journal on these questions: What kind of patroning do I need at this time? From whom? What kind of patroning can I give? To whom?

  3. Work on patroning (*Note:* This assignment requires extra time because it involves getting together with another person. Those who take the time to do this find it extremely valuable.):

  a. Choose one other person in the group who has completed the list of "doings" (explained in #4 of last session's individual work). Allow at least two hours to work together.

b. Depending on your time, use all twenty "doings" or your ten most important ones. The following is an example of how to proceed. George goes over his list of "doings," explaining each one and why it was important. Mary listens and helps George elaborate, and as this happens, writes down items under this heading, "George is happy when he is

• innovating;
• up front and on stage;
• walking in the woods alone," etc.

After George is finished describing each item on his list, Mary reads the list she has made and asks George to confirm, clarify, or modify it. For example, George might say, "Yes, I'm happy walking in the woods alone. Actually, I love being alone in all sorts of situations—outdoors, inside with a good book, etc." After Mary's list, "George is happy when . . .," is refined by both, then Mary, with George's help, tries to name and identify some of the gifts indicated by the list. For example, "You have a gift for solitude," or "You seem to love to be a pioneer," or "You are an occasion maker," or "You have a gift for relaxing and helping others relax." When you have completed that process, reverse it and let George become the patron-listener as Mary describes her "doing" list. Be sure to budget half your time for each person. It is disappointing if a disproportionate amount of time is used on one person.

c. After you part, reflect more on your overall impression of your partner's gifts. Summarize your impressions in a note to be mailed to your partner or given at the next session. Notice any consistent abilities that flow through your partner's life—e.g., "Bill, your love of adventure comes through in a lot of situations." These notes are an important part of the process and are usually cherished by the recipients.

4. At the end of the week, summarize in writing your work with this assignment.

Notes

1. Elizabeth O'Connor, *Eighth Day of Creation* (Waco, Tex.: Word Books, 1971), p. 34.

Session 3

Which Piece of God's Vision Is Mine?

Where and how can we use our gifts most effectively to help the Reign of God happen? Needs are all around us. Which are ours to address? Do the contributions of one person matter in this complex world? One way to approach these questions is to reflect on God's vision coupled with our own experience and see how they tie together.

Walter Brueggemann has made God's vision the subject of his book *Living Toward a Vision.* In his opening passage, Brueggemann describes God's vision in these words:

> The central vision of world history in the Bible is that all of creation is one, every creature in community with every other, living in harmony and security toward the joy and well-being of every other creature. *In the community of faith in Israel,* this vision is expressed in the affirmation that Abraham is father of all Israel and every person is his child (see Gen. 15:5; Is. 41:8; 51:2). Israel has a vision of all persons being drawn under the lordship and fellowship of Jesus (Mt. 28:16-20; Jn. 12:32) and therefore into a single community (Acts 2:1-11). As if those visions were not sweeping enough, the most staggering expression of the vision is that *all persons are children of a single family,* members of a single tribe, heirs of a single hope, and bearers of a single destiny, namely, the care and management of all of God's creation.
>
> That persistent vision of joy, well-being, harmony, and prosperity is not captured in any single word or idea in the Bible, and a cluster of words is required to express its many dimensions and subtle nuances: love, loyalty, truth, grace, salvation, justice, blessing, righteousness. But the term that in recent discussions has been used to summarize that controlling vision is *shalom.* Both in current discussion and in the Bible itself, it bears tremendous

freight—the freight of a dream of God that resists all our tendencies
to division, hostility, fear, drivenness, and misery.[1]

In the scriptures, God is portrayed as entrusting this vision to all
people. Peter made this clear in explaining the meaning of the Pentecost
event. In his sermon, he used these words from the prophet Joel:

And in the last days it shall be, God declares,
that I will pour out my Spirit upon all flesh,
and your sons and your daughters shall prophesy,
and the young shall see visions,
and the old shall dream dreams;
yea, and on my manservants and my maidservants in those days
I will pour out my Spirit; and they shall prophesy.

(Acts 2:17,18)[2]

Peter used this passage to show that God wants to pour the Spirit on
everyone: young and old, male and female, rich and poor. When that
happens, people see visions, dream dreams, and are able to embody and
articulate God's vision of *shalom*. Scripture describes individuals who
implemented particular aspects of this all-encompassing vision of love
and justice. For example, Peter and Paul emphasized the importance of
individuals' knowing God and therefore carried on intensive evangelistic
work. Luke focused on the healing and wholeness available through
God's love and wrote from that vantage point. John fostered the idea that
the risen Christ can live with us in the same sort of intimacy that Jesus
has with God.

It seems that we are given the ability to understand the completeness
that God's *shalom* implies, but are called to implement a specific aspect
of that vision in light of our own gifts and experience.

If indeed God has entrusted a part of the *shalom* vision to each of us, it
is important to try to discover what it is. By definition, if it is part of
God's vision it will be large, all-encompassing, and perhaps impossible
to conceive in human terms. It will express biblical themes that contain
the vision: love, justice, wholeness, reconciliation. But because we are
human beings and therefore limited, our particular piece of the vision
will often be specific and suited to our unique experience, makeup, and
abilities. It will take shape out of the combination of who we are and

what we have experienced.

In addition to seeing how our piece of the vision relates to God's vision, it is also clarifying to see how we differentiate vision from call (which has already been mentioned in the first and second courses and will be dealt with at length in the next session). Unlike vision, which is usually large and perhaps seemingly impossible, call is specific, imaginable, feasible. Vision is seeing or believing something; call is doing something. Vision is often fairly consistent over long periods, even perhaps for a lifetime, whereas call changes with circumstances. Vision is seeing the big picture; call is the way we can implement the vision in a particular time and place. Examples will clarify the difference.

Fran Campbell has a vision that retarded children will have a religious education uniquely suited to them. Years ago Fran's retarded child was prepared for the reception of the Eucharist by a friend in her parish. Through this process, Fran saw her child come to know and respond to God in faith even though he was intellectually limited. Inspired by this, Fran felt called to explore possibilities for bringing the Good News to other developmentally disabled people. She began in her parish. As her children grew and she had more time, she extended her involvement first to other churches in the diocese and eventually to a national organization dedicated to special religious education. What fuels her long commitment to this vision and vocation is the memory of developmentally disabled children and adults living on the periphery of parish life, often not taught about God's love for them, and her subsequent gratitude and joy as she now sees this need and challenge being met.

Mike Mapes' vision has to do with world peace. He describes his concern in personal terms. "I'm working for my grandchildren, even though I don't have any yet, trying to make it possible for them to get to know *their* grandchildren." When the chance came to make a vocational change and work full time for an organization that implements his vision, he jumped at it. He is the Executive Director of the National Peace Academy Campaign, whose purpose is to found the United States Academy for Peace and Conflict Resolution. The establishment of the Academy will commit the United States government to a long-term program of research, education and training, and public information in the ways and means of peace. It will develop the emerging social science of conflict resolution and the field of peacemaking as well as train people in techniques of nonviolent domestic and international conflict management.

Sometimes our commitment to an aspect of God's vision comes to us through becoming personally gripped by a world issue, as happened with Mike Mapes. Other times, our initial stimulation occurs much closer to home and in circumstances that initially seem to carry more darkness than illumination, as it did for Fran Campbell.

How do we discover which part of God's vision is ours? Insight comes when we reflect on what evokes our most passionate criticism, our deepest grief, or energizes us to new possibilities. Certain situations or events make us more angry than others; certain pictures or articles in the paper touch deep chords; certain visions draw our allegiance. When we pay attention to them, we begin to get glimmers of the aspects of God's vision that may be ours to carry out. These clues can sometimes enable us to voice a central concern that has gripped us over a long period or a dream that will not let us go.

Understanding God's vision and discovering an aspect that is ours to implement in this complex world is not an easy task. First, we are subjected daily to philosophies that are antithetical to the vision of *shalom*. "Take care of yourself." "Me first." "Don't trust 'em." "We need to retaliate." These are commonly heard sentiments about personal and national life. Secondly, even those who are committed to a religious view of life do not often agree on the specifics of *shalom* or how to realize it. This is evident in matters related to peacemaking. For example, there are people of faith who sincerely believe in peace through strong defense and who devote themselves to building more sophisticated weapons. Then there are people like Elise Boulding who dedicate time and energy to "imaging a world without weapons" and helping others to do that.

A vision is not easily sustained; it must be nurtured. A good example of how this can happen occurred when one family was involved in a church group that was renovating some substandard housing. Each Saturday when the crew assembled, the pastor would gather the workers for a brief discussion of why they were there. The vision was that every resident of the District of Columbia would have adequate housing. Their piece of that vision was to rehabilitate one section of the city. Reflecting on that vision with others made the grime and cockroaches more bearable, and it bound them together as a group.

Often people have a sense of vision when they are starting a new venture, but it can dissipate if left untended. At a seminary workshop the faculty and students were asked to remember the vision that first brought them to the seminary. They reflected on how their vision was fostered by each of the courses they were taking or teaching. After sharing these perceptions with one another, they felt refreshed and renewed. Said one, "I came to this lunch-time gathering frantic with pressure, but I'm leaving deeply touched by what I found within myself and heard from others about why we're here together at seminary."

Our vision can be nurtured not only by sharing it with one another but by finding new ways to articulate it. Certain business people realize this well. When some railroad companies began to visualize their purpose as fostering better transportation, not simply better railroads, their re-formed vision gave new energy and focus to their activity. Learning about people of vision nourishes our ability to see more compassionately. That is why a study of historical and modern-day saints is motivating. And really seeing a person act because of a vision can also inspire our own. Those who stood with Martin Luther King, Jr., at the Lincoln Memorial when he gave his "I have a dream" speech will always remember that day.

Failure to nurture our vision can cause burnout. This phenomenon is receiving increased attention in all spheres of life. *Time* magazine described the work of Pehr Gyllenhammar, the President of Volvo, Scandinavia's biggest industrial combine. Beginning in his own company and then going around the world, he is trying to address what he feels is a growing problem for industrial nations, "the mismatch between people and jobs." People need to know why they are doing a particular job and the value it has in the larger scheme of things. Says Gyllenhammar, "The problem today is not just to pay people, but also to help them feel they can identify with something in society." *Time* ends the article by noting that what may sound like idealism has had concrete results at Volvo: Productivity there between 1976 and 1978 jumped 20%, whereas in the same period in American private business it rose 2.4%.[3]

Being aware and responsible for part of God's vision need not involve long-term commitments to a certain institution or work. An example of this is Jessie Daniels, a woman in her sixties. Making God's love and care available to others in each situation of life would be one way of summing up her vision. She sees herself as wanting to be available to persons as concrete needs arise: a ride to the hospital, sharing a meaningful book or article, a comforting phone conversation, a meal out or at her home. Jessie is ready and delighted to be this kind of companion and helper to all kinds of people who cross her path.

Furthermore, what we are talking about need not involve doing something different, but rather seeing differently what we do. The well-known story of the two stone masons is pertinent. When one is asked what he is doing, he replies, "Laying stone." The other says, "I'm building a cathedral."

Our marriage, job, relationships—all aspects of life take on a different hue when we see them as part of God's vision. It is easy to fall into a sort of "tumbleweed philosophy": We come into the world by accident and drift along, bumped by the vicissitudes of life, until we drift out. Biblical vision has a good deal more purpose than that. Indeed, biblical writers insist on the importance of knowing and embodying God's vision personally, economically, politically, and socially. As Proverbs 29:18 puts it starkly, "Where there is no vision, the people perish."

Our awareness of God's vision and our willingness to be responsible for part of it can determine our life work and color every aspect of life. Allowing all of life to reflect this vision is a process that takes time. It is unwise to rush the process or to oversimplify it. People in our groups sometimes are disappointed that they do not know "their vision" by the end of the six-week course! We, on the other hand, are happy if people only *begin* to be aware of and explore this tremendous concept within that brief time. People tend to want to reduce "their vision" to a phrase that will do for all time. We feel, though, that part of the task of becoming people of vision is naming that vision and pondering it in a variety of ways, so that the exploration of vision is a constantly enriching search rather than a static find.

Some of us may never feel that a particular piece of God's vision has our name on it. But what we can all do is bring God's vision to every endeavor in which we are engaged. Our sense of God's vision can be heightened through reading, prayer, scripture study, being aware of current events and circumstances, and examining our own experience.

One thing we have found in our groups is that most people do not lack vision at all. And they enjoy the challenge to ponder and share their vision.

Group Design

Purpose: To become conscious of and share our sense of vision.
Materials: Candle, wooden matches, low table.

A. Gathering Time   (10 minutes)   Large Group
Put on a perky jazz or ragtime record. One person acts as Simple Simon and does motions to the rhythm of the record, one consistent motion for about thirty seconds, then changing to another motion. The group imitates. The purpose of this is simply to loosen up and have some fun together. With a stretch of the imagination it can be seen as related to vision in that it depends on picking up visual cues from Simple Simon, and Simple Simon has to have a vision of the group as fun loving as well as serious minded.

B. Sharing Groups   (20 minutes)   Groups of Four
Share your experiences with patroning. Exchange patroning notes and, if you like, read them to one another.

C. Vision Exercise: "I Have a Dream. . . ."   (60 minutes)   Individuals and Groups of Four
1. *Journaling:*   (15 minutes)   Individuals   Each person get settled and quiet in a comfortable position with journal and pen ready. The leader may give a very short review of the session material on vision and then invite people to jot down any glimmers they have about their own sense of vision. To stimulate this, the leader can read the following material slowly and meditatively, pausing at length where pauses are indicated, and giving people plenty of time to think and write.

"How can we figure out which piece of God's vision is ours? This is what we want to begin to do right now. While I'm talking, jot down in your journal what occurs to you.

"What is it that concerns you very much, has concerned you for a long time, perhaps even from childhood or teen years? (Pause.)

"What excites you to great joy, hope, possibilities . . . but also causes high frustration, even pain, or envy? (Pause.)

"What is it that makes you angry, moves you to tears, keeps you awake at night? (Pause.)

"Look at your choice of reading—books, magazines, newspaper articles. What subjects move you the most? Which do you turn to most frequently? (Pause.)

"If you were to look at the area that concerns you most and have a dream about how that could be better or different or new, what would your dream be?"

2. *Sharing:*   (45 minutes)   Groups of Four   Now we will have a chance to share our vision and dream in a special way, so move into groups of four (we suggest people you have not been with before). For this time of sharing, we suggest that you find a place in the building where you can lie down on the floor, each on his or her back, with heads touching in the middle like spokes of a wheel. (An alternative is to sit in chairs, back to back in fours, but the former position is preferable.) Depending on the space, if you are crowded, you might like to have groups in different rooms. Here are the instructions for sharing:

a. Settle yourselves, relax, enjoy this position, ask God for guidance, and be silent for a few minutes.

b. As you feel moved, share your vision briefly. You may have something quite definite, you may have only a glimmer or a hint. Share what you can.

c. Each of the others receive that sharing, listen, reflect, and then each in turn walk into the other's dream as if it were a reality. Participate in it. Don't discuss it, give advice, or say it's impossible. If you as a listener need clarification about the nature of the vision, ask for that, but then simply in a few words affirm the dream in any way that's genuine. You may find this challenging. It isn't easy to get out of yourself and into another's dreams. Here is an example of how this might work out:

First Person: "I have a vision about the elderly in our suburbs. When I go to the city, I see lots of older people walking, shopping, talking together, and being more a part of things. But in the suburbs that is not evident. The elderly seem isolated. My own mother is that way. She's alone in an apartment, and I'm the only one who visits. I have a dream that our church could figure out a way to make a different life possible for our suburban elderly people, perhaps by making more of an effort to include them and use their gifts too. I'm busy myself, and involved, and I don't know what could be done about this vision, but I'm sure God doesn't want these people simply on the shelf, and I'm willing to do something about it. I'm just not sure what."

Second Person: "I know what you mean. I've noticed the same thing too. I'm not sure how I could help, but if you ever do anything about this, I want to know about it, and perhaps I could support you. Or if not, I could be an encourager because I know something could be different."

Third Person: "Yes, my elderly parent lives with us and is becoming dependent on us for just about everything, but he has a lot to offer others as well. I think he would love to be a part of anything that got started in the church. He just won't go to the county programs, though."

Fourth Person: "I feel I have my hands full being a board member. I know I can't take on anything else, but if you do want to do something, I'll do all I can to obtain the backing of the board."

d. When you have had the first round, go to the second person, and so on, until each is finished. Allow about ten minutes for each round, and try to budget the time for each person. It's tempting to concentrate on the first one and not have any time left for the last. When you're finished, be in silence and wait for the other groups, or take a break if that doesn't disturb others.

3. *Journaling:*   (5 minutes)   Individuals   Briefly record any new insights concerning your vision as a result of this sharing.

4. *Group Sharing:*   (15 minutes)   Large Group   Whole group reconvene around a lighted candle, either on the floor or on a low table. Beside it are some wooden matches. One by one, each person take a match, light it from the candle, and, while the match burns, briefly describe the vision that he or she shared in the group of four.

D. Closing   (10 minutes)   Large Group
Choose one or two of the following suggestions as appropriate for your group: evaluation of session, discussion of details for next session, prayer, and/or song ("This Little Light of Mine").

Individual Work

Purpose: To reflect on scriptural passages related to vision and to do further personal work on vision, patroning, and gifts.

1. Meditate on what scripture says about vision:
* its importance (Prov. 29:18);
* who receives it and how (Acts 2:14-24);
* having a piece of a vision (Acts 10);

- its substance (Is. 58);
- its breadth (Ps. 117).

2. Further work:

a. *On vision.* Reflect further on the vision you shared in the group. Continue the journaling you started in the session. Add further insights. Try to record how the others "walked" into your dream. What of significance did they add to it? Did anyone's response deflect you from your vision? What can be learned from that?

b. *On patroning.* Give the note you wrote on your partner's gifts to that person if you have not already done so.

c. *On your own gifts.* Ponder the note you received and any other insights as you review all your work on gifts: the sketch you did in the first group design; your own list of "doings" and what came out of that for you; your patron's responses and discoveries; the labels from the group session of patroning. Summarize all your findings and journal on the following:

My strongest gifts are. . . .

The ones I enjoy most are. . . .

3. Now that you have experienced several ways to identify gifts, you may have experienced delight as well as difficulty. For a greater understanding of what blocks the evoking of gifts in self and others, read the following paper "Why We Bury Our Talents."

4. For further clarification of how a Christian community can help or hinder the process we are describing, read "The Gift-Evoking Process in the Community."

5. Summarize in writing what you did with this assignment.

Why We Bury Our Talents

It is no secret that gifts are often not evoked by ourselves or others. There are many reasons for this, and it is wise to know about them and to learn ways to meet them. If you are feeling stymied in this regard, here is a checklist to consider:

1. Do you have another person or a small group of persons who will listen to you and give you the warmth, acceptance, and encouragement necessary for evoking gifts?

2. Have you taken the time and solitude necessary to look at and listen to

yourself?

3. Are you afraid of rejection if you use your gifts or even try them out? Are you allowing only those gifts you think will be accepted to be named and refusing to name the core gifts?

4. Does your envy of others focus you on their accomplishments rather than allowing you to develop your gifts?

5. Are you afraid of provoking envy and thus exposing yourself or your gifts to the negative feelings of others?

6. Gifts imply specific commitment to use them and accountability for them. Are you avoiding commitment? Why? Do you have a naive view of creativity as "fun and games," and do you back off from the pain and work of creativity?

7. Are you aware that the new, the innovative, may be threatening to others and put you in tension with them? Are you willing to move through that tension?

8. Are you unwilling to exercise a gift until you are mature in it, an expert? If so, is it because you are taking your gifts too seriously? Are you afraid of experimenting, failing, playing, looking silly?

9. Are you more concerned with higher wages, another rung on the ladder, and recognition than with a sense of self-worth, growth?

The Gift-Evoking Process in the Community

The Bible assures us that if we wish to accept gifts, the Spirit gives them to each of us. They are within us, but several things have to happen before we can use them well. Here are things that both the individual and the community do.

Our gifts must be *called forth*. We have practiced and described several ways to do this. As individuals, we place ourselves in situations where this can happen. As a community, we work on a continuing basis with each person in the "calling forth" process, constantly doing this for one another.

Our gifts must be *identified*. The more specific we can be in this, the better. I might have the gift of writing; but what kind of writing? I know it is not fiction or freelance writing. I realize that I get the most fun out of writing on demand for groups who will work with my writing. Another person has a good way with people. More specifically, he finds he has a gift for working with them on the telephone.

Sooner or later our gifts, if they really are of the Spirit for the building up of the community, need to be *confirmed* by the community. When the community asks me to write something for it, my gift is reconfirmed and I am newly gifted with creativity. Likewise, the community's lack of confirmation may be a signal to me to go back to prayer, to listening, to discovery. Sometimes the community is not ready for my gift and can confirm it only later. Sometimes the gift is not yet ready for the community: It needs more development, more polishing.

The gift needs to be *owned and accepted* by the gifted person. There are powerful personal and social forces working against our owning of gifts. Personally we have been taught not to be proud, not to brag. Socially, people have been in subordinate positions—for example, black people, persons who are handicapped, women. These people have been conditioned to hold back.

The gift has to be *offered* by the owner. It is difficult to react to a gift in the abstract. My community may ask me to write, but they cannot deal with the gift until they have an actual piece of writing to which to respond. Who knows? There might be someone whose gift will be called forth by mine. I offer my first piece of rough work to the community and find that someone else has the gift of editing!

The gift eventually must be *received* by others. One woman who owns a store made room on her premises for exhibiting a collection of paintings done by a talented friend. She announced the opening, planned a reception, and in this way fostered the gifts of the painter and created a way for others to do so as well. Receiving another's gift requires openness and thought, even ingenuity. It is an essential part of gift evoking.

Notes

1. Walter Brueggemann, *Living Toward a Vision* (Philadelphia: United Church Press, 1976), pp. 15, 16.
2. Inclusive Language Lectionary Committee, *An Inclusive Language Lectionary* (Philadelphia: The Westminster Press, 1983), Pentecost 1.
3. Marshall Loeb, "Ideas from a Matchmaker," *Time*, December 17, 1979.

Session 4

What Is God Calling Me to Do?

"Moses! Moses!" He answered, "Here I am." "Come no nearer
. . . I will send you to Pharaoh to lead my people, the Israelites,
out of Egypt."

(Ex. 3:5,10, NAB)

We have seen that each of us is uniquely gifted by God, immeasurably
helped by those who act as patrons, and often particularly attuned to a
piece of God's vision of *shalom*. Scripture indicates further that God
calls us to specific ways of implementing our piece of the vision. It is to
this idea of "call" or "calling" that we now turn.

Scripture uses these terms in two ways. God calls everyone to be a part
of the overall vision, to live a life of grace, to be "the beloved" of God
and an "ambassador" of Christ. In addition, scripture portrays God as
calling individuals to specific roles, tasks, or ways of implementing
parts of the vision. Some are called to be apostles, others teachers, and
so on. Moses was called to lead his people out of oppression; Jeremiah
was called to voice the word of God in a troublesome political situation.

In our groups we focus on God's specific calling to each one of us.
There are two aspects to this: God calls us to a particular work; and then
we ourselves often issue a call to others to participate in this work. In this
session, we will discuss God's call to us. In the next, we will discuss our
call to others.

The question is often asked, Does God call everyone? Isn't the call of
God, or a sense of that calling, reserved for the few? What about the
verse in Matthew (22:14, RSV), "Many are called, but few are chosen"?
Doesn't that mean just a select few are called in a vivid way?

When we examine that verse in context, we see that it was attached at
the end of the parable of the wedding feast. Being in the realm of God is
compared to the joyful, festive, fulfilling experience of a banquet to

which all are invited—those known by the host and then (when they
refuse because of other interests or commitments) unknown passersby.
The Jerome Biblical Commentary clarifies the meaning of that confusing verse:

> . . . the invitation to all who pass on the highways and byways, even
> "the good and the bad" (as contrasted with Luke's beggars,
> destitutes, blind, and lame) is clear. All these are called; the chosen
> are those who accept the call and do not reject the invitation, like
> the first guests, or who do not accept it fully, like the man who
> comes to dinner but is too much of a boor to dress in the proper
> manner.[1]

It is a shame that this verse is sometimes seen as saying that God
disqualifies those who want to respond, when the very opposite is true.
Matthew used it to underline God's open-door policy but also to point to
our responsibility to respond to God's gracious invitation, rather than
ignore it or put it aside till later.

Indeed the total biblical revelation moves from the chosenness of a
particular Hebrew tribe to the call to all nations. Isaiah expressed it in
Chapter 55:1 (NAB):

> All you who are thirsty,
>   come to the water!

These words from Psalm 22:27 (JB) are another example:

> The whole earth, from end to end, will come back to Yahweh.

A similar universality is expressed by Jesus in his commission to the
apostles in Mt. 28:19 (RSV): "Go therefore and make disciples of all
nations. . . ."

While presenting God's call as being offered to all, the Bible does give
colorful and informative details as to why we may not feel as if we are
included in that call. God is not portrayed as being careful about going
after the best qualified for a particular job. The youthful, inexperienced
David was called to fight the terrible giant Goliath; Mary, an obscure
young woman, was called to be the mother of Jesus; Paul, a ruthless
persecutor of the Christians, was called to carry the message of a loving
Christ to the Gentiles; wobbly, impetuous Peter was called to a ministry

of fearless preaching, witness, and healing. The stories of these and other unlikely candidates for call seem to be ample proof of the words Paul attributes to God: "My grace is enough for you; for where there is weakness, my power is shown the more completely" (2 Cor. 12:9, Phillips).

Sometimes the person called is overcome with a sense of unworthiness. Peter's first response to Christ's call was "Leave me, Lord. I am a sinful man" (Lk. 5:8, NAB). Isaiah felt much the same way: "I am lost, for I am a man of unclean lips" (Is. 6:5, JB). At the news of his own calling, Jeremiah protested, "Ah, Lord Yahweh; look, I do not know how to speak: I am a child!" (Jer. 1:6, JB).

Further, the called person doubts the genuineness of the call, particularly when implementing it brings resistance and opposition. Never has this feeling been more poignantly voiced than by Jeremiah.

> For the word of God has become for me
>   a reproach and derision all day long.
> If I say, "I will not mention God,
>   or speak any more in God's name,"
> there is in my heart as it were a burning fire
>   shut up in my bones,
> and I am weary with holding it in,
>   and I cannot.
>
>   (Jer. 20:8-9)[2]

In contrast to these doubts, John Henry Newman expressed the biblical message clearly when he wrote: "God has created me to do Him some definite service. He has committed some work to me which He has not committed to another. I have my mission." If that is true, how can we know what our mission is? How can we hear God's call to us personally?

We cannot hear God's call unless we are in relationship with God. Many ways to cultivate and nourish that relationship have already been described—e.g., prayer, scripture pondering, retreat, spiritual direction, listening. And there are other ways to hear and clarify God's call.

Recording insights received through prayer and working with our dreams in a personal journal are also helpful. In these ways we will get hunches or glimmers of direction that we can test out. Often we seem to be led one step at a time and do not see the next step until we take the one first indicated. Paul's experience illustrates this (see Acts 9). On the road to Damascus he was first given a vision of the reality of the risen Christ; then he was directed to go to the city; there "you will be told what to do" (NAB). Ananias, who was also following the guidance he had received in a dream, indicated the next step for Paul.

Speaking to people currently active in our area of call in order to get the facts can bring real illumination. We can read about our area of call in current publications and can see through the eyes of those who have worked there in the past. For example, someone called to work with the inner-city poor can profit by reading material by and about Dorothy Day, who gave her life to working with the destitute.

Circumstances shape our call. Limitations may not always block our call; they may shape it. For instance, one of our participants who had terminal cancer knew when she took this course that she had only a short time to live. She felt God was calling her to work with doctors to raise their awareness of how individuals deal personally with their coming death. Again, several young mothers who lived in a garden apartment area that had a common playground and sandbox felt their call at that time was to facilitate a caring and sharing among young mothers in matters of faith and parenting. They could do this while watching their children at play.

Our call can be further clarified through talking with friends, counseling with particularly helpful people, and submitting our yearnings and hopes to a community of people. It is surprising how often the calls described in scripture not only involved the hearer but also a helper. Ananias was a healer of Paul and an articulator of his call. Eli counseled the young Samuel to answer God in prayer and openness.

The timing of call differs from person to person. For some there is an instantaneous sense of clarity and rightness about it. This happened to several of us with a call to Christian unity in the sixties. Circumstances were propitious; there was a climate of openness and eagerness for ecumenical sharing. We knew this was the time to develop a way for Catholics and Protestants to come together for study, prayer, and fellowship. All kinds of "happy coincidences" helped this develop quickly, effectively, and with a great deal of spirit.

But this does not always happen. Some calls take a long time to clarify and develop. Several individuals at one church felt the need for extended retreat for that community. It took five years of pondering, praying, meeting people, reading, visiting retreat centers, and making retreats before they felt a definite call to build their own retreat center and offer retreats to the community. The building of the facility and development of the program took many more years. In considering timing we should also remember that some people, like Abraham and Sarah, do not hear a call until late in life. We cannot pin down the process of call into a neat, predictable pattern.

Feelings about call also vary a great deal. Sometimes it fills us with delight; other times it frightens us. It is surprising how often people say, "I want to hear and respond to a call from God, but I'm afraid I'll be asked to do something I really don't want to do." Certainly, suffering is a part of call, but there is much evidence that an authentic call is something we really want to do, something that expresses what is deep within us.

Surely the God revealed by Jesus is like a parent who desires the very best for us, who wants us to develop fully and use our gifts in ways that give joy and help to others as well as to ourselves.

Group Design

Purpose: To reflect on the experience of call in scripture and today.
Materials: Marking pen, newsprint.

A. Gathering Time   (15 minutes)   Large Group
Large group stand in a circle. Turn to the right and massage the shoulders of the person in front of you. After a few minutes, turn in the opposite direction and do the same.

B. Sharing Groups   (30 minutes)   Groups of Four
Choose from these suggestions for sharing:
• your learnings from scripture;
• insights or questions that came from reading "Why We Bury Our Talents" and "The Gift-Evoking Process in the Community";
• any personal discoveries you made about patroning, vision, and call.

C. Experiences of Call in Scripture and Today   (30 minutes)

Small Groups
1. Divide the large group into six small groups (two or more to a group).
   2. Each small group select a scriptural description of call. Choose from the calls of Samuel (1 Sam. 3:1-18), Moses (Ex. 3, 4:1-23), Isaiah (Is. 6), Jeremiah (Jer. 1:4-19), the disciples (Lk. 5:1-11), Paul (Acts 9:1-30), or other scripture persons of your choosing.
   3. Read over the passage together silently and then discuss these questions:
• In what circumstances did call happen?
• To whom?
• What did it feel like?
• What did it involve?
• What kinds of reactions were evoked when the called person tried to implement the call?
   4. Each small group then prepare to present to the larger group:
• the name of your story and a quick summary of it;
• learnings about call from your story that you find relevant for you today.

D. Group Presentations on Call   (30 minutes)   Large Group
1. Each small group share its presentation of the story summary and learnings about call.
   2. Optional: After each presentation, consider writing learnings about call on newsprint.

E. Closing   (15 minutes)   Large Group
Choose one or two of the following as appropriate for your group: evaluation of session, discussion of details for next session, song and/or prayer of thanks for those who have heard God's call and for our own openness to that call.

Individual Work

Purpose: To meditate on Jesus' experience with call and to ponder your own call and possible next steps.

1. Read and meditate daily on Luke 4 to gain insight on how Jesus

clarified and issued his call and how people responded to it.

2. Clarify how you now feel about call by doing some journaling. Begin by using one or more of the following responses, then expanding on how you feel.
• I don't want to think about it.
• It's exciting.
• It's scary.
• I don't believe God has a calling for me.
• I'm not good enough to receive a call.
• I'd like to feel called, but I don't hear any.
• I hear a call but don't know what to do about it.
• I'm confused.
• Other.

3. Consider possible next steps regarding your call. *If you don't feel a call:*
• Is there a block to your hearing it?
• Are you devoting enough time to listening for it?
• Are you rejecting the call that is there in favor of something more to your immediate liking?

If you do have a sense of calling:
• Is there something further you should be doing about it?
• Is this a time to ponder or clarify more?
• Should you take a step alone?
• Is now the time to go public?
• Is there something else you could do?

4. In the light of these reflections, decide on an appropriate next step, write it out, and tell your patron about it.

5. Summarize in writing what you did with this assignment.

Note: Have a try at all these questions or concentrate on those that seem particularly appropriate for you. Remember there are no "right" answers. The important thing is to deal honestly and openly with the material. Don't be too concerned about your feelings. Some people feel encouraged in this course; some discover envy as others have "breakthroughs" and they don't. Remember that God works within you in the timing and manner that best suits you. Often people take these courses but nothing hits them at the time. Later, however, as their life and circumstances change, material from the course reappears and becomes relevant. If you respond to the questions during the course and deal with them personally, no matter how you feel, the chances are good that the insight that is most important to you will recur when you need it.

Notes

1. *The Jerome Biblical Commentary,* Raymond E. Brown, S.S., Joseph A. Fitzmyer, S.J., Roland E. Murphy, O. Carm., eds. (Englewood Cliffs, N.J.: Prentice-Hall, 1968), 2:100.
2. Inclusive Language Lectionary Committee, *An Inclusive Language Lectionary* (Philadelphia: The Westminster Press, 1983), Pentecost 5.

Session 5

Is There a Communal Expression for My Vocation?

"He named twelve as his companions whom he would send to preach the good news."

(Mk. 3:14, NAB)

If we have a particular vision and sense of calling, several factors might make us want to have more people involved. Maybe we need and want the support of companions in the same mission. Or we might wish to do more and have greater impact than an individual could have. We may wish to make a corporate Christian witness publicly.

Those were some of the reasons why Jesus gathered others to join him in his call. He wanted to be with companions to extend his ministry beyond his own place and time, and to make the light of the new order visible, not hidden under a bushel basket, so it could give "light to all in the house" (Mt. 5:15, NAB).

Suppose we want to gather others to develop ways to implement our calling. How can we organize the effort?

Of course, there are many ways to do this. One that we have found effective but not often tried is what can be called the servant community: "servant" because it offers a particular service, and "community" because it develops concrete ways of caring for and nurturing each person in the group. These are very much like the basic communities in Latin America that were mentioned earlier.

In our work we see the servant community as one vehicle through which ministries involving a group of people can be carried out. This form of organizing combines these important ingredients:
- spiritual nourishment that will develop and sustain the people and their ministry;
- personal caring among those involved so that each one can feel known, loved, and supported as she or he engages in the hard work of ministry;

221

• mission or service developed out of the vision of the group and expressed through the gifts of the members.

This type of organizing is a way to address the fragmentation and over-extension that seem to plague so many people. What sometimes happens in churches, for example, is that people may go to a Bible-study group for spiritual nourishment, to a life-sharing group for companionship, and to a task force for service. As a result, many dedicated Christians are away from home every night.

Others, who want to cut down on the number of meetings, choose one thing—either a service opportunity or a meeting for nurture or sharing—but find these meetings unsatisfying and ineffective. We frequently hear frustrated people saying, "Members of the task force don't know one another personally"; "We're too busy with the agenda"; "We have a perfunctory prayer at the beginning and end of each parish board meeting, but we really don't feel nourished spiritually by that"; or "All our group does is pray and study the Bible; we never *do* anything."

Another problem that servant communities can help address is the frustration that occurs when committee systems are unwieldy. For example, a person wants to develop quality adult education in his parish, but has to go through several hoops before he can actually start working. First, he must serve on both the education committee and the adult education subcommittee. All decisions have to go through these two bodies plus the church council. That takes a minimum of three nights a month, and still he has done no adult education. He is exhausted before he can give what he wants to offer. So next time he refuses to serve and says, "Sorry, I'm not a committee person."

In contrast to this fragmented, partial way of living the committed life, the servant community attempts to integrate spiritual, communal, and ministry dimensions into one group. It is like a church in microcosm, with a life of prayer, caring, and service integrated into one effort. One minister, when discussing these ideas, said excitedly, "Then the local church becomes a community of servant communities!" Indeed, that describes a congregation that organizes in this way.

What we are describing, of course, is nothing new but simply how Jesus and the disciples operated together. St. Paul gave a metaphorical description of how the church functions. Instead of organizing a church in a democratic fashion where the majority rules, he suggests organizing it around the gifts and vision of its members. The analogy he uses is that of the body (Rom. 12 and 1 Cor. 12). He suggests that the body runs harmoniously when each member recognizes his or her gift (or unique role or ministry) and exercises it to the full. Harmony and effectiveness do not come when the head and several other prominent parts of the body form a coalition and vote that the toe should do what they would like done.

The Book of Acts is replete with stories of how people acted out of vision (Peter and Cornelius) or a dream (Paul and Ananias) or a call ("Come to Macedonia"). We are exhilarated when we read of the confidence, boldness, and sense of urgency of these early Christians. They were not required to submit their program to several committees for approval.

Moreover, people in church history who excite our imagination are those who had a vision, a call, certain gifts, and a desire to involve others: St. Francis of Assisi in former days, Dorothy Day in recent times.

Members of growth groups sometimes think they can develop a common ministry based on the friendship, love, and nourishment they have developed in the group. We have rarely seen this kind of metamorphosis occur. Usually each person in the group discovers a different calling. Then the group finds itself trying to make each person's individual calling fit into a common ministry.

In our experience, servant communities usually evolve when one person clarifies a personal calling and then issues an invitation to others to join in the work. Responses to call vary from eager participation to seeming indifference. There may be many reasons for this. However, it seems that public calls to action that do evoke the response of others have several characteristics.

First, the call sounded is the result of serious inner work on the part of the person called; it is not issued off the top of the head. There is a sense of excitement about the call because it is coming from deep within and has been a matter of reflection over a period of time. Second, it expresses in some way the broad vision of God and articulates the specific piece of that vision that is important to the person sharing the call. Third, it is issued at a catalytic moment when the called person is ready for action and seeks others who want to be involved.

Finally, a public call for action is most successful when it is freeing—

i.e., when it seeks those with similar calls and does not coerce anyone to respond. This point is frequently misunderstood. When we feel called and motivated, it is easy to assume that others will find the same calling equally motivating. In reality, only a few usually share the call. Sometimes we are tempted to appeal to people's feelings of guilt: "The old people in our neighborhood are suffering. We need to respond. Let's all meet next Tuesday and discuss it." The problem with this approach is that although everyone wants to see the suffering eliminated, not all are called to be directly involved. It is better to state the call completely and clearly and then say, "All who feel a similar sense of calling or who are drawn to working with the elderly, please meet with me." We want to find those who bring the same kind of excitement and commitment that we have. This approach may get a smaller response, but two called and committed people can often do far more than a large committee of well-intentioned people, many of whom really don't want to be involved.

A call of this sort can be issued in many forms. It can be written as a letter or as a paragraph in a newsletter. It can be spoken casually in conversation or formally in a short announcement or in a longer talk. The length and style of such an articulation are less important than the deeply felt conviction of the person issuing the call.

Jo Magno is a medical doctor from the Philippines who had the idea of opening a hospice for the terminally ill in our area, as we mentioned in Course 1. Those who heard her issue a call to establish the hospice experienced an unforgettable moment. She had done a great deal of personal work, had met regularly with a praying group of friends, and had come to the point of wanting to develop public interest and involvement. By sharing some of her own story, she showed the deep roots of this vision within her own life, how it was an outgrowth of her personal experience and her faith that Jesus cares for each person at every stage of life. Giving examples of how hospice care worked in Britain, she outlined a vision of how to help people die with dignity, without pain or loss of control, and in surroundings that are personal and attuned to each one's individual need.

The response to this kind of specificity and clarity has been outstanding. Hundreds of people with a wide variety of gifts are involved. Because the Hospice of Northern Virginia is a public facility, it has gained municipal support and participation from people of many backgrounds, some of them not specifically Christian, although Jo has never hidden her own deep roots in the Christian tradition. This kind of momentum can snowball in effective, inspiring ways. Billie Johansen, an interior designer, heard Jo Magno's call and offered her unique gifts for the project. Billie then issued her own call, through the local American Society of Interior Designers newsletter, for other designers to participate. It is a splendid statement of call that is motivating, specific, and personal. Here is a portion of it:

Community Relations Hospice
of Northern Virginia

Last week the administrative staff of Hospice of Northern Virginia moved into their new quarters. Murphy's law was running true to form, and as most Designers understand—time alone will bring those four lost special ordered chairs, or will help replace nicks, bruises and breaks. The project, overall, though, has been gratifying because the planning committee and the people associated with Hospice are so special, and the idea of Hospice is so right and so timely.

The original Georgian school is really delightful. It includes some marvelous architectural features like 14 foot ceilings and high mullioned window bays for the patient lounge, and for one of the multiple patient rooms. In addition to the lounge and other patient rooms, there will be a library/conference room and a chapel.

Bids are out now, and construction for Phase II is scheduled to start as soon as possible for a completion date in the spring of 1981.

It is a heady thing to watch this project rise like the phoenix from the ashes. It is a project with soul and heart. If I sound enthusiastic—I am. The Woodlawn Design Committee would welcome other designers to a challenge that brings fulfillment. If this sounds fascinating to you, and you would like to join us, give me a call.

Billie Johansen, 821-2593

Once a person's call is heard by others and a small group gathers, how can they develop their life together? We suggest starting very simply by asking who in the group feels motivated to develop the spiritual nourishment, community support, and ministry dimensions of the group's life. Depending on how many people are involved, one or more could be responsible for each of these three dimensions. It is best to agree on the frequency and length of meetings and on the approximate time that will be devoted to each dimension. Then each subgroup is responsible for developing ways to make the best use of its allotted time.

Most ministries start very small, in the hearts of one or two people; some mushroom to impressive size while others do not. One servant community, for example, might see its ministry as faithful intercession for the vitality of one congregation, and might always be appropriately small. Another might see its mission as enabling intercession for the entire world. Such a mission did begin, in the 1970s, within the hearts of two New Zealand women, Joy Dawson and Sheilagh McAlpine. It resulted in the Lydia Movement, a dynamic network of intercessory groups in many cities of the world. The size is not what counts but rather the faithfulness of each servant community to its own sense of ministry in its own setting.

There are simple ways to get started. The following group design on the Servant Community Lab gives some details that are helpful as you begin.

Group Design

Purpose: To prepare for and run a simulated first meeting of a group of people who have responded to a common call and intend to develop a servant community devoted to that call.
Materials: Newsprint, marking pens.

Necessary Preparation: Two members of the group agree ahead of time to think about and prepare to articulate a call to ministry that has particular relevance for this group. Others in the group can help with suggestions, but the two ultimately must decide on what particular call to issue and how to articulate it in as clear and appealing a way as possible. This group design is most effective when the call is really on the minds of some of the people involved. Therefore it is hard to give more specific help other than listing some of the calls given in our groups. The situations that these calls addressed include:

- how to welcome and integrate newcomers into our congregation;
- how our congregation could most creatively respond to the challenge of major highway construction that will split the parish in two;
- how to minister to and with the elderly in our area;
- how to foster world peace;
- how to nurture and encourage the spiritual life in our parish.

A. Gathering Time   (10 minutes)   Large Group
Gather the group in a way that is appropriate for you. Consider going around the circle and speaking about one aspect of Session 5 text that caught your interest.

B. The Servant Community Lab
Because this lab takes up almost the whole session, it is suggested that any small-group discussion of individual work be eliminated unless you choose to budget an extra half hour for that purpose.

1. The Call   (10 minutes)   Large Group   The pair who have prepared in advance issue the call. Tell the whole group how it is related to the simulation. For example:

- "You are the congregation of our church on a Sunday morning, and we are making an announcement."
- "You are the Social Action Committee of the church, and we have asked for a few minutes to speak with you."
- "You are an informal group in our living room, and we are sharing our dream with you."

After you have given the setting, articulate the call in a way that is most appropriate for that setting. Here is an example of a call that was issued in one of our groups:

"I'm concerned about the growing number of Central American and East Asian refugees in our community. Many are having a hard time learning English, obtaining good jobs, and finding places to live. And when they do attain a certain level of success, I find they threaten the longtime residents who are having a hard time keeping good jobs and making rental or mortgage payments.

"Jesus taught about reconciliation. I'm excited about the prospects of making that come alive right in our midst. I believe we have a lot to offer these refugees, but they can broaden our horizons as well.

"If you'd like to join me in thinking about how we could work with the refugees arid residents for the benefit of each group, please meet me after church so we can plan a time to meet together."

2. Group Instructions   (10 minutes)

Large Group   (Someone read these instructions or say them in your own words.)

"In this simulation, each of you in the room is asked to pretend that the call just issued really grips you personally, and you want to respond. Each of you is asked to join one of three subgroups devoted to a specific dimension of the life of the new servant community that is being formed: spiritual nourishment, support, and ministry.

"Who feels most drawn to working on the ministry or task that this group will be tackling? Your job will be to develop ways to study the situation and eventually to do something about it. Please go to one corner of the room to form the *task subgroup.*

"Who is concerned and willing to develop the spiritual dimension of this group's life, to work on how to keep the inspiration going, and to see how it can be nurtured through prayer, scripture, or other resources? You are asked to go to another corner to form the *spiritual nourishment subgroup.*

"Those who want to help the members of the new servant community to know and care about one another personally, form the *support subgroup* in another corner of the room."

Each subgroup will have 30 minutes by itself to prepare its part of a simulated first meeting of the budding servant community. After the preparation time, the whole group will come together again for the actual meeting, which will be roughly 45 minutes long. This allows 15 minutes for each subgroup to lead the larger group in an activity designed to begin a life together of mutual support, prayer, and ministry.

Allow for some discussion as each one moves into a subgroup. If the numbers in each are badly out of balance, do some trading to assure that there are at least two people in each subgroup.

3.   Subgroup   Preparation   Time   (30   minutes)   Subgroups Each group begin by reading the following instructions for your role in the simulated meeting to come:

a. *Instructions for the support subgroup:* You are to prepare and then lead the larger group in 15 minutes of activity that will involve everyone and begin to build community. Building community means to help group members to know one another, keep in touch with what is happening in one another's life, care about one another, and share thoughts and feelings about the life and work of the group and the individuals in it. Naturally, this is a broad, long-range description. For your 15-minute segment, be prepared to initiate caring within the group. You might begin by including an exercise that helps people know one another in a specific way (e.g., each naming your hometown) and to share feelings regarding the call to which you have responded.

b. *Instructions for the spiritual nourishment subgroup:* You are to prepare and then lead the larger group in 15 minutes of activity that will involve everyone and provide spiritual nourishment for the group. Spiritual nourishment, broadly seen, includes receiving God's love, inspiration, energy, direction, and vision for the group's life and work. This can be done through scripture, journaling, prayer, song, nonverbal exercises, and so on. For this particular meeting, you are to initiate the group in receiving some spiritual nourishment related to the opening stages of its life and work.

c. *Instructions for the task subgroup:* You are to prepare and then lead the larger group in 15 minutes of activity that will involve everyone and begin to address the ministry of the group together. Over the long range, your subgroup will help the whole group define the task more specifically, identify resources to help solve the problems involved, and find ways to carry out the ministry. In your preparation time, we suggest you use about 15 minutes to brainstorm on ways to do the above very briefly, be prepared to give the large group a brief summary (5 minutes) of your own brainstorming, and then use 10 minutes to guide everyone in the larger group in offering ideas and energy for tackling the task. Your job as ministry subgroup is not to do the task entirely by yourselves but to guide the whole group in tackling it together.

4. Simulated First Meeting of the Servant Community   (45 minutes)   Large Group   One of the leaders call the group together, remind each subgroup of its 15-minute time limit, and then invite each subgroup in turn to lead the group for its segment. The best order we find is: support, prayer, task. But feel free to proceed in another order if that suits the group.

C. Closing   (10 minutes)   Large Group

Choose one or two of the following suggestions: evaluation of session, discussion of details for next session, song, and/or prayer. If you have time, an evaluation can be particularly helpful here. Speak about what went well, what could be improved, implications for other situations.

Note: This design may seem a bit complicated at first. Also you are creating an "artificial" situation in simulating a first meeting. However, we find that when people freely enter into an experience like this, they can design a simulated meeting that has reality, aliveness, and power. The time limits may seem constraining: You have to move right along or you cannot finish in the allotted time. But this pressure can create a lively, fun atmosphere where some real creativity can occur. Our word to you: Enjoy yourselves and see what happens!

Individual Work

Purpose: To reflect on the corporate dimensions of your calling.

1. There are many scriptural descriptions of how a servant community lives and works. (For example, see Acts 4, Rom. 12, and Phil. 2.) Use one of these or another selection to work with this week. What would you like to incorporate into your own life from these descriptions?

    2. Go over the Session 5 text and do some journaling on the following questions:
- Where am I, and where would I like to be as far as ministry is concerned? Am I called to an individual ministry, a corporate ministry, or to no particular mission?
- Do I feel supported in ministry? How? Do I need more support? What would that look like?

    3. Evaluate your area of service in the light of the three dimensions of Christian life (support, prayer, and task):
- Are you offering this service more because you feel called, or because you feel you ought to do it?
- Is there a balance of support, prayer, and task?
- Are there adjustments of time and emphasis that you would like to make? For example, "I'd like more time devoted to spiritual nourishment in our

parish board meetings, not simply an opening prayer."

4. In the light of these reflections, consider taking one concrete step regarding your own area of service this week, and share this with your patron. For example, "I'll bring this up at the next board meeting to see what we can come up with."

5. For additional ideas on how to begin a servant community, read the following "Forming a Servant Community." If you feel moved to organize such a group, consider journaling on the points raised in the article.

6. Summarize in writing what you did with this assignment.

Forming a Servant Community

You think you have a call. It is too big for you. You need others to join in it. You issue the call in conversation, in writing, or perhaps before a wider audience (e.g., a committee, a congregation).

Then what do you do with the people who are drawn by the call? Here are some suggested next steps to think about.

1. *Get the non-negotiables out on the table.* These are the dimensions of the group's life and ministry that are essential for you. Perhaps you mentioned them when you shared your call. But now you must share them again because they are crucial for the vitality of the group. For example, it may be essential for you to build regular prayer into the group life, or to meet only in the daytime, or to be committed to multicultural membership. It is better to start with fewer people who agree on the essentials than to include a larger number who disagree or are unclear about the non-negotiables.

2. *Begin right away to discern, evoke, and organize around the gifts of each member.* This is a never-ending, always changing, and infinitely rewarding process. When a gift is confirmed by the group members, go ahead and exercise it wholeheartedly. Don't wait for each one to be sure of his or her gifts. That day may be long in coming. But remember that a group is working at less than full capacity when any member is not exercising his or her gift.

3. *Gradually open yourselves to reordering your lives to make room for the new priority of your call.* Realize that people will do that at different rates, and this can cause some tension. Patience and understanding need to balance eagerness and excitement as you embark on the demanding task of

deepening your awareness of God's love and your ability to extend God's care.

4. *Submit plans and communicate developments to the larger community for confirmation.* It is necessary to go through the decision-making bodies of the larger community (e.g., the parish) for their input, encouragement, and ratification and to stay in communication with them. But don't devote too much time and energy to this process. Constant checking and control can be draining to all concerned. The response of the larger community is what confirms your group in its life and work. Its enthusiastic acceptance or resistance should be taken seriously.

Session 6

How Do My Gifts and Calling Tie in with the Larger Community?

"God has arranged the body so that . . . each part may be equally concerned for all the others."

(1 Cor. 12:25-26, JB)

We have said that the purpose of this course is to enable us to experience a process of discernment that can be used for the rest of our lives. A secondary purpose is to learn about one way of "being or doing church," i.e., the servant community.

We believe that the six discernment questions are best addressed together and in relation to one another:

1. What are my unique, God-given gifts?
2. How can I be a patron of another's gifts?
3. Which piece of God's vision is mine?
4. What is God calling me to do?
5. Is there a communal expression for my vocation?
6. How do my gifts and calling tie in with the larger community?

This course has accomplished its purpose if we have learned the value of asking these questions throughout our lives, and if communities become places where we are encouraged to ask and address these same questions.

Surely answers come at different times for different people. Some find clarity during the course; others discover it much later. It would be sad if the course itself were the only favorable setting in which to deal with these questions. Ideally the groups and communities to which we belong will become places where these questions are continually addressed. Those who take this course can learn concrete ways to help groups continue the process of discernment and discovery.

The questions are designed to be dealt with by individuals within a community. Alone, we rarely can identify, much less use, our spiritual gifts. They are given for the community. We discover our piece of God's vision as we hear others talking about theirs. We discover our call from God within our own hearts, but the awareness that God might be calling us is nurtured as we hear the stories of God's call in history and in the lives of those we know personally. Whether our calling could be expressed in a common ministry requires reflection with others on what is needed in our area, how we might fit in, and how others might help.

In this session the term *community* refers to either the small group or the larger congregation or organization to which we belong. Vital connections with our community are like the veins carrying the lifeblood of Christian experience to us. When a community is sensitive to its role in calling forth the vision and in using the gifts of its members, creativity is released. When the opposite is true, discouragement and resentment can set in.

Jo Magno's experience illustrates what can happen when the connection with the community is strong. For years, Jo has been a part of the Cursillo Community, an international renewal movement begun among Catholics but now spreading to other denominations. It was to some of her friends in the Cursillo Community that Jo first brought her dream. When the time came to "go public," she approached the churches. With their support, she went to local municipalities, who, impressed by the existing support, offered further help. Each of these communities has had a vital part to play in developing the mission of the Hospice of Northern Virginia. In addition, the involvement of these diverse people and groups has drawn the larger community together.

To show how to develop fruitful interaction between individuals and the communities to which they belong, we will use the parish as an example, although the approaches we discuss can be applied in other settings as well.

What are some things a parish can do to call forth and use the gifts of its members?

1. It can provide basic *training* in the three areas that these courses emphasize: spiritual nourishment, community support, and ministry. People need training in how to work out a program of spiritual nourishment that sustains their particular calling and gifts. Training can also help us become more effective in supporting one another and in extend-

ing God's love through various ministries. We would like to see communities offer training that incorporates some of the components we have found so vital: leaders who feel called to design and offer courses; coordinators who support participants through prayer and caring; courses that include cognitive content and experiential approaches; material that fosters movement in participants as they grow from inquirers to committed sharers of God's love.

2. It can offer various kinds of *retreat* opportunities where people can take time apart to listen to God and to reflect on their lives. These experiences can be offered initially through half-day or day-long periods of reflection held in the local church. Gradually people can be encouraged to spend more time in longer retreats away from home.

3. It and other communities can encourage *a wide variety of small-group life* so that people will have many ways to grow and develop their vision and gifts. Here are some of the ministry groups that can exist happily and creatively side by side in any community:

• *Servant community:* This is often the most efficient way to organize for those committed to a common mission. It can be life-giving for those who are ready for it.

• *Ministry support group:* It provides prayer and caring support for people whose mission is carried out individually either on the job, in separate areas of church life, or in the wider community. Such groups may be bound by a covenant and engage in common spiritual disciplines.

• *Prayer and sharing group:* This is for busy people who want support and inspiration but do not want to tackle a new ministry or to study. These groups generally use a book or scripture passage as stimulus for reflection and sharing and pray for one another during the week.

• *Prayer partners:* These are two people engaged in mutual prayer, support, study, and inspiration. This arrangement is often good for busy people who do not have time for involvement in a larger group.

Our experience is that encouraging a variety of groups suited to the different needs of members is more effective than trying to make one type of group fit everyone—e.g., "Let's organize the whole congregation into neighborhood sharing groups" or "What we all need to do in this community is to form Bible-study groups." Each of the types we have mentioned (and there are many more that can be helpful) provides a slightly different kind of support for the prayer, support, and mission dimensions of our lives.

On the other hand, the absence of tangible human support can motivate us to develop our relationship with God apart from human companionship. It is tempting to think that a supportive community is an absolute necessity, but this simply is not so. Those times when we lack the support of others can be periods of profound growth.

4. It can foster the creativity of people by providing *seed money* for the training and mission of members. One church has established a Cutting Edge Fund. It helped one member attend the Sixth Assembly of the World Council of Churches in Vancouver, British Columbia. Another person was given money for a week of discernment in a desert retreat in New Mexico. By granting this money for the growth of its members, the church as a body is saying, "We believe in you. We believe that your searching is important," or "Your attendance at this event will enhance you and us." This practice of granting seed money can be extended to all areas of service or mission. A soup kitchen, bookstore, or craft co-op in a poor area can become a realizable dream. Such tangible and psychological support can be critically important to people embarking on something new or untried.

5. By its leaders' *attitudes* it can encourage people to use their gifts and develop their mission. Welcoming ideas that are new or different encourages people to share dreams, issue calls, or perhaps take a sabbatical from doing in order to focus on being.

6. *Inspiration* nurtures vision and can come from sermons and from hearing individuals and groups report on their work and life during community gatherings. Books and pamphlets available for borrowing or buying can provide nourishment and inspiration on many topics of interest.

7. *Support, recognition, and blessing* given either in conversation or during liturgies cost very little in time but can make a big difference. Biblical people often blessed one another. Why don't we do it? Short appropriate ceremonies, a word or letter of support, public prayer over a person—these are some of the forms a blessing can take. Ray, an ordained minister, went to a conference discouraged and ready to quit his work. Through the love of persons in his group, he was renewed. Just before leaving, the group invited Ray to kneel in the center while each one laid hands on him and prayed for his renewed sense of ministry. This

little ceremony probably took ten minutes, but several years later Ray, encouraged by the blessing of that little group, is still going strong.

8. Leaders and people can foster *creative interaction and communication between traditional and new ways of living our faith.* There is no one way that is right for all. We know this, yet it is easy to distrust or at least ignore the group of people who espouse a way different from ours. However, if communication is encouraged, we can enhance one another while freeing one another to be different.

These are some of the ways we can create an atmosphere in our communities that encourages discovery of gifts and vision. When listed in this fashion, these approaches seem obvious. Yet it is surprising how often we hear the assumption that one course, one week of renewal, or one inspiring talk will unleash the creativity of people, whereas using many approaches is what contributes to a milieu that continually nourishes and fosters creativity in all its forms.

Likewise, there are behaviors that hinder the creative Spirit among people, that foster attitudes of discouragement, resentment, or fear of trying anything different. We are painfully aware of how this happens:

Squelching: The unanswered phone call or note, the interrupted conversation that is not resumed—these are little ways the budding sprouts of an idea are killed through lack of encouragement, listening, blessing. One person sparkled when hearing about mission. Someone said, "It sounds as if you're thinking about something wonderful. What is it?" He replied, "I am. I've always wanted to establish a listening and caring ministry in our local hospital."

"Why don't you do it?" he was asked.

"Well, I told my pastor about it, and he just didn't seem interested, so I dropped it."

Here was a capable man who could have established this ministry on his own. All he wanted was a word of encouragement that would have taken five minutes of the minister's time and no further involvement on his part. When he sensed the pastor's lack of interest, his own enthusiasm was squelched for a long time.

Over-control: Some communities take so much time making sure everything is cleared, coordinated, and controlled that people are exhausted before they begin. Communication and official blessing are important, but frequently they can be accomplished without the red tape so often involved.

Mistrust: Communities sometimes require more assurance of success for a project than business does. Business talks about risks and seizing the moment. "Why not?" could often be the church's stance. But too often it stops at "Why?" and requires the person to answer that "Why?" for so many people that enthusiasm wanes.

Over-organization: This often happens in democratic organizations. Instead of saying to two people, "Run with the ball," we appoint a committee of ten that cannot find time to meet or that has so many absentees that action is delayed.

The responsibility for fostering gifts and vision does not rest with the community alone. The individual can do a lot. If we need support from our community, we must make that known specifically and not expect people to read our minds. For example, if we need money for training, an official blessing for a project, a certain kind of nourishment from homilies, rest from existing responsibilities, or opportunity for retreat, we need to let people know. If we would like the support of a small group, we can find one that is right or create a new one. Communities are not always responsive the first time they are approached, but gradually they can come to know how much their support means and how to offer it more effectively. The more clarity and specificity individuals bring to their communities about what they can offer or the support they need, the more likely it is that the communities will be responsive.

As individuals and small groups of people become clear about their own gifts, vision, and calling and go to their communities for concrete support and encouragement, together they can trigger renewal on all levels of life.

In the opening words of *The Prophetic Parish,* Dennis Geaney describes the impact of this renewal. He speaks in terms of how it could start in the parish. His words apply as well to prophetic organizations of any kind:

> This book promotes what may appear to be a ridiculous proposal: that the parish is an ideal place to start a peace and justice movement, not only to renew the local church community, the neighborhood and the city, but to renew the total American and universal church establishment—not to mention local, state, and federal

governments and the entire world that is held together by TV satellites.[1]

This is not a pipe dream. We see it beginning to happen with the basic communities in Latin America, tiny prophetic groups addressing local problems. Their leaders go to regional institutes for training and to national gatherings for inspiration and exchange. Visits among the communities are promoted. Regional and national leaders listen carefully to the learnings of these grassroots people and pass them on through writings and courses. Members and leaders of these basic communities are active in trade unions, political parties, and many other aspects of national life.

One pastor commenting on Geaney's vision says, "My experience . . . tells me this proposal isn't ridiculous. Geaney articulates what I think is possible. Parishes [and we might add, other prophetic organizations] can be the base communities through which the Spirit renews the world."[2]

We began these courses with some of the first words of scripture, "God creates." It is fitting to conclude with some of the last. The writer of the Book of Revelation describes the vision we have been talking about. He sees a new heaven and a new earth and calls us to build the new city "where God dwells." He reminds us that we are not alone but are linked to God in covenant—linked to the God who lives with us and invites us as one people to join in making "all things new" (Rev. 21:1-3,5, NAB).

Our courses offer tools with which to build the new city. We build from the ground up, starting with each person's response to God's love.

Group Design

Purpose: To summarize and clarify our learnings from the course and to discern and share where we are in relation to each part of it.

A. Gathering Time   (10 minutes)   Large Group
Choose a way of gathering and settling the group that is appropriate to

the spirit the group has developed—e.g., a song or prayer together, quiet music, or each one briefly stating how you feel about coming to the last session.

B. Sharing Groups   (20 minutes)   Groups of Four
Share the learnings from the individual work that were most important to you. Work out a way to have closure with your small group.

C. Taking Stock and Going On   (30 minutes)   Individuals
1. Each one look over notes and use about 15 minutes to respond in writing to these statements:
• My strongest gifts are. . . . The ones I enjoy using most are. . . . The ones I would like to offer our community are. . . .
• My experience with patroning is. . . . About being a patron I feel. . . . About needing a patron I feel. . . .
• My glimmers of vision are. . . . The way I feel about my vision is. . . .
• At this point, my awareness of call is . . . and I feel. . . .
• Regarding the corporate dimension to my calling I have learned this:. . . .
• About community, what I would like to offer is. . . . What I need from the community is. . . .
• In summary: How have you grown from this experience? What are the implications for you as you leave the course?
    2. Silent Walk   (15 minutes)   Take a walk through the building and look for an object that symbolizes the growth or challenge you have received through the course.

D. Closing Celebration   (30 minutes)   Large Group
Devise a way to celebrate the ending of this course. You might like to place a candle in the center of the group. Then one by one each one share the object you selected and how it symbolizes what has happened to you in the course. Decide together how fully you want to share.
    Another way to end would be to share informally on these topics:
• I'm grateful for. . . .
• I wish that. . . .
• I'm disappointed about. . . .
• I learned. . . .

• What I want to do now is. . . .
  If there is time, have informal conversation over refreshments.

Notes

1. (Minneapolis: Winston Press, 1983), p.1.
2. Norman Rotert's review, *National Catholic Reporter*, March 23, 1984, p. 17.

Epilogue

Our courses are over. Yet they are just a beginning—doorways through which we enter into deeper experiences of God's love.

Have you noticed the circular nature of these courses? We come close to the heart of God in reflection and then are thrust into the world of action. And when we are involved in committed witness and ministry, we recognize more deeply the need for spiritual support and nourishment. As we learn to know ourselves within, our consciousness of the world outside enlarges, and we are drawn by compassion to serve.

The emphasis in these courses the first time we experience them is often personal for many of us. But then with the enlarged awareness that results, we can work with them again from a different perspective. For example, the Exodus story can first help us understand our personal places of freedom and oppression. Then, approaching that story with a deeper awareness of our own calling to compassion and justice, we see its relevance and power for all marginalized and oppressed inhabitants of the earth.

Dorothy Day was one who lived the life of faith with extraordinary commitment. Remarks on the jacket of the book of her selected writings summarize her life work:

> A co-founder in 1933 (with the French peasant philosopher Peter Maurin) of the Catholic Worker movement, and for almost fifty years editor and publisher of its newspaper, she applied the Gospels to a sweeping radical critique of our economic, social, and political systems and addressed the most urgent issues of our time: poverty, labor, justice, civil liberties, and disarmament. She saw the movement as an affirmation of life and sanity, and a way to "bring about the kind of society where it is easier to be good."[1]

What was striking about Dorothy Day, according to the editor of her writings, "was not what she wrote . . . nor what she believed, but the fact that there was absolutely no distinction between what she believed, what she wrote, and the manner in which she lived."[2]

How did the life of faith begin for Dorothy Day? She relates that an important influence was her childhood friend, Mary Harrington, a twelve-year-old with whom she often talked and dreamed. One evening Mary told Dorothy the life of some saint. Dorothy later wrote this about the incident:

> I don't remember which one, nor can I remember any of the incidents of it. I can only remember the feeling of lofty enthusiasm I had, how my heart seemed almost bursting with desire to take part in such high endeavor. One verse of the Psalms often comes to my mind: "Enlarge Thou my heart, O Lord, that Thou mayest enter in." This was one of those occasions when my small heart was enlarged.[3]

This is the hope we have for these courses: that they may be occasions when our hearts are enlarged so that we may welcome God's love more deeply and share it more fully.

Notes

1. Dorothy Day, *By Little and By Little: The Selected Writings of Dorothy Day,* Robert Ellsberg, ed. (New York: Alfred A. Knopf, 1983), jacket.
2. Ibid.
3. Ibid., p. 12.